Breaking Tradition to Accomplish Vision

TRAINING LEADERS FOR
A CHURCH-PLANTING MOVEMENT:
A Case from India

By

Paul R. Gupta

and

Sherwood G. Lingenfelter

For Further Contact:

Dr. Paul (Bobby) Gupta
HBI Global Partners
P.O. Box 584
Forest, VA 24551
bobbygupta214@aol.com
Phone : 614 - 598-8317

BREAKING TRADITION TO ACCOMPLISH VISION
TRAINING LEADERS FOR A CHURCH-PLANTING MOVEMENT

Copyright ©2006 by Paul Rajkumar Gupta and Sherwood G. Lingenfelter

ISBN 10: 0-88469-305-8
ISBN 13: 978-0-88469-305-5
Printed in the United States of America

Published by BMH Books
BMH Books, P.O. Box 544, Winona Lake, IN 46590 USA
www.bmhbooks.com

TABLE OF CONTENTS

DEDICATION

In honor of the faithful grassroots missionaries
and church planters of India
who have taught us so much about
reaching this nation and have
faithfully served to fulfill
the mission of our Lord.

Acknowledgements

This work involved the collective efforts of many who join me in serving the Lord toward fulfilling His mission in India. I owe very special thanks to Dr. Sherwood Lingenfelter who was a great inspiration, encouragement, and mentor from the beginning and then later collaborated with me to produce this book. Without his partnership and encouragement, I do not believe we would have seen this work completed. It has been a great honor to work with him.

I'm grateful to the Board of Directors of Hindustan Bible Institute. They encouraged me and were willing to step "outside the box" along with me to pursue an opportunity that would require significant changes in the HBI program. I am especially indebted to Dr. Robert Moses, chairman of the board, who was a mentor and father to me as I started my ministry at HBI. When I was unsure of what I was doing, Uncle Moses called me daily to encourage me as I took leadership of the mission. I know without his and the board's support, it would not have been possible to pursue all the changes.

I want to acknowledge the Administrative Leadership Team at HBI who have given extra effort toward implementing the project. Rev. Samuel Visuvasam was our first training coordinator to move "out of the box." Rev. E. Sundaraj, director of the program, and later Dr. Isac S. Raja worked hard and found ways to implement the new ideas as they emerged. I also acknowledge Dr. Jim Montgomery who birthed the vision of the Council On National Service (CONS) and Dr. Lamech Inbaraj who took it to a new level in mobilizing the church toward a vision of discipling the nation.

I want to thank and acknowledge my administrative assistant Malini Asir for her consistent efforts in gathering and loading the data and typing the manuscript. She helped me tirelessly and faithfully in seeing that the drafts and manuscripts were completed.

I am very thankful to the heroes of this book—the national church planters in the field who work to see the vision become a reality. Their passion, faithfulness, and commitment to Christ and the Great Commission always encourage me.

My heart is filled with gratitude to my mother and father who had such a great influence on my life, ministry, and commitment. I am thankful to my wife Linnet for her full support and prayer to see the work completed. I want to thank my children Mythraie, Sushil, and Deepak for their encouragement and support.

Most of all, I thank my Lord Jesus Christ for His grace, provision, wisdom, and leadership. Without Him I would not have started or completed this book. I thank the Lord for the vision and mission He has entrusted to me to join Him to see India discipled for Christ. This book is all about Him, and I know everything we learned in the process was from Him by the Holy Spirit's work in our lives. I want to praise and thank Him for trusting simple people to do incredible things that will result in bringing glory to our Heavenly Father.

Paul Rajkumar Gupta
Chennai, India
December 2005

FOREWORD

I first met Bobby Gupta at the inaugural celebration of the Consortium for Missiological Education (CIME) in India in June 2002. The board of CIME gathered in Bangalore, India, to inaugurate Dr. Siga Arles as the new dean of the consortium. Dr. Paul "Bobby" Gupta is one of six presidents of schools in India who had agreed to work together to equip Indian faculty with the Ph.D. in Missiology. These leaders are committed to mobilizing a new generation of mission leaders for the task of discipling the whole nation of India.

At the conclusion of the inaugural ceremonies, Dr. Gupta and I rode in a taxi together to the Bangalore airport and flew to the city of Chennai, where I would depart for the United States and he would return to his home at Hindustan Bible Institute (HBI). During our journey together I asked Bobby to tell me the story of HBI and God's work through the school to equip leaders for evangelism, church planting, and mission. The fact that Bobby and his colleagues at HBI had released two of their faculty and supported them financially to study full-time in CIME convinced me of their commitment to mission.

Over the two hours of our taxi ride and flight to Bangalore, Bobby related the highlights of the story of Hindustan Bible Institute. First, he told the story of his father, Paul Gupta, a high caste Hindu whose family banished him after he received Christ. After years as an itinerant evangelist, God miraculously took Paul to the Bible Institute of Los Angeles to prepare him to found a school to train Indians to reach India for Christ. That school, Hindustan Bible Institute, produced hundreds of leaders from its founding in 1952 until Paul's untimely death in 1977. Bobby then described how HBI lost its vision, until the Board invited Bobby to return to lead the school in 1984.

As I encouraged Bobby to tell me more, he described how God opened his eyes to their programs' failure to produce evangelists and church planters. Then, through encounters with Dwight Smith and Jim Montgomery, God expanded his vision and forced him to think about what it would take to reach all of India for Christ. Accepting Montgomery's challenge that his vision was too small, Bobby organized a consultation of Indian leaders in 1987 to consider the question, "What will India look like when we have fulfilled the Great Commission in India?" Out of this meeting these leaders articulated a vision for India, and formed the Council on National Service (CONS) to begin the work of mobilizing a church-planting movement in India.

At the same time, Bobby began to experiment with new programs at HBI, and he told how God led them to create a mission, and to recruit and train hundreds of evangelists and church planters to reach India for Christ. He told of designing new kinds of programs, learning from mistakes, correcting direction mid-course, and seeing God work in incredible ways to empower a church-planting movement in India.

By the end of this airplane flight I was so moved by Bobby's testimony of God's work in India that I said, "Bobby, you must tell this story to the world. You need to publish this for the wider mission and church community." Bobby turned to me and said, "I would love to do it. But I need somebody to mentor me. I am so busy and have so much to do that I just can't do it unless I take the time apart and have someone work with me."

At that point I told Bobby about the Global Research Institute (GRI) at Fuller Theological Seminary, founded by Dr. Walter Hansen, to help national scholars and leaders find time away from their busy schedules to live in the Fuller community and work in the Fuller library to write and publish works of benefit to the church and mission communities. Hansen, professor of New Testament at Fuller, had taught in Singapore and other two-thirds world seminaries and recognized how difficult it was for scholars to find time to pull away to write.

Bobby said, "I would love to come to Fuller and write. Is there anyone there who could mentor me?" Reflecting on the compelling story I had just heard, I said to Bobby, "If you come, I'll mentor you."

This book is the product of that relationship. Bobby Gupta came to Fuller in October 2003 with a first draft nearly finished. Over the next three months we worked together revising the manuscript, adding new material, and doing background research. We produced a draft, which we then submitted for review to his leadership team at Hindustan Bible Institute and to a select group of mission scholars and leaders. After receiving many constructive and helpful comments from reviewers, I went to India in August 2004 to conduct interviews with HBI leaders and to do documentary research in the records of CONS and the mission department of HBI. We have benefited greatly from both questions and challenges of the reviewers and the research support of the HBI leadership team.

In this book we tell two compelling stories. The "big picture" story is how God has worked through committed mission, church, and educational leaders to mobilize the whole church of Jesus Christ in India for church planting. From about 1985 to the present, God has moved in a very significant way. Millions of people have responded to the gospel, and hundreds of thousands of new churches have been planted. This movement has involved every denomination, every mission, and many, if not most, of the grass roots pastors and local churches in the nation. In every state and district in India Christian leaders have organized for prayer and responded to a vision to plant churches in every village and town. This book tells how the Council on National Service has sought to equip many of these pastors and leaders for this task.

The second story, the "training leaders" account, is about how Hindustan Bible Institute changed its programs and focus to play a significant part in that dramatic church-planting movement. It is the story of how Bobby and his colleagues at HBI saw God at work, saw the need to train leaders, and sought to respond to that need. The narrative describes how they experimented with different kinds of strategies, how they learned from their mistakes, and how they continued to fine-tune and revise, always seeking to get people back into ministry where they could make disciples and plant churches for the Lord Jesus Christ.

Bobby, who has been a key participant in each of these stories, serves as narrator in each of the chapters, providing a personal commentary on events while drawing extensively on the input from his partners in ministry. I have sought to provide documentation for his narrative from the records of CONS, the departmental records and annual reports to the Board of HBI, and from interviews with leaders and church planters involved in the movement. We are deeply indebted to our colleagues at HBI: Dr. Lamech Inbaraj—National Coordinator of CONS and Director of the Church Mobilization Department, Rev. Isac S. Raja—Mission Director, Rev. Biju Sajan—Director of Regional Centers, Dr. Dayanandham Francis—Principal of the College, Mrs. Linnet Gupta—Director of Networking, Mrs. Swarnalatha Felix—Director of Evangelism Follow-up, Mrs. Malini Asir—Director of Personnel, Mr. Mark Kaushik—Director of Maintenance, and Mr. Thuthi—Coordinator, Social Development. Each supported us with significant data from his or her area of ministry responsibility, and each gave constructive and helpful commentary on parts of the story. We are also grateful to Dr. Roger Hedlund, Dr. James Montgomery, Mr. David Guiles, and Mr. Daniel Kim for reading a draft manuscript and providing helpful and constructive feedback.

We acknowledge that the story of God's work in India extends far beyond what we are able to relate in this book. Other indigenous church-planting movements, such as Gospel for Asia, the North India Harvest Network, and denominational movements such as the Assemblies of God, have been used by God in profound ways to reach India for Christ. In telling this story, we hope that others will be stimulated to tell how God has transformed their ministries to establish the church of the Lord Jesus Christ in this vast nation.

I count it a privilege to have encouraged Bobby Gupta to recount the story of God's work through CONS and HBI to multiply His church in India. At the end of each of the chapters I provide a short reflection on leadership training that draws principles from the stories Bobby has told. In chapters 10 and 11, Bobby and I are writing together about issues of training master trainers and the effectiveness of global partnerships for mission in the twenty-first century. The use of "I" in the text always refers to Bobby unless specified "I" (Sherwood).

Sherwood Lingenfelter
Fuller Theological Seminary
November 2005

INTRODUCTION

In October 1983 I (Bobby) returned to India after many years of study and preparation in America to serve the Lord and His mission to establish His church. I just had turned 30 and was still growing in the Lord, but excited to return. I knew God had a plan for my life but was not sure exactly what or how it would unfold. I knew it had something to do with equipping leaders for the task of evangelism and a dream of planting a church in every village of the nation.

I remember that I could hardly wait to be in India. I was ready to do anything the Lord had in store for me. After almost ten years it was time to get out of the classroom and do something with my life. Perhaps because I had been a rebel, God seemed to take a long time to mold me for His service. I know I was (am) strong-willed, so God had to break me, so I would learn to hear Him and follow His voice.

Later in the book I will tell you more of the story of how the Lord worked in my heart and prepared me for this task. But as you read through these pages the underlying theme of the book is to understand that life and ministry is all about God! God's mission for the church is to make disciples of the nations, and God insists on accomplishing that mission through us. We need to learn to listen to the Holy Spirit, and when we do listen, God will transform us and direct our lives toward implementing His mission for the church, and the peoples of the world.

LEARNING TO DISCIPLE A WHOLE NATION

This book is about how God called, prepared, and used me and a team of Christian leaders at Hindustan Bible Institute in Chennai, India, to serve Him in developing a church-planting movement in India. The story is about a time when the school was at a crossroad in its mission of equipping leaders for the church. It is the story of our journey of listening to God, learning from our mistakes, and developing practical strategies to equip leaders to take on the task of discipling the nation of India.

Indian Christianity shares with other world Christians the challenge of preparing its leaders to fulfill the mission of God. One of the ironies of this task is the inherent tension between shepherding a flock of new believers, and mobilizing church planters to take the good news to those who have not yet heard. Our challenge centered on this tension—how do we prepare leaders to do the work of evangelism with the vision of making disciples of the whole nation? As God made the goal clear to us—a church in every village and colony of every town and city of the nation of India in one generation—we discovered that our training programs did not produce the kind of people who were motivated and adequately prepared to achieve that goal.

This book details the story of our journey, learning to listen to the leadership of God, and to becoming willing to do things outside the box. We had to break many traditions to accomplish the vision the Lord had given us. We learned from the theories of missiologists like Donald McGavran and Paul Hiebert, from the experiments we designed to implement these theories, and from the stories of individuals God touched and used to fulfill the mission of the church.

Throughout our journey we saw that our work and the movement in the church was part of a larger picture of historic transitions in the worlds of national and international politics, economics, and the history of God's church. We detail the importance of observing the trends and preparing the church to capture the opportunity and to anticipate the consequences of the changes. The story reveals how we lost many opportunities, lagged behind and tried to catch up, and endured the consequences of the delays. We hope that in telling our story, mission and church leaders in other places will be encouraged to reach beyond their traditions and discover their "outside the box" opportunities to keep the church on task, fulfilling the mission of God.

THE CONTEXT: HINDUSTAN BIBLE INSTITUTE, 1952

My father, Dr. Paul V. Gupta, founded Hindustan Bible Institute (HBI) in 1952. A high caste Hindu convert to Christianity, Dr. Gupta perceived before independence that the door to missionaries would be closed and he heard the Holy Spirit calling him to train Indian evangelists and church planters to carry on their work. Out of his own dramatic meeting with Jesus Christ (See Appendix 1), he had a lifelong passion to proclaim the good news of a God who forgives sinners to every person in India.

Paul Gupta established HBI with the purpose of giving every Indian an opportunity to hear the Gospel, respond, and be reconciled to God. He sought to equip Indian men and women so that one Indian could lead another Indian to Christ. Under his leadership HBI evolved a rather complex evangelistic strategy that involved crusade evangelism, personal evangelism, literature distribution, radio ministry, and other social efforts to serve the cause of bringing people to the knowledge of the Lord Jesus Christ.

Hindustan Bible Institute, the first of its kind to be started by a national, was born in the context of nationalization. The board and founder led from their vision to develop national leaders and serve the church in the context of nationalization. The enrollment of students at HBI, while modest in the beginning, grew rapidly and has had a significant impact, graduating thousands of leaders for the church in India. As we will see later in the book, HBI followed a western educational model and developed limitations in the process of institutionalization.

A RADICAL TURN IN MISSION: LAUSANNE, 1974

In 1974, twenty-two years after the independence of India, a very important event took place that changed the course of the nationalization process for the church throughout the world. Dr. Billy Graham, the evangelist of the century, called for a conference on world evangelism in Lausanne, Switzerland. To his surprise he found that more than 85 percent of the members present were expatriates and fewer than 15 percent were nationals.

He looked at the hundreds of mission and church leaders and graciously rebuked them. He called them to accountability for failing to develop national leadership. He challenged the nationals to go back and start movements to contextualize the task of discipling the nations and develop national leadership to take responsibility for the Great Commission.

Graham's comments set the tone for the conference, and from this the Holy Spirit led the resource people to address major issues related to the process of nationalization and indigenization of the leadership in mission and the church. Among the many speakers, Ralph Winter (1981) challenged the conference about the thousands of unreached people groups, and the practice of sending most missionaries to places where churches were by that time well established. Others, such as Donald McGavran (1970, 1981), spoke of the failure of missionaries to communicate the message and frame the church into the cultural medium of the people they sought to reach. Many attending the conference realized that methodology had to change, and that the national church and movements had to take on indigenous forms and methods to communicate the gospel effectively to the people. They spoke of contextualization of the church, its leadership, and its methodology.

Amidst many other factors, the conference gave birth to the realization that the Great Commission is not about proclamation and presence, but about making disciples. Unless the church focuses on the task of making disciples and planting churches, we will not fulfill the mission of God for our generation. This truly marked a turning point in the history of mission and the expansion of the church.

My father, Dr. Paul V. Gupta, attended the conference and when he returned to India he began to teach and implement the changes the conference addressed. To raise awareness and initiate a church-planting movement, he invited Dr. Donald McGavran to address the pastors in the city of Chennai. Out of this meeting the pastors agreed to plant 100 new churches. But this was the last major initiative for my father. Before he could do much more, he became ill in 1975, and in 1977, the Lord called him to Himself.

MY JOURNEY AS AN EMERGING NATIONAL LEADER

By the time of Lausanne 1974, God had touched me, a rebel who had run away from my father's faith and ministry, and transferred my father's vision for India to me (See Appendix 2). As a student at Talbot and Fuller seminaries from 1977 to 1983, I learned what it means to focus on making disciples among the unreached, using contextual means in the context of nationalization to communicate the message. I remember sitting in a class in 1978, dreaming of things our movement would do to disciple the nation of India. God was at work in my heart. I was eager to see how I might engage in this ministry for which God was preparing me.

I studied under Dr. Donald McGavran at the School of World Mission at Fuller. Dr. McGavran influenced me greatly as he served as my mentor in writing my Th.M. thesis. I remember how he insisted that evangelism was a process and he described how people of India made decisions differently from Americans. I understood that if we Indians wanted to see a larger number of people respond to the gospel, our methods had to accommodate to their decision-making process.

In 1979 God led me to step out of my comfort in the USA and return to India for a short-term ministry trip. It had been five years since I had left India and two years since my father had gone to be with the Lord. Carrying my church growth material from McGavran, I taught these principles with trembling and courage everywhere I was invited to speak. Each time I taught the seminar, God stretched and shaped me, the potter working the clay on His wheel for the mission of equipping leaders to share the gospel and plant churches. He helped me to understand that if evangelization was going to make progress, we needed to develop indigenous methods that were contextual to the various people of our nation. This required a serious evaluation of the methods we were using, and then making changes so the task could be accomplished.

My father had developed a curriculum for HBI modeled on his experience as a student at the Bible Institute of Los Angeles from 1948-52. The course in evangelism taught students that a decision for Christ must be independent, autonomous, and individualistic. In contrast, the large majority of Indian people made multi-individual, mutually interdependent, consensus decisions. Our graduates used these foreign methods and forms to conduct evangelism. Consequently, we lacked effectiveness in fulfilling the Great Commission. As nationals, new to the task, we eagerly shared our faith, but we did not understand missions. Missions and evangelism were synonymous for most of the leaders. In 1979 I met with a number of national ministry leaders in India to learn what they were doing. As they described their evangelistic work, I saw they lacked a vision for making disciples and planting churches. As I traveled I saw many villages without a church or Christian presence. God helped me to understand that evangelism without church planting would not enhance the process of discipling the nation. As I traveled, looking out of the window of a car or down from a plane, I saw thousands of villages with shrines, temples, and mosques, but no churches. God gripped my heart for the absence of His church in these villages in the nation. I began to pray with tears for a church in every village of India.

A RADICAL TURN FOR HINDUSTAN BIBLE INSTITUTE

Near the end of my trip in 1979, God opened the door to bring transformation in the way HBI taught and practiced evangelism. A few weeks before I returned to the USA, the Board of HBI invited me to attend their meeting. They gave me a warm welcome and an open invitation to attend any of the meetings. At the end of the meeting, the board chairman invited me to share what God was doing with my life and what He was putting on my heart in preparation for His service.

While I did not expect this and was not prepared, God prompted me to share my burden for contextual evangelism that resulted in making disciples. The board asked how this was different from what HBI was already doing. Being young, impetuous, and understanding little about leadership. I responded with a question: "Can you show me one person in a church that our students have led to

Christ? We must have led no fewer than 25,000 people to the Lord." I asked, "Where are the converts?" For the first time, it dawned on us that evangelism without disciple making resulted in nothing. Early the next day I had a call from the chairman asking me to meet with him. He asked me to explain exactly how I would do evangelism that would result in making disciples. While I had very little experience in making disciples, I explained what I understood from those who had taught me at Fuller. Within 10 days, HBI organized a meeting of its leadership to discuss the tension. They accepted the need for a change and committed to do evangelism that would result in making disciples. We defined disciple making as evangelism that results in planting new churches where churches do not exist, or entrusting the new converts to the existing churches.

I returned to the USA to finish my preparation, not knowing or expecting that in 1983 God would call me to lead HBI. Between 1979 and 1983 the evangelistic efforts of HBI resulted in planting 10 new churches in and around the city of Chennai. I cannot describe the immense satisfaction of the chairman of the board. For the first time he began to see how God could use His people to disciple the nation. There was new excitement in the mission, but we were far from ready to take on the nation. That story is the focus of this book.

PART I

HOW CAN A SCHOOL TRAIN CHURCH PLANTERS?

FORMAL, NON-FORMAL, AND INFORMAL STRATEGIES

GOD RESTORES
A VISION FOR HBI

This chapter describes how "formal education" gradually cripples and derails a school originally founded to produce church planters! This happened because Indian church and educational leaders imitated what they had learned in schools in Europe and America. The theological schools emerging from the reformation, such as the Yale of Jonathan Edwards in New England, had one fundamental purpose—preparing men to pastor established churches. Teachers and congregations measured the stature of graduates by their mastery of biblical languages, logic, and great preaching. The great theologian, Edwards, sought biblical answers to the major questions of the Reformation church without a theology of mission or church planting. Few Reformation leaders imagined the essential questions of modern mission—evangelism, making disciples of new believers, and planting new churches.

Mainline theological schools established accreditation in the Twentieth Century to define standards of quality and to distinguish themselves from many newly established evangelical Bible schools and seminaries. It became an instrument in the United States and India to defend the status quo in theological education. As many evangelical schools like HBI became accredited, they had to conform to standards as the price of approval.

In the grace of God, Bobby and the board of Hindustan Bible Institute awakened to this lost vision,

*and took steps to restore the school to its mission.
The tragedy of missionary-founded Bible schools and
seminaries is that most do not recognize how they
imitate "seminary education" roots, and lose their
vision to equip leaders for church planting.*
—Sherwood Lingenfelter

When I (Bobby) returned to India in 1983, I found HBI a
very different school than the one I attended in 1971-1974. The
trainees thought first about getting a degree. They were not concerned about evangelizing the nation. The faculty pushed students
to achieve scholastic awards from the university, but not to plant
churches. The management struggled to meet all the standards of
the university. Neither faculty nor students gave time or invested
energy in the ministries of evangelism or church planting.

In this chapter it is my purpose to describe how institutionalization threatened the founding vision (see Appendix 1) and
national impact of HBI. I will show how improper implementation of institutionalization led to the near death of the founding
vision and mission of HBI. I will look closely at some of the forces
and decisions that led HBI down this path and then document the
events that led to the restoration of the vision and the development of new strategies to achieve it.

Institutionalization is a necessary process in any movement
that grows rapidly and serves increasingly larger numbers of
people. However, when it blurs God's purpose and vision for the
movement in order to meet the needs of growth, please individuals, or increase one's sphere of influence, the organization runs the
risk of losing its reason for existence. Institutions can turn their
focus from doing what God intended through their founders to
what others or the next generation values.

THE PURPOSE AND IMPACT OF HBI

My father founded Hindustan Bible Institute in 1952 with a
purpose of giving every Indian an opportunity to hear, understand, and respond to the gospel. The vision was to see nationals

equipped and sent to every part of the nation. Others joined him and shaped a strategy to accomplish the vision of equipping national leaders with skills, character, and information to develop committed, competent, and matured transformational leaders to disciple the nation.

Each year as students graduated and demonstrated their ability as evangelists, teachers, and missionaries, the faculty equipped and released them for the task of fulfilling the mission of the church. By the year 1974, HBI became the largest theological training institution in Asia. Many spoke with regard about the effectiveness of the training. The college had graduates serving in every state of India, in the neighboring countries, and as far as Europe and the United States of America. Most of the major organizations, denominations, and mission societies had our graduates as pastors and missionaries serving in the movements and, in some cases, leading these organizations.

HBI had grown from being a Bible Institute to a Bible College, yet it also launched an evangelistic movement that was proclaiming Christ through literature, street preaching, crusades, radio, and many other means. Its social development programs served the poor and cared for the sick. In a short period of 22 years God did incredible things through my father before he went to be with the Lord in 1977. Men and women were effectively trained, the gospel was proclaimed, souls were saved, and the poor were served.

HBI became so effective that mission, church, and parachurch organizations sought its graduates. The founder had a vision and imparted it to the students. Many young people dedicated their lives to go to unreached parts of the nation. Students who came to HBI were so close to the leader that his faith, prayer life, and passion for lost souls influenced their lives and affected their ministry.

Many organizations sent their recruits to HBI to be equipped for leadership for the mission of the church. As the number of trainees rapidly increased, the organization looked at ways to expand and increase its sphere of influence. The opportunity to equip more students, however, brought pressure from various sections of the church. They said, "If you want us to continue to send candidates, the institution must consider affiliating with the university." Having a desire to serve the need and increase its impact, HBI leaders agreed to meet Serampore University standards of affiliation, but little did they know how this decision would affect the purpose and sacrifice the vision and strategy of HBI.

THE THREAT OF INSTITUTIONALIZATION

Responding to pressure from church leaders to seek accreditation of its degrees, in 1967 HBI applied for affiliation with the Serampore University, the school established by William Carey, which at that time accredited all theological education in India. The university senate welcomed the application, informed HBI of its standards, and set a date to conduct an evaluation. HBI staff made numerous internal changes in structure and curriculum designed to satisfy the standards for accreditation. When the evaluation was completed, HBI received a provisional affiliation for three years.

Serampore University, in accord with its mission to develop academic quality and improve standards of operation, issued HBI a number of recommendations to be fulfilled during the three years of provisional status. In addition, they imposed regulations and changes that caused the institution to move away from its priorities, purpose, and value. The administration worked to meet the standards, and to implement the changes suggested in the recommendations. HBI's newfound prestige and recognition excited administration, faculty, and students.

As soon as the word of affiliation with Serampore spread, prospective students from all over India applied for admission. HBI leaders were greatly encouraged and motivated. Within four years the student body doubled. This forced the college to invest in development of the institutional infrastructure to serve these students and achieve continuing accreditation. These investments supplanted HBI programs for evangelistic outreach that had been a central focus of its early mission.

As we all worked hard to meet the standards of the university, in a very subtle way we turned from our original purpose. HBI started serving a new purpose without knowing it. The priority to develop godly, mature individuals, skilled in sharing their faith and proclaiming God's Word to the unreached, took second place to the development of individuals of knowledge who could serve in the professional ministries of the church.

The evangelistic program of HBI was designed to facilitate the preaching of the gospel and to build practical skills to preach and share one's faith. But after affiliation with Serampore the students and faculty attracted to HBI's programs lacked the interest and desire for those skills and ministries. They held other values, priorities and purposes, those associated with the church establishment in India. As a result HBI lost its ability to educate people for the evangelistic and church-planting movement envisioned and established by my father.

In the end HBI lost its cutting edge. By acceding to the desire of church leaders for accreditation, and to the attraction of becoming the largest training center in the nation, HBI's leaders sacrificed the mission and vision of its founder. When the process began, Serampore allowed HBI to maintain two different programs and curriculum. The first, a four-year Graduate in Theology degree (G.Th.), maintained the priorities of our founding mission and vision. The second, a three-year License in Theology degree (L.Th.), served the priorities of the university. Both programs attracted mature candidates, and together they allowed both the university and HBI to each accomplish their respective purpose and vision.

As time passed, the university senate chose to change its program to a Bachelor in Theology (B.Th.), first offered as a three-year program, and later as a four-year program. The students qualifying for this four-year program needed a tenth grade equivalent. At that same time the Serampore faculty re-evaluated the G.Th. program of HBI and decided it was inferior to their B.Th. degree. Any student wanting to get the B.Th degree had to proceed from the G.Th. and do an additional one year of studies. These changes affected the number of students joining the G.Th. program.

With the decline of enrollment in the G.Th., the HBI administration decided to drop its original program, and offer only the B.Th. degree of the university. We did not realize it, but when we lost our curriculum, we stopped serving our mission. The original curriculum and program were designed to build character and provide skills to study, interpret, and teach Scripture. We sought to graduate individuals who would do the work of an evangelist and facilitate the development of faith and character in new believers.

The Serampore curriculum centered upon scholastics, and intellectual and current issues, and it ignored the issues of character development and skill building for ministry. The graduates had gained much knowledge, but lacked skills and often the character to serve the people and the church. Many of the students lost the vision they had received from the Lord as new believers to evangelize the nation. The training did not prepare them to evangelize, but instead equipped some as urban pastors to fill empty pulpits, and others to lay a foundation for further study and theological teaching. Most graduates grew intellectually, but they were not equipped to evangelize the rural parts of the nation where the largest numbers of unreached people live.

MISSION DELAYED AND PASSION LOST

In the old program we attracted mature adults, often new believers, called by the Lord to ministry. They came because they wanted to be equipped to serve the Lord in evangelism and church planting, and after graduation they went directly into evangelistic mission fields.

After affiliation with the university, the majority of students came because they sought a recognized degree. Most of the persons we attracted to the program came straight out of the tenth grade, too young to be effective in ministry. Some came because it was an opportunity, not because they had a call. The new standards for admission focused on whether or not the person was eligible to be admitted into a university program. The average age of the student entering the program dropped from 22 to 17 years. The Bible College became the place they came to buy time and determine whether or not they were called to the ministry, a place of extended childhood.

A sad outcome of this process was that many students, after spending four or five years of study at HBI, found they were not fully qualified for ministry. The graduate needed the next level degree before the church would accept him in the urban professional ministry. So instead of entering the ministry, most graduates enrolled for further education. While our training was professional, the individual graduates were often too young to proceed to ministry. Because of this delayed entry, many individuals lost their passion for ministry.

THE COST OF INSTITUTIONALIZATION

The university senate continued to impose standards to develop the college. One particularly crucial area was that of faculty appointments. The university had a list of approved institutions from which HBI could recruit new faculty. And HBI had to submit all faculty appointments to the university senate for its approval. These requirements made the task of recruiting new faculty who understood and supported the mission of HBI especially difficult, and led to the compromise of historic values in recruiting faculty. To maintain university affiliation, HBI compromised its standards and employed faculty who were not committed to the evangelical thrust of the institution.

The institution, in its effort to develop faculty, sent individuals to colleges openly in conflict with the theological stand of the founder's mission. Instead of developing faculty committed to evangelical Christianity and leaders for evangelism and biblical theology, HBI unconsciously nurtured a theology opposite the ethos of the organization.

The more we evaluated the programs and policies of accreditation, the more we realized that we had sold our birthright. HBI was now serving the purpose of the university. Our leaders had compromised our historic commitments to the Word of God, to building leaders of character and passion for reaching the lost, and to expanding Christ's church. We had sacrificed our vision to disciple the nation on the altar of establishment interests for the legitimacy of programs and degrees.

THE EVENT THAT OPENED OUR EYES!

It was a night in April 1985, eighteen years after the college affiliated with Serampore University. In the tradition of HBI, the president and director host a celebration for the graduating class in which the graduates share what God is calling them to do. Linnet and I were hosting our first graduation banquet. The chairman of the board and his wife were our special guests. Excited to have the class and distinguished guests in our home, we looked forward to hearing God's plans for this group. After a time of fellowship and dinner, we gathered into a circle and I asked the question "How has HBI helped you and what are your plans for the future?"

As the graduates shared their stories, and we listened carefully to each of them, our hearts sank. Instead of feeling prepared for ministry, they confessed how they felt inadequate to enter the ministry. I remember that all, with the exception of one, were leaving for further education.

With shock on his face, the chairman of the board turned to me and said, "Bobby is it for this reason we are running the college?" Standing to speak to the graduates, he expressed his extreme disappointment that only one graduate was going out to serve. As the graduates departed that evening, we together grieved over the loss of our vision, asking ourselves, "Why do we exist? How did we let this happen?"

Institutionalization is a natural outcome of success, a process in which organizations improve their effectiveness to fulfill their mission. HBI had to be institutionalized to make continued impact. But if institutionalization is improperly implemented the organization will lose sight of its purpose for existence, sacrifice its values and begin implementing programs that have little or no impact on the purpose and vision of the organization.

HBI had stopped fulfilling its mission. We were demoralized, had compromised our values, and had fallen into a maintenance mode. Praise God! He showed us the handwriting on the wall and gave the leaders the will to make the changes before HBI moved to its own death.

RESTORING THE PURPOSE:
A CHURCH-PLANTING MOVEMENT

The graduation ceremony in 1985 forced us to come to grips with the fact that training people for further graduate study was not the answer for discipling the nation. I must confess we tried hard to make the program fulfill the vision. We altered the curriculum, introduced additional courses, and took out courses, but found great opposition to the changes. We were unable to restore the purpose and mission of HBI through the university-approved degree. The B.Th program set a high standard, but it attracted the wrong candidates who did not contribute to the purpose, vision, and strategy of Hindustan Bible Institute & College.

In 1987, shortly after we joined our efforts with other Indian church leaders in a national movement to mobilize for church planting, we decided to end our affiliation with Serampore and replace the B.Th. with a program and degree that would serve the missional purpose for which God had led my father to establish HBI. We graduated our last class with a B.Th. in the year 1990.

Through the 1987 consultation of national leaders on church planting, we understood that the majority of India's people need Christian leaders who understand rural communities and have skills to minister contextually to the needs and culture of rural people. The complexity and focus of formal training left most graduates inadequately prepared to work in rural environments. Evangelists and church planters to rural India must be equipped for the uniqueness of the task, requiring a different form and process of training.

As God opened our eyes to the challenge of discipling a whole nation, HBI found herself at the crossroads of having to make a major change. We recommitted to our founding purpose—equipping servant leaders to give every Indian an opportunity to hear, understand and respond to the message of the gospel, and to form new communities of believers where converts may become disciples of Jesus Christ. To achieve this purpose leaders and faculty had to make changes in programs and curriculum to equip committed, competent, mature, servant leaders. We decided to rethink our education at HBI to produce graduates ready to join and lead in a church-planting movement.

Did this mean that formal theological education is not necessary? No! While as part of a wider network we sought to launch and sustain a national church-planting movement, we understood that sound theology must provide a foundation for developing such a movement. Every people group will have cultural realities that will enhance and limit their understanding of God's Word. Formal education equips people to gain a deeper understanding of God's Word, and wrestle with the more complex issues of how to contextualize faith in a growing church.

FORMAL AND NON-FORMAL THEOLOGICAL TRAINING

Classical theological education, emerging in medieval European societies where the total population was either Catholic or Protestant, was not designed to equip leaders for the church and its mission in the pluralist societies of the twenty-first century. As we struggled with the challenge of the peoples and religions of India, God helped us understand the need for several types of leaders to fulfill the Great Commission in India. The different situations and leadership requirements often demanded a different structure and method of training.

At first, we faced the great temptation to end the formal training program. It was costly, high maintenance, and low return. But after we began developing the church-planting movement, the Holy Spirit showed us the need for mature trainers for our front line evangelistic force, and theologians to contextualize the Word and serve as theological faculty. As we reviewed our personnel needs, we realized the value and function of developing theological leaders as well as church planters.

We decided that if we terminated the formal program, we would hinder theological development in the nation. Fewer and fewer persons in India between 35 and 50 years of age had the skills to interpret Scripture and effectively serve the church. Given the probability that rapid evangelism and church planting would lead to the compromise of Scripture and theology in the process of contextualization, we agreed to keep preparing Indian leaders to think deeply about these issues and address possible future distortions.

In our conversations we observed how graduates of classical theological programs also have a broad range of ministries for the church. Many of the best graduates serve as teachers in Bible colleges and seminaries. Others minister to sophisticated urban families who prefer an educated pastor who understands how to make God's Word relevant to their lives. Such leaders must have substantive theological foundations to serve the professional and elite classes of the cities. We also realized that these leaders were better served with training at the graduate level rather than at the undergraduate. Urban pastors, ministering to complex communities, required a background that included the secular and religious. To best serve the urban context, a pastor needs an undergraduate training in a secular context as a foundation to understand his audience and generation. Combining undergraduate study and a graduate theological program, the pastor is equipped to minister in such communities.

After much reflection and some experimentation, we agreed to proceed on two fronts. To fulfill our purpose of equipping leaders for a church-planting movement, we turned to non-formal training strategies. That story is told in detail in the next chapter. At the same time we agreed that HBI would continue to offer degrees and formal theological education. To meet the need for accreditation we turned to the Asian Theological Association, which gave us more freedom and flexibility to determine our curriculum and hire the faculty we needed for our mission.

MAKING FORMAL THEOLOGICAL EDUCATION RELEVANT

Today, in an effort to graduate pastors and leaders for urban churches and Bible schools, we have developed a Master of Divinity degree (M.Div) designed to develop committed, competent, and capable leaders with maturity to understand and teach God's Word. The program requires every student to study Greek and Hebrew. We believe that men and women need to use the original texts and develop a biblically-based theology for the church. Every student must master and practice ministry skills while pursuing his degree. Faculty members mentor these students in the practice of ministry, and engage them in personal discipleship to ensure that each is growing in his or her relationship with God and in character development.

We have reduced the total number of students in our formal programs with the purpose of assuring the quality required to accomplish the vision. More recently we have enhanced the formal programs by introducing a Master of Theology program, and in a consortium relationship with five other schools, offering a few select students the opportunity to pursue a doctorate in missiology.

Our goal is to continue to grow, developing formal programs that meet our vision for missions, the need of ecclesia, and evangelical Christianity. While other institutions will serve other needs in theological development, our contribution will be founded on pastoral leadership, missions, and biblical theology. Through this process, HBI seeks to use formal and non-formal programs to serve the purpose of developing leaders for the church at large in India.

SHERWOOD'S REFLECTIONS ON LEADERSHIP TRAINING

As a lifelong participant in American higher education, and as the chief academic officer of a leading theological seminary, I was not surprised by Bobby's story about the loss of vision at HBI. Yet it has provoked me to engage in very serious reflection about the strengths and weaknesses of accreditation and formal theological education. In my career I have served as member and chairperson of evaluation teams, visiting Christian and secular institutions to assess their capacity and effectiveness for the reaffirmation of their accreditation. I have also served as a member of the Senior Commission of the Western Association of Schools and Colleges that accredits colleges, universities, and graduate schools in California and Hawaii. Through this experience and participation in the accreditation process, I have learned that accreditation is a powerful force that reshapes institutions, regardless of their mission.

Accreditation for a college or seminary provides many significant benefits, the most important of which is the legitimacy of the degree. Students enroll in accredited institutions because they have assurance that when they have completed a program of study, they will receive a degree or certification of learning that will open doors to a career or to advanced study. Other benefits include transfer of credit, assurance of the quality of faculty and program, financial responsibility by the institution, and reasonable student services. Yet all of these guarantees come with significant cost.

Accreditation sets very clear limitations on the kinds of students one may admit to a program. Without a high school diploma (see

Appendix 2) Bobby Gupta would have been excluded from most accredited institutions. Accreditation forces an institution to spend money to develop systems that are "standard" for approved institutions, money that must be diverted from other aspects of its mission. Accreditation places limits on the kinds of people who may serve on the faculty, on the time that one must spend in class, on the structures of courses and programs, and so forth. Further, the peer review process insures that every institution will in some way be pressured to conform to existing practices in the wider academic community. These are the kinds of pressures that Bobby described so graphically for HBI, pressures that in the long term diverted HBI from its original vision and mission. The processes of accreditation, conservative by nature, suppress innovation and change in education.

Formal education is the teaching and learning that happens in schools. Schools have a calendar, curriculum, faculty, and standards for admission, successful performance, and graduation. Students are required to attend classes, study subject matter, and pass examinations to demonstrate their knowledge. Formal education takes students out of life experience, suspending their engagement in work and living for a period of intense study and learning. This type of training has very significant benefits and very significant limitations. Bobby's story of HBI illustrates both in a profound way.

I have concluded that formal education is ill suited and cannot effectively equip evangelists, church planters, and apostolic leaders for ministry. We are limited for the same reason that we do not train carpenters, masons, and airplane mechanics through formal education. The skills and the work of the evangelist, church planter, and apostolic foundation-layer can be understood and mastered only through practice, through experiential learning. Some formal study may be helpful, but it cannot take up the larger time frame of the student. Students who spend most of their time in formal theological education become teachers and scholars, which is precisely what the educational program is designed to produce.

The story of HBI is not unique. After reflecting on my experience with students over the last thirty-five years, I can say with confidence that every evangelist who has graduated from Talbot or Fuller seminaries, where I have worked, came into the seminary as an evangelist, and by God's grace escaped with the calling and gift intact. None learned to be an evangelist in these schools, although they may have taken a course or two on the subject. Many have been diverted from this calling into more prestigious teaching or pastoral ministries.

Finally, both Paul and Bobby Gupta have demonstrated that vision, mission, and courage are critical factors in leadership training for a church-planting movement. Each man received a compelling vision from God to equip men and women to preach the gospel to those who have never heard. Out of this compelling vision they took steps of great social risk and personal cost to identify the right people, and to bring them into the right relationships where, as disciples of Jesus Christ, they engage in the practice of evangelism and church planting. Driven by their calling and a commitment to the mission of God, they have kept the goal, the end product of training, in very clear focus. Bobby, after evaluating the graduates of HBI, acted with great courage to withdraw HBI from accreditation. Then he engaged in a process of continuous evaluation, and course correction, always with the end in mind—a church-planting movement to accomplish the mission of God. The chapters that follow describe the process of experimentation, evaluation, correction, and pressing on toward that goal.

CHAPTER 1. RESEARCH AND REFLECTION QUESTIONS:

Research Exercise: Interview a person who has planted a new church and ask the following:

1. How did you learn the basic knowledge and skills of evangelism?
2. Is it important to you to have a degree from an accredited school? Why or why not?
3. What aspect of your education and experience contributed in significant ways toward meeting the challenges of church planting?

Reflection:
4. What value did accreditation add for the ministries of evangelism and church planting?

CHAPTER TWO

A NEW PARADIGM: NON-FORMAL TRAINING

What do you do when you discover that none of your graduates are evangelists or church planters, and that your training program produces completely different results than you intended? What do you do when you discover that you have recruited the wrong people for the mission you want to accomplish? Most institutions respond by making changes to curriculum and programs, hoping to recover their mission. This rarely, if ever, works, since the cause lies in the fundamental design or paradigm of learning in the institution.

This chapter is about radical change, recruiting a completely different kind of student, inventing a new method of training, adopting a radically different system of finance, and learning how to improve by evaluating your results and experimenting with new ways of training.

—Sherwood Lingenfelter

Korasa Paul, a Koya convert from the state of Andhra Pradesh, shared with his pastor that God had called him to the ministry. His pastor saw that, even though Paul was not educated, he had a great commitment to ministry. His conversion was a miracle. He had lived in such darkness and so far from God that no one imagined he would ever turn to God. But one day he and his wife accepted Jesus as Lord, and thereafter Pastor Raju found Paul in church at every opportunity.

Paul followed his pastor everywhere he went in ministry and repeatedly expressed a desire to serve the Lord the rest of his life. Since Paul could not read or write, Pastor Raju was not sure how to help him. He informed our mission of the problem. In our investigation we learned that his wife was able to read, and so we invited them to come together for the training.

We did not know that Paul was a very ill man. In the debauchery of his past, he had nearly destroyed his liver. Never for a moment complaining of his physical problem, he and his wife attended each of the ten-day training sessions to learn all they could about the Lord and serving Him. Then they worked daily to share their faith and develop a community of believers. His wife would read for him and he would teach. God helped them minister to the people. As people responded to the gospel, he built a temporary shed where the 30 people who came could meet.

As God established this local church, Korasa Paul lived his last days serving the Lord with great joy. Many came to the Lord, including several members of his family. When he died his nephew Rajarathnam took on the responsibility of the church Paul founded. Today Rajarathnam pastors several churches and Paul's wife serves as a Bible woman.

If we had refused to admit Paul to our non-formal training because he could not read, or had not gone to school, the many churches emerging from their ministry among the Koyas would not be there today. The flexibility of the non-formal paradigm enables HBI to equip men and women like Korasa Paul, whom God calls to ministry in spite of their limitations.

In this chapter I (Bobby) will tell the story of how God led HBI to design and implement a new paradigm to train leaders for a church-planting movement. This paradigm evolved over several years as we listened to the leadership of the Lord, experimented with non-formal training, and evaluated the results. You will see that our program changed over time as we adapted to the people we served, and to their effectiveness in ministry. Finally, I will explain why we need to look at alternative methods to equip a church-planting task force to build and serve the body of Christ.

THE CHALLENGE OF THE MISSION

God had given me a vision for the whole nation. Taking seriously the words of Scripture that God is not willing that any should perish, I understood that our task was to take the gospel to every person, and to provide a church for every people group in India. This soon became the vision of the leadership of HBI, and we began to think about establishing a church-planting movement. In the course of our journey the Lord led us to adopt a strategy called Discipling a Whole Nation (DAWN).

The DAWN strategy, emerging from the Lausanne movement, envisions a church for every people group, social structure, and geographical location. The strategy recognizes the complexity of each people group, economic community, and social structure. It makes provision within those contexts to see that the message is contextualized and people are discipled into a personal relationship with the Lord Jesus Christ. When the task is completed the nation is saturated with churches.

To understand the immensity of this task, you must imagine a country like India, with more than a billion people, living in more than 600,000 villages with more than 4,693 people groups. To plant a church in every village and colony of every town and city of this nation, a church for every thousand people in every people group, we needed an additional million churches and a minimum of a million mature pastor leaders. To develop the leaders to accomplish such a task using formal education would take generations—the formal method of equipping leaders trains only a few, and at far too slow a pace.

I remember going through seminary and thinking of the need to have a church in 600,000 villages and wondering how this could be a reality in my lifetime. But we worship the God of the impossible, and the Holy Spirit began working on my heart so I would see how He would do this. I never for a moment thought it was possible. But the Holy Spirit led us to think outside the box, to take risk, and to listen to the Spirit. After working on the process for 20 years, I am convinced it can be done in our generation.

GOD UNVEILS A NEW PARADIGM

In 1983, when I first returned to HBI, I found the influence of the formal paradigm filled with challenges. I tried to change the curriculum, adding new courses to build skills and values so the students would catch the vision. No matter how we tried to bring about change, we felt we were running into a brick wall. We finally recognized that our program attracted the students who were interested in degrees, not in church planting.

This frustration was good for us! We had to understand that the formal paradigm had its weakness and limitations, before we were willing to trust God for a better way. We had to accept that we needed a different kind of student and a new kind of training to accomplish the task, independent from the formal context.

Once we were ready to hear God and follow, He began to unveil the process of multiplying leaders. The first principle was to find students who had a passion for evangelism and church planting, like Korasa Paul, and provide training for them that did not take them away from their villages and people group. We learned to bring the trainees to HBI for ten days of training and send them back to live and minister in their villages. We established the Missionary Training Institutes with the flexibility to equip individuals within the context of their own community, and thus avoid the dislocation students experienced in a formal training program. Once every three months we brought them to HBI for ten days of training. They came for eight modules over a period of two years (see Table 2.1).

A second principle of the training is repetition. We learned that our trainees had varying educational backgrounds, and most came with little or no biblical knowledge. We organized the program with five different tracks, repeated each time the trainees came to HBI. Through this repetition the trainees gained progressive mastery of foundational information on the Bible and biblical theology. In the evangelism and special ministries course they learned the methods and skills of Bible study and how to share their faith. In the Christian life and work sessions, we helped them develop and practice the personal disciplines, essential for growth in character and ministry. In the beginning I taught these training modules. Today we have a core group of six full-time trainers who have been through the program and have successfully planted several churches. In addition we have 75 part-time teachers, all of whom are graduates of the Missionary Training Institute and are successful church planters.

A third principle of the training is application by teaching others. We required all trainees to teach immediately what they had learned to those they are reaching and discipling in their villages. When they returned to HBI for the next training session, they reported on how they had carried out the ministry assignments during the three months of ministry.

TABLE 2:1
MISSIONARY TRAINING INSTITUTE 2003

FIRST YEAR:

Module I	Module II	Module III	Module IV
Bible Survey	**Bible Survey**	**Bible Survey**	**Bible Survey**
OT Pentateuch NT Gospels	OT Pentateuch Part II NT Gospels Part II	OT Historical NT Books of Acts	OT Historical Part II NT Books of Acts – II
Bible Theology	**Bible Theology**	**Bible Theology**	**Bible Theology**
God – Trinity & Revelation	Man	Sin	Christology
Evangelism	**Evangelism**	**Evangelism**	**Evangelism**
Definition and need for Evangelism	Biblical Basis, Models and Steps	Various types of Evangelism E1, E2	Various types of Evangelism E3, E4
Christian Life and Work	**Christian Life and Work**	**Christian Life and Work**	**Christian Life and Work**
Understanding the Bible	Devotional Life	Character Building	Stewardship
Special Ministries	**Special Ministries**	**Special Ministries**	**Special Ministries**
Bible Study Methods Preaching Technique	Bible Study Methods Preaching Technique	Christian Education	Strategic Planning

SECOND YEAR:

Module V	Module VI	Module VII	Module VIII
Bible Survey OT Poetical & Wisdom NT General Epistle and Apocalyptic	**Bible Survey** OT Poetical & Wisdom NT General Epistle and Apocalyptic - II	**Bible Survey** OT Prophetical NT Pauline Epistles	**Bible Survey** OT Prophetical Part II NT Pauline Epistles – II
Bible Theology Salvation	**Bible Theology** Holy Spirit	**Bible Theology** Church	**Bible Theology** Satan & Angelology
Evangelism Methods of Evangelism	**Evangelism** Mass Evangelism	**Evangelism** Contextual Evangelism	**Evangelism** Guidelines for Effective Evangelism
Christian Life and Work Family	**Christian Life and Work** Missionary Biography	**Christian Life and Work** Leadership Skills	**Christian Life and Work** Life in Contemporary Society
Special Ministries Spiritual Warfare	**Special Ministries** Cross-cultural Ministry	**Special Ministries** Bible Translation	**Special Ministries** Adult Literacy, First Aid

During the two years of the Missionary Training Institute we challenged them, while developing skills and character, to share their faith with as many people as possible, and teach those who respond how to become disciples of Jesus Christ. They learned to recognize people who are receptive to the gospel, and receptive areas where they might locate their first church. We encouraged them to identify five other locations of people receptive to the gospel. At the end of two years trainees knew how to share their faith, understand and study their Bible, lead Bible studies with others, and prepare sermons. As they returned for each of the training sessions, we added to their skills and ministry assignments.

Finally, we had to rethink the financial basis of this training. In the formal programs students pay tuition, which provides substantial revenue for faculty salaries and the operation of the school. If a person wants to earn a degree from HBI, they must enroll for that program and pay the normal fees. The Missionary Training Institute, however, is free to anyone who wishes to enroll, and we welcome students from all over India. The Missionary Training Institute has as its primary goal the equipping of evangelists and church planters.

One of my tasks was to raise support in India and abroad for Indian evangelists and church planters. Early in the movement we agreed to provide financial support for these national missionaries, funding about 50 percent of what they needed to live and serve in a village community. They, in turn, were responsible to earn or raise whatever else they needed. In 2003 we were supporting church-planting missionaries with a stipend of Rs 700 a month.

Recognizing that we needed a different structure to support our church-planting initiatives, God worked in our hearts to form a movement, parallel to HBI, that would implement our vision for contributing as much as we could toward discipling the whole nation. We called this movement the Indian National Evangelical Fellowship (INEF), and through this fellowship we raised support and sent out evangelists and church planters. The churches planted by this task force were known as INEF churches until 2000, when they formally organized as the Indian National Evangelical Church (INEC).

THE IMPACT ON TRAINEES

To recruit leaders to disciple a whole nation, we attracted many who were newborn believers. They could hardly explain their faith. Most of them had a theophany (a visible manifestation of God). God had touched them in such a way that they decided Jesus was their God. They did not understand even a basic theology of salvation. In the HBI program we first taught them the basics of the gospel, and then how to share their faith with others in many contexts and ways. The gospel became a high priority and value, a natural part of their purpose for living, and they developed a high value for evangelism. After two years of equipping, these young trainees readily shared their faith and led many people to the Lord as a natural part of their life. They also acquired a bird's eye view of the Bible, an exposure to the key doctrines, and skills to study their Bible, conduct Bible studies, and prepare sermons.

Over several months, as these candidates learned how to study the Bible, they immediately began to teach others. The local people learned the same Bible study methods and some foundational principles to interpret Scripture that the trainee had learned. Many learned to lead others in Bible study. This teaching experience was revolutionary for the student, especially as he led others in Bible studies. The simplicity of the program enabled him to unearth deep truths from the Word of God, which transformed him personally, as well as those he taught. We found the students reading the Word, teaching it to others, and experiencing its powerful impact on their own lives and on those they influenced.

CASE STUDY: THE KUVI BARE FOOT MISSIONARIES

Sarat Jana, a student in one of our formal training programs called the Asian School of Evangelism (ASE) (training associate pastors and junior leaders to help build church-planting movements), caught a vision to multiply churches. He excelled in raising leaders with a vision to plant five churches and train five leaders. Three years into his program among the Kuvi people groups, God gave him so many new believers, he was not certain what to do with the ministry. He asked if we could help him train these people. We gladly accepted his request, developed a partnership with his mission, and over the next three years the whole group joined INEF.

The Kuvis live in the state of Orissa in the district of Rayagada. This tribal community made their living by hunting, growing crops, and collecting sticks that they sold to generate revenue. They spoke Kuvi and Oriya, but were not literate. Because of the nature of our training we accepted 56 of them into the Missionary Training Institute to equip them for the ministry.

The first time these men and women came to Chennai for training, they had not seen a train and knew nothing about how to travel by train. We arranged for them to be chaperoned and transported to our campus. It was a great shock for them to leave their forest area and come to the urban city of Chennai. One day during their first training week, they did not come to class. We found them sitting on the sidewalk with their mouths open and in shock watching the buses pass by our gates. The crowds stretched their imaginations, and the cultural learning for them continued over their first year of training.

Five years into the non-formal training they had learned to read the Word of God, interpret the Scriptures and preach sermons. They had led Bible studies and worship, had become key leaders in their community, and had recruited others into the movement, which in 2002 had grown to 120 bare foot national missionaries. Each of these missionaries planted a minimum of five churches, often guiding people movements to faith in Christ, and teaching for transformation in their villages.

While we are astonished to see their abilities and achievements, God is the architect of the impossible. Through the HBI non-formal programs, God equipped them to do evangelism, study the Word, plant churches, and lead the church and the people in the community. A number of them serve today as state coordinators.

FROM EVANGELISM TO CHURCH PLANTING

One of the primary goals of the MTI training was to equip trainees to start their first church in their home village, then to identify five unreached villages around them that were receptive to the gospel, and begin evangelism in those villages with the objective of planting new churches. Most of the trainees planted one church and could not progress any further. When the director of missions and our team of trainers evaluated the success of our trainees, we discovered that many had difficulty planting more than one church. As the number of church planters grew from 17 to 117, the average number of churches planted dropped from 2.4 to 1.5 per church planter. While we observed incredible growth in our trainees, the training was not sufficient to launch a movement of saturation church planting. So the Lord led us to the next level of the training, teaching the evangelist to plant and grow churches.

I am often asked what the church is. When I think of the church I am reminded of the words of Jesus to His disciples, "Upon this rock I will build My church" (Matthew 16:20). These are the words of Jesus in response to the confession of Peter, "Thou art the Christ, the Son of the Living God" (v. 16). The Church is a community of two or three individuals who affirm that Jesus is the Christ and gather together in His presence, under His lordship, to worship, and to study God's Word. Members exhort, equip, serve, and edify one another and seek to be transformed, incarnating Christ in all of His love and glory in communities so the world in seeing them will see the Father who is in heaven.

We learned that planting churches required skills different from doing evangelism, and without those skills we had only a proclamation ministry. So the director of missions, the training coordinator, and I developed a second level of training to equip the trainees to plant churches. This on-site training program (OST), on-the-job and field-based, engaged students for two more years of learning by observation and participation.

In the on-site program the training coordinator gathered the trainees in groups of 8-10 and organized training for them on the field in five-day training segments (See Table 2:2). He began by reviewing the methods taught in the MTI training and reinforced the training by showing them how to use various methods of evangelism more effectively. The trainer then demonstrated in practical ways how evangelistic efforts might be employed to plant churches.

Our most successful method of planting churches used the Jesus film in a strategic way to develop contacts. In 1990 we organized a special Jesus film ministry team at HBI to support the evangelistic outreach of local churches. The evangelists projected the film in the streets in three stages so people came back to see the movie each day. At the end of each day the team called people to respond for prayer, but not for a decision to be saved. Many individuals would come, and God used this to stimulate faith in individuals and collectively.

The morning after showing the first reel of the Jesus film the trainer and trainees visited the homes of those who responded for prayer. They encouraged them to talk to other members of their families, explain the story of the gospel, and invite them to come see the rest of the movie over the next two days. The trainer stressed that the evangelist should never call for a decision, but simply allow the people to see, hear, experience, process, and understand. Generally by the end of the week people were asking how they could become followers of Jesus. Through this process the instructors showed the trainees how to develop an initial group and take the next steps to see a church planted. The trainee who organized the film outreach in the village had responsibility to see that those who responded were nurtured and discipled to the Lord.

As they debriefed every day, the mentor repeatedly emphasized the process and the key dynamics involved beginning with the showing of the film. He explained about watching the response, praying for those who indicated a need for prayer, and why we call for prayer and not a decision. He also guided trainees daily in debriefing their visits to families, reviewing how to respond to return invitations in order to facilitate group responses to the film and decisions to follow Christ. This process allowed the mentor to interact with the students and coach them in how to plant a church.

TABLE 2.2
THE ON-SITE TRAINING PROGRAM

Practicum	Theoretical Training
1) Screening of Jesus Film First day – Screen reel one Second day – Morning visit houses for prayer Second day – Evening screen reel two Third day - Morning visit houses Third day - Screen reel three and call for commitment Fourth day – Visit those who responded Fifth day – Gather them in one place for worship.	1) Review methods of evangelism taught in MTI and discuss which ones work in their context and the results of implementing methods.
2) House visiting	2) Understanding and identifying spiritual gifts
3) Street preaching	3) Identifying and developing leaders
4) Literature distribution	4) Equipping them to teach a course on "Called to Shepherd" to the lay leaders
5) Prayer walk	5) Theory of church planting
6) Evening crusade meeting	6) Strategies for church planting
7) Counseling and prayer	7) Understanding how to be contextual

The on-site training had a major impact on our church-planting efforts. Soon many of the successful evangelists had gained skill and experience in planting more than one church. The following case studies illustrate some of the dynamics of the training and how God worked in each situation to establish His church.

CASE STUDY: ON-SITE TRAINING AMONG LAMBADIES

One of the trainees who worked among the Lambadies, a tribal people group, reported that he had shared his faith in a particular village and people listened with a lot of interest, but had not responded to the message. The trainee suggested that we do the on-site training in the village. He believed God had prepared this village and that many were ready to receive Jesus, but some obstacle kept them from responding. Sam Visvasam, the on-site training coordinator, organized a group of ten trainees to approach the village with the Jesus film. After the team projected the first reel of the film and witnessed to people in the streets, the leaders of the village met and discussed what influence the Jesus film might have on their people. That evening they instructed the religious leader to confront the team the next day and ask team members to leave the village.

On the second day the spiritual leader of the village met them in the public street to inform them they were not welcome in the village. Sam Visvasam and the trainees had never experienced such open opposition. But they sensed the power of the evil one confronting them like a wall, stopping them from preaching or entering farther into the village. Sam gathered the trainees in a corner of the village and simply began to pray. They called on the Lord and asked God to enable them to do His work. To their surprise the transparent wall they could not penetrate came down, and the spiritual opposition evaporated. People gathered to see the second reel of the film, and the local spiritual leader could not stop them. The elders who had opposed them were amazed at the spiritual power of the team. That day the whole village made a decision to become followers of Christ. The rest of the week they carried out the training, screened the rest of the Jesus film, preached in the streets, visited homes to explain the message of the Lord, prayed for the sick and conducted a village crusade. By the end of the week they planted a church with the whole village.

On that day we experienced real spiritual warfare and the great value of the on-site training. God demonstrated to these trainees that He would plant His church, and Satan could not stand against Him. In two years these trainees observed this process eight to ten times. They participated in the process and developed knowledge and skills of how churches are planted.

CASE STUDY: N. SUDARSANAM

N. Sudarsanam was born in a high caste Hindu family. His parents worshiped the Goddess Ellamma. He also worshiped idols while living in a village called Agraharam in the district of Kurnool in the state of Andhra Pradesh. He heard that Jesus is a great God and was the only God, but he said to himself, "Jesus is the God of the untouchables, how can He be so great?" Yet all he heard about Jesus fascinated him. So he got a gospel portion and began to read. His appetite increased and led him to save his money to buy a Bible. However, he avoided the local untouchable church, lest someone see and report him to the leaders in his village. After reading the Bible he gained courage to attend church, but came late, sat in the back to remain unnoticed, and left quickly before anyone could talk to him.

One day he became ill and doctors could not help. In desperation he prayed to Jesus who heard his prayer, and he was healed. He told his parents that Jesus healed him, and encouraged them to trust Christ. They resisted because they knew they would be thrown out of the village. Sudarsanam had a speech impediment, and had not done well in school. Since he was the only son of his parents, they tolerated his behavior, even though they called Jesus the god of untouchables.

Sudarsanam earned his living by caring for a herd of sheep. One day while watching his sheep, he sensed God's call upon his life and prayed that God would equip him for the ministry. In answer to his prayer God sent a believer into his life and Sudarsanam shared his story with him. This believer, whose son worked at HBI, told him, "HBI will certainly help you get equipped."

I remember Sudarsanam when he first came to HBI—timid, stuttering through every sentence he spoke, but very certain God had saved him and called him for His ministry. He had finished high school, but like any village shepherd, he had a very simple outlook on life. I watched him gain confidence as he went through the training. Today one would hardly know he is the man who had a speech impediment.

He started the training in 1985, barely staggering through the MTI program, and then he struggled to plant a church. The on-site, hands-on training, however, transformed Sudarsanam's leadership. After he worked on a team with others to plant a church, he found he could do it. Since then he has planted a total of 20 churches, constructed 12 church buildings, trained eight other pastor leaders, and is now a church-planting coordinator helping others to do what God helped him to accomplish.

The two cases above illustrate clearly the power of training through practical, on-site experience. Adults learn far better when they see and do ministry. God reinforced the process and practice of ministry in the minds of these individuals, and they had confidence to step out in faith. I observed that the curriculum each year did not change much, but the trainees gained a deeper understanding of what they had learned. We added only what was necessary to help them go to the next level of ministry effectiveness. We saw an immediate impact of the on-site training. From its inception in 1991 we saw an increase in the average number of churches per church planter each year. In 1991 we averaged 1.5 churches per missionary. By 1996 we averaged 3.0 churches per missionary, and by 2003 we averaged 4.5 churches per missionary. (See Table 2.3)

Some years into the program we expanded this experience to include the making of disciples and training leaders. We helped trainees to identify giftedness and leaders to equip them for leadership. During the two years of on-site training the trainees teach their local leaders a course entitled "Called to Shepherd." Developed by a veteran missionary to help pastors to train lay leaders in

TABLE 2:3
IMPACT OF NON-FORMAL TRAINING AND TRAINEES

Year	Non-Formal Training	Missionary Task Force	Churches Planted	Membership
1986	Indian National Evangelical Fellowship (INEC) started			
1985-86		2	12	
1986 – 87	Field training began	17	40	280
1987-88	**Missionary Training Institute (MTI) started (December 1987)**	36	81	380
1988-89		49	104	579
1989-90		74	131	723
1990-91	**On-site Training Started**	117	172	3068
1991-92		125	196	5612
1992-93	**Mobile Bible Institute (MBI) started (January 1993)**	146	249	8600
1993-94		158	280	13207
1994-95	**Pre-MTI started**	216	587	18716
1995-96		223	658	21373
1996-97		242	815	24746
1997-98		307	1091	38851
1998-99		342	1154	50427
1999-2000	**Training for Discipleship**	376	1463	66555
2000-2001		412	1652	86622
2001-2002		488	2117	102281
2002-2003		502	2346	108379

the local church, this course achieved a two-fold objective. First, it helped the national missionary to equip lay leaders. Second, it reinforced the knowledge and skill trainees had been exposed to in the first two years at MTI. By training the lay leaders for their church, they built a stronger foundation for themselves.

SHERWOOD'S REFLECTIONS ON
NON-FORMAL LEADERSHIP TRAINING

The lessons in this chapter have profound implications for mission and church leaders who have a vision to equip leaders for a church-planting movement. Bobby has clearly shown that non-formal training produced the leaders needed to fulfill his vision. As we conclude this chapter, I (Sherwood) will recap some of the themes that Bobby has presented and highlight some of the most important contributions of non-formal leadership training.

1. Non-formal training vastly expands the potential recruits. HBI's non-formal programs trained men and women who could never have been admitted to the formal degree programs. Further, some of their most successful church planters would not have succeeded in a formal program, even if they had been admitted. For those who seek to equip leaders for a movement, this is absolutely crucial.

2. Practical engagement quickly sifts out those who are not wired for, or committed to, the ministry. While Bobby did not emphasize this in the case study, those who dropped out because they would not or could not do the work saved the movement from a poor investment of people and resources. In formal education many persist who can do the academic work, but then fail in ministry. Since ministry is the main thrust of the non-formal, those who do not have the aptitude for it drop out early.

3. Experiential learning has powerful results for adult learners. This was illustrated in the case most powerfully through the addition of the on-site training for church planting. Table 2.3 shows how the addition of the on-site training had a multiplication effect on the number of churches planted. Once these evangelists experienced with others how to multiply churches, they did so with enthusiasm and effectiveness. While the MTI program of study at HBI helped evangelists to become more effective at nurturing new Christians, the experiential on-site training transformed the church-planting movement.

4. Evaluation and correction with reference to goal increases positive learning outcomes. Bobby and the HBI team have an

impressive record of evaluation and mid-course correction in their training programs. Each major adjustment they made over a fifteen-year period contributed in a significant way toward their goal of multiplying churches. In addition to these major corrections, they made smaller corrections to produce more effective leaders. Because they had a clear idea of the kind of leaders needed, they were able to adjust the training to achieve the goal.

5. The variable pace and repetition of learning serves the diversity of trainees, so that most succeed. The great diversity of trainees (illiterates to high school graduates, new converts to established lay leaders) would challenge any training program. Part of the genius of the repetitive series of trainings lies in their flexibility for the learner. Each phase of the training takes a student deeper than the previous one, yet the exact depth varies with each student. Individuals who progress rapidly become coaches for those following at a slower rate. Repetition enhances learning at every level, so all participants grow in their understanding and effectiveness. The data presented suggest that all who stayed with the program succeeded in planting and pastoring at least one church. Some of the most handicapped students at the outset actually exceeded the performance of better-prepared or more gifted peers.

6. On-site mentoring advances student learning. Mentors play an important role in all the training components. Trainer mentors and peer mentors assist trainees in the development of spiritual disciplines, character, and skill for ministry. The on-site mentoring for church planting seemed to have the most powerful impact on student learning. The faith and obedience to God of a mentor has a profound effect on trainees, as was illustrated in the case study of Sam Vivasam among the Lambadies.

7. Empowerment of trainees to train others serves to multiply leaders and followers. The practice of teaching trainees to teach their new converts and teaching new converts to teach their families had a profound multiplication effect when it was implemented well. This most powerful strategy of the MTI

and on-site trainings led to the multiplication of leaders in every one of the cases recounted in the chapter. When a trainee produced other leaders, these leaders added new converts and started new churches.

CHAPTER 2. RESEARCH AND REFLECTION QUESTIONS:

Research Exercise: Find a dynamic growing church in your community and interview one of the pastors to learn about its ministries:

1. How many of the ministries are led by people with formal training?
2. How many of the ministry leaders have only a high school education?
3. How were these leaders without formal training equipped for ministry?

Reflection:

4. Can you find examples of "non-formal" training in this local church?
5. What similarities and differences do you see between training in this local church and the programs of HBI?

CHAPTER THREE

Assessing Impact: Mid-Course Corrections

How do you know when you have achieved your goal? Starting with some clear ends in mind makes the task much easier. HBI had very clearly defined ends— recruiting people with a passion for evangelism, five or more churches for each church planter, and churches that reproduced other churches. But even with clear ends in mind, one must gather statistics and use qualitative measures to evaluate the impact of the training.

Radical change has its risks, and without ongoing evaluation the flaws in any plan will surely lead to unintended consequences. Very early in the implementation of the non-formal paradigm, Bobby and the team committed to continuous evaluation of the performance and impact of their trainees. In this chapter, we learn of some mid-course corrections that led to greater effectiveness of the ministry.

—Sherwood Lingenfelter

In chapter two we described how HBI developed a non-formal training program to produce leaders committed to evangelism and the multiplication of churches. At that time we agreed to support and send out these trainees to plant churches under the umbrella of the Indian National Evangelical Fellowship. As these men and women planted churches, their disciples planted other churches and the fellowship of local churches grew. In 2001 these churches organized together as the Indian National Evangelical Church (INEC), a denomination founded with a vision to fulfill the Great Commission of making disciples.

Non-formal training, like formal training, also has its weaknesses. After five years of training leaders in MTI and two years of on-site church planting, we began to observe weaknesses. INEF church planters spent all their energy and time planting churches and discipling new believers. This left little or no time for reflection or developing skills at interpreting Scripture. Because they are oral learners, they often listened to others and developed inconsistent and sometimes erroneous interpretations of Scripture. As a result they lacked strong biblical foundations, and could not give foundational teaching. After training these evangelists to be church planters and watching them plant many churches, we saw the need to train them further as pastors.

One illustration of this problem came from an MTI graduate serving as a pastor, who developed an idiosyncratic interpretation of the Good Samaritan story. According to this pastor, the traveler on the donkey represented "the lost," the thieves that attacked him represented Satan and his power, the Levite and priest represented the religious leaders in the church, and the Good Samaritan was Jesus. The oil the Samaritan poured on the wounds of the traveler was the Holy Spirit, the inn was the church, the innkeeper the pastor, and the two coins represented the two sacraments of the church. When I heard this kind of interpretation, I realized the need for our pastors to have a clearer understanding of how to interpret Scripture.

At first we invited our pastor/evangelists to attend a formal, residential type of training for a year or two. But we had an interesting problem! They all had congregations and did not want to come. So we had to develop a non-formal process of advanced training, the Mobile Bible Institute (MBI) programs, which we launched in 1993 (See Table 3.1). We aimed to equip these leaders to teach accurately the Word of God and develop in their church communities a deeper understanding of the Scriptures so believers would grow in the grace and knowledge of Christ.

The Pastoral Stage: The Mobile Bible Training

MBI provides three years of training, organized into five-day training sessions, six times a year. The training increases the depth of the pastors' understanding of Scripture and interpreting the text for ministry. Teaching them both biblical and systematic theology reinforces their theological understanding. A course in interpreting Scripture, along with a course on the religions of India, enables them to contextualize the message and make relevant applications to their local congregations. To advance their pastoral skills we train them in advanced sermon preparation, counseling, management, stewardship, and building a disciple making church.

We give these leaders every opportunity to finish the program, and when they finish, they have the equivalent of a Bible college diploma. For those who complete the program, the Indian National Evangelical Church (INEC) examines them for ordination. Each candidate attends an ordination review course, and then a council of multi-denominational pastor leaders interviews the candidate and his wife. This council examines their confession of faith, understanding of Scripture, and call to ministry. They also inquire into their reputation in their local community and church and review the significance of their ministry. The council confers ordination only if the wife agrees with her husband in his call and the state coordinator supports the application.

TABLE 3:1
MOBILE BIBLE INSTITUTE

Year	Course 1	Course 2	Course 3	Course 4	Course 5	Course 6
First Year	Introduction to the OT	Introduction To The NT	Biblical Theology	Contemporary Religion - Hinduism	Cross Cultural Ministry	Developing a Disciple-Making Church
Second Year	OT Survey	NT Survey	Systematic Theology	Contemporary Religion- Islam	Leadership & Stewardship	Developing Small Groups
Third Year	Hermeneutics	Advanced Sermon Preparation	Management Skills	Contemporary Religion – Animism, Jainism, etc.	Pastoral Counseling	Managing and Multiplying Disciple-Making Churches

Training for the pastors never stops in a non-formal context. We have observed that if a leader moves on before the equipping process is complete, or if the roots of the church are not deep, the church may not survive. Training is very important to bring the church to where it can sustain and become reproducible. For example, Mr. P joined our program and went through the first two years of the MTI training. At the end of the training he felt he could sustain himself and decided to separate from INEC and continue on his own. Within a very short time we found that his church stopped meeting and the pastor was no longer involved in building the church. We have found that it takes at least four years of mentoring a non-formal trainee to develop stability in a church. While other church-planting movements in India discontinue training and support after two years, we believe that is not long enough. In the non-formal process continuing training is a non-negotiable if the new churches are to mature and reproduce.

One of the strengths of the non-formal paradigm is its flexibility. As we watched and listened to our church planters, we learned to evaluate their effectiveness, discover what was needed, and make alterations in the training modules. Over a fifteen-year period we made many small changes in what has become a seven-year program for church planters (MTI, On-site, and MBI). Yet we still found it necessary to make two more major adjustments in the process. The first we called the Pre-MTI and the second a training on Making Disciples.

PRE-MISSIONARY TRAINING INSTITUTE

In 1993 the missions department noticed that placing all the new recruits into MTI was not working well. Some came as new converts; others had spent years being nurtured in a local church. As a consequence, they progressed at very different rates, so that some trainees planted churches and developed leaders before they finished their first year of training. Others lacked biblical foundations and lagged far behind their peers in MTI.

Another challenge came from the increase in applications for these programs. By 1993 applications were coming from all across India and our recruiting process had to be streamlined.

Third, the INEC church was growing and the local pastors wanted HBI to provide a short training for the leaders in their local churches. Many of the trainees who came from the INEC churches subsequently applied to the mission and were recruited into the task forces and the training teams.

To address these concerns, in 1994 we introduced the Pre-Missionary Training Institute to prepare new converts for the MTI training (See Table 3.2). During these thirty days of intensive study, students learn basic Bible, doctrines, evangelism, and spiritual disciplines to grow in Christ. They memorize key biblical passages that relate to the major doctrines of Scripture, recite the books of the Bible, read their Bible systematically, do simple Bible studies, and appreciate the uniqueness of the Scriptures. They practice communicating their personal testimony and leading a person to the Lord. When students complete the training they must share their faith and the clear message of the gospel. The Pre-MTI program gives the trainee and the trainer sufficient informa-

TABLE 3:2
PRE-MISSIONARY TRAINING INSTITUTE

Week I	Week II	Week III	Week IV
Introduction to the Bible Inspiration and the Unity of the Bible	The Unique Books and Sections	History of Translation and Different Translations of the Bible	The Relationship Between Old and New Testament
Introduction to Bible Doctrine Definition- Doctrine	Doctrine and the Bible	Doctrine of God, Man, and Sin and Salvation	Doctrine of Church and Mission
Spiritual Growth– Discipleship Importance of Personal Bible Study Methods of Bible Study	**Spiritual Growth– Discipleship** Methods: Church/Group Individual/Personal Family	**Spiritual Growth– Discipleship** Techniques and Tools Employed in Personal Bible Study	**Spiritual Growth– Discipleship** Importance of Prayer Discipleship- Introduction
Personal Evangelism Definition of Evangelism The Need for Evangelism	**Personal Evangelism** Evangelism and Bible Methods of Evangelism	**Personal Evangelism** Methods of Evangelism-cont.	**Personal Evangelism** Jesus the Evangelist and Different Steps to Evangelism

tion before HBI/INEC selects candidates to join the ministries or serve as leaders-in-training for the mission.

CASE STUDY: OSBORN SOI

Osborn Soi is from a tribal group called Mundas in the state of Jharkand in North India. Every day for 18 years he saw his wife lie in bed with debilitating sickness. She continued to deteriorate and the whole Munda village was expecting her to die. In August 2002, Soi visited a nearby town on business. While in the marketplace, he heard a man who spoke with authority about Jesus. He said, "Any of you can ask Jesus to help you with any of your problems and sickness. He will answer your request because He is the true and living God."

With these words ringing in his ears Soi traveled back to his village by bus. He was wondering who this Jesus was? He knew that his wife would die anytime. That night he decided to call on the name of Jesus and said, "Jesus, I don't know who you are, but that man stood in the market street and said that anyone can ask you and you will help. Please heal my wife!" This became his daily prayer.

Over a period of three months, his wife became progressively better. After three months she got out of bed and people saw her on her feet for the first time in 18 years. This surprised the entire village and everyone asked him which doctor treated her and how did she get well? He had to think about it, but then proceeded to tell them that he did not take her to a doctor. Instead he said, "One day I heard a man in the market who said to ask Jesus to solve our problems and he will heal our sickness. That night I began to call on this name Jesus and every day and night I kept calling him and realized that my wife was getting better."

Many of the village people wanted to know who this Jesus was, because they, like Soi, had never heard the name of Jesus. Soi told them he did not know who Jesus is, but he believed that Jesus is a god who can do anything. People began to bring their sick to Soi to pray and ask Jesus to heal them. To his surprise, Jesus kept answering his prayers.

Into this context, the director of missions and the associate director responsible for the cross-cultural missions program of HBI visited Soi's village. They asked God to lead them to an unreached people group, and God led them to Soi. When they listened to the whole story, they were awestruck at how God had led them to this village and people group. Soi wanted to know more about Christ, so they shared the gospel with him, and he accepted Christ as his personal lord and savior. He quickly expressed his desire to know more, so they invited him to come to the Pre-Missionary Training Institute (Pre-MTI).

After 30 days of training, Soi asked to join our missions program and serve the Lord. Today Soi is ministering in his own village, sharing the good news of Jesus, and continuing in the MTI training for ministry. By the end of his first two ten-day training sessions, Soi started his first worship center and began evangelism in seven other villages. As he listened to others he met in the movement, he learned how to identify other leaders, and he started training them in the things he was learning. These men have now become as committed to evangelism as Soi.

Pre-MTI fills a key need for people like Soi. Through this one month "head start" they are better prepared to implement the ministry training of MTI. The flexibility and the focus of the training helped us to make the design work for the diverse training needs of our students.

TRAINING FOR DISCIPLESHIP

From the beginning in 1987 we trained INEC workers to mobilize the body, identify gifts, and equip the new leaders. Within the first five years of ministry we set a goal that an INEC church planter identify, equip, and enable 30 leaders to do the ministry of the church. Through this process 500 apostolic type leaders have facilitated the planting of more than 2,300 churches from 1987 to 2003.

Through these years of church planting we learned a hard lesson about the difference between church planting and church growth. In the early years we focused on planting new churches. Our leaders were very successful in planting churches, but they could not grow churches. In reflecting on this problem, we discovered that our church planters did not make disciples of new believers. Our teams planted many churches but they were not growing. This discovery led to a second major change in the non-formal program—discipleship training. In 1999 Bob Gilliam, a consultant, shared with us that churches do not grow because they do not make disciples. He helped us see that the only way a church will grow is when the church planter takes time to make disciples and empower others intentionally to help him in the process.

Bob shared with us how Jesus took His disciples through a four-stage process: "Come and see," "Follow me," "Learn from me," and "Remain with me." Bob partnered with us in July 2000, teaching our pastors to enable their churches to grow by making disciples of new believers. We applied this process and in the first year those who went through the training began to see growth. By the second year they had doubled the numbers of people in their churches. So at this stage in the training we now equip our trainees to make disciples.

When we learned to develop leadership in the local church, and empower these leaders to disciple others in the body of Christ, the churches grew and Christ was exalted. In the first 12 years of INEF our churches grew from 20 members to about 60,000 believers. But after these believers were equipped to make disciples, the churches grew from 60,000 to about 110,000. Through this experience we have learned that when the local church takes responsibility to develop leaders and disciple its people, the church will grow. (See Figure 3.1)

INEC has set a goal to develop 2,000 pastors in the movement by 2020, and to encourage each pastor to plant five churches and train five leaders. We seek to mobilize the INEC churches to plant a total of 10,000 churches and disciple 1,000,000 believers. In order to accomplish this task it will be necessary for the INEC pastors to be intentional in their vision to make disciples and develop leadership in the local church by equipping them to serve the Lord.

The New Testament is clear that the mission of the church is to be God's instrument to disciple peoples of the nations into reconciliation with Him. Jesus said, "I will build my church" and it is

He who is building the church. It is clear that God has given people with diverse gifts to the church, and the leaders have responsibility to equip them for the various ministries to fulfill the mission of the church.

FIGURE 3:1
IMPACT OF TRAINING TO VISION AND PURPOSE

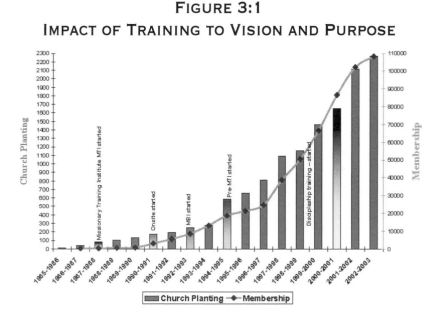

ASSESSING OUTCOMES OF FORMAL AND NON-FORMAL EDUCATION

Most formal training programs give the student volumes of information. An average undergraduate student will read about 500 pages per course and a graduate or postgraduate student will read on average 2,000 to 3,000 pages per course. This provides a great foundation and knowledge on the subject. This is truly the strength of the program. The weakness of formal education is the absence of experience within which to process the data. The formal method provides information without context and with very little practice, so the student does not see its relationship to life. Too often students go into a job thinking they know the essentials, only to learn later what they really did not know. Information without character or skill development can lead to a very frustrating and dangerous end.

I remember during my seminary days I was given an opportunity to do practice preaching, a one-time chapel sermon, for which I was given a grade. I gained some basic tools but when I had to apply them, I was overwhelmed, lacking a mentor to whom I could go for help. Given the option to sink or swim, I sank, because I was in a context where I could not seek help.

As the Lord led us in the implementation of this new paradigm, we discovered that the trainees acquired skills and accomplished the objectives for which they were trained. We also observed how God transformed their lives, strengthened their character and self-esteem, and motivated them through biblical values to minister to others and lead many people to Jesus Christ.

The contrast between the students in the non-formal and formal programs at HBI is striking. The 482 students who had spent two to five years in our theological development program had degrees, but few pastoral skills for ministry. A less-educated trainee enrolled in five years of non-formal training had learned to share his faith, developed 25-30 leaders in a local church, and often planted three to five churches where churches did not previously exist. The more than 500 non-formal graduates had planted an average of 4.5 churches each and were supervising ministries that they had watched the Lord develop through their efforts in a number of locations and people groups (See Table 3.3).

The church in India can never develop enough pastors in a formal context to fulfill the task of discipling India for Christ. The task is so complex it will have to be done by those who remain in their villages, who are comfortable with their context and accepted by those local people. If discipling the nation of India is to take place, it is my belief that the large majority of leaders must be trained through non-formal and informal methods of leadership training.

SHERWOOD'S REFLECTIONS ON NON-FORMAL LEADERSHIP TRAINING

One of the significant strengths of Bobby's leadership of this training and church-planting movement is his commitment to continuous assessment of outcomes in reference to their clearly defined "ends." They collect and analyze data in each training cycle to discern how well each individual is performing, and to discern the impact of the movement. One of the most remarkable parts of this story for me (Sherwood) is the record of "course corrections" and the impact they had for the overall movement.

TABLE 3:3
COMPARISON OF FORMAL
AND NON-FORMAL GRADUATES

Year	Formal					Non-Formal		
	B.Th	MDiv	MBS	M.Th	ASE* DTE	MTI	Church Plants	Members
1986-87	30					17	40	280
1987-88	29					36	81	380
1988-89	22					49	104	579
1989-90	31					74	131	723
1990-91	23					117	172	3,068
1991-92	26					125	196	5,612
1992-93	7				18	146	249	8,600
1993-94	5				13	158	280	13,207
1994-95	4				8	216	587	18,716
1995-96	-				46	223	658	21,373
1996-97	-	6			97	242	815	24,746
1997-98	-	11			102	307	1,091	38,851
1998-99	-	16	23		129	342	1,154	50,427
1999-00	25	17	13		159	376	1,463	66555
2000-01	21	21	19	3	118	412	1,652	86,622
2001-02	22	25	15	5	170	488	2,117	102,281
2002-03	16	18	22	7	187	502	2,272	108,379
Total Grads	261	114	92	15	1047	502		

*ASE is a formal diploma program started in 1992 by the HBI church mobilization department in partnership with Evangelism Resources, Louisville, Kentucky, to equip young church pastors and associates with vision and skills for church planting. DTE is a formal diploma program for discipleship training started in 1995. HBI offered this training at eight different centers in 2003.

As Bobby shared in his evaluation of some of the mature pastors in this movement, non-formal training also has its weaknesses. As with most aspects of leadership, areas of strength always have some inherent weakness. A careful review of each of the strengths identified in Chapter 2 will also reveal an area of potential failure. Bobby has focused upon three of these weaknesses that I will recap here.

1. Quality control is dispersed in non-formal training, requiring frequent repetition to impart patterns. The fact that so many are engaged in the training of leaders insures that the process will be sloppy, and many will not be trained well. We know that some change occurs in any message each time it is passed from one person to the next. While the repetition in the long cycle of trainings works to correct this type of error, nothing will assure sound doctrine and right interpretation as well as formal training.

2. Reflection and deep thinking are sacrificed to activism. Bobby noted that the veteran pastors in the movement were too busy to take a year off for formal training. This also is typical of "movement" leaders. Nurtured in an activist paradigm, and then extended to capacity by their success in training others, they no longer have time for essential reflection and self-evaluation. Movement leaders, as a consequence, fall into habitual patterns of teaching and practice that may distort Scripture and become self-serving in the practice of ministry.

3. Error or omission can have a major impact on outcomes (e.g. making disciples). The last weakness Bobby identifies is in the effectiveness of the non-formal training paradigm. Bobby notes how over the fifteen years they employed a continuing process of evaluation with reference to their goals. Along the way they discovered numerous flaws in the training that they then attempted to correct. However, even with this serious commitment to evaluation and adjustment, they missed a fundamental flaw in their church-planting efforts. They had not trained their leaders to make disciples of new believers effectively. Fortunately, God led them to invite a consultant to critique their ministry, and through Bob Gilliam they discovered this problem.

Bobby has made it clear throughout this story that God is the author of the vision and the power for its implementation. Therefore it is important to acknowledge that the non-formal paradigm has no power of its own. It is merely a tool that allows us to equip a diverse group of people who have been called of God to serve as leaders in His church-planting movement. The most important command is the one Jesus gave to His disciples, "If anyone would come after me, he must deny himself and take up his cross and follow me." (Matt. 16:24) To equip leaders for a church-planting movement we must begin with some very basic questions: Where is God already at work? Whom is God calling to serve? How can we serve God's purpose to make disciples and support those He has called? How are we blinded by our habits and thus fail to discern God's purpose or plan of action? Who is God sending to teach us what we cannot see on our own? Only as we listen to God and learn from God, and only then, will we accomplish God's purpose.

CHAPTER 3. RESEARCH AND REFLECTION QUESTIONS:

Research Exercise: Interview a missionary who works as a church planter in his or her home country or abroad. Ask the following questions:

1. What kind of training does his organization provide for church planting?
2. How does she evaluate the impact of the training and mission strategy toward the achievement of her goals?
3. What evidence does the missionary see of the movement of the Holy Spirit among the people he is trying to reach?

Reflection:

4. What are the similarities and differences between the evaluation processes of that movement and the HBI/INEC movement?
5. What balance do you see between assessment of training and practice, and the work of the Holy Spirit in leading to effective evangelism and church planting?

CHAPTER FOUR

DEVELOPING CROSS-CULTURAL MISSIONARIES

One of the most common mistakes of church leaders is the temptation to export success! In this chapter Bobby confesses that, rejoicing in the fruit of their non-formal training, they fell into this trap. Knowing that India has so many unreached peoples, in their excitement of God's blessing their church planters in South India, they decided to send some of these evangelists to other language groups in North India.

Planting churches outside their own language area proved far more challenging that anyone imagined. Indians found cross-cultural evangelism in their own nation as difficult or more so than going to Europe or Africa. Bobby and his team discovered that HBI's non-formal training for church planters working in their own cultures failed utterly to prepare cross-cultural missionaries. To meet this challenge, they had to develop a completely new training program and recruit more highly educated couples to equip for this task.

—Sherwood Lingenfelter

The non-formal training at HBI produced evangelists and church planters who, after returning to their home communities, achieved our expectations and goals for church planting. We learned early, however, that the program did not produce missionary evangelists capable of moving into other cultures in India. In a missions conference in 1991, the Indian National Evangelical

Fellowship (INEF) stressed the need for missionaries to North India. The conference adopted a vision to identify unreached people groups in North India and establish church-planting movements among them. Several pastors and young people indicated a willingness to go. INEC leaders organized them into teams and commissioned them to serve in various locations outside of India, including Indonesia.

In 1992 two young men shared their desire to work in the state of Maharashtra among the poor. With the support of the leaders and their church, they went to the largest slum in Asia on the outskirts of Mumbai in the city of Thane. In two years the team developed a cell group that had the makings of a church. They requested INEC to help build a church building. Excited about the success of the team, we raised the money and God helped us build the building.

On completion of the building the team invited me to speak at the dedication service. In the fall of 1995, I flew to Mumbai for the celebration. As the people gathered for the service I realized that these missionaries pioneered a church plant in an unreached location, but the people in the church were culturally identical to the team. These two dedicated servants did not know how to work outside their own language and culture. They planted a church among a people group that originated from their home state. They were church planters, but not cross-cultural missionaries.

At this point I realized that our training had not been adequate. These committed people, sent without preparation to work cross-culturally, did what came naturally to them. After they settled in Thane, they made friends with unbelievers who spoke their language, led them to Christ, and planted a church. They were not prepared for the challenge of learning a new language and culture, and sustaining a cross-cultural witness. In this chapter I will tell how we learned to equip leaders for cross-cultural evangelism and planting churches among unreached people groups.

THE NEED AND CHALLENGE

Today India has more than 4,693 distinct people groups (K. S. Singh 1998). The Indian Missions Association has estimated that only 10 percent of these people groups have any significant Christian witness among them. When we map the demographics of Christianity in India, we find that 80 percent of the Christians live among 20 percent of the population and 20 percent of the remaining Christians live among the 80 percent of India's population. Unless Christian workers make an intentional effort to move into these unreached communities and become cross-cultural witnesses, much of India will remain unreached.

To reach these distinct groups, India must equip and mobilize a large number of cross-culturally trained missionaries. Only in the last 15 years has the church become seriously aware of this reality and acted to target unreached people groups in the nation. We learned from the Mumbai experience that unless the team is intentional from the outset to reach a specific unreached people, they will not succeed. To do cross-cultural church planting they must begin with a vision to reach a sizable community in the new language area, with the goal of establishing an indigenous church and enabling a church-planting movement.

Second, unless we prepare a team with the right expectations, they will become discouraged, and either be tempted to shift their efforts to a more receptive group, or leave the field and return home. For example, many missionaries who went to Rajasthan became discouraged because of their inability to penetrate and establish a Rajasthani church, and so they started a work outside the Rajasthani people. Missionaries must be equipped to face resistance, to accept a slow response, and to overcome the temptation of losing sight of the targeted group.

Third, without proper skills and tools to enter and live effectively in another culture, missionaries are likely to dislocate themselves and the people. The church they plant will not be contextual to the community and will struggle to become indigenous. We must equip teams with the proper tools and skills to be effective. I have observed that most of the mission and church organizations working in India remain unaware of the cultural complexity of its unreached peoples. Indian national mission organizations have yet to understand the need and process of training workers to cross cultures. Until we grasp this reality, we cannot fulfill the desire of the Lord to have worshipers around His throne from every language and people group.

Fourth, the role of the missionary is not to plant churches but to facilitate a church-planting movement by identifying and enabling the giftedness of the people being discipled in the community. He should encourage the community to use forms and styles of worship, music, leadership, communication, community, and learning that are contextual to the culture of the people. As a result, the church will look like a worshiping community that is culturally relevant to them and not like the church culture of the missionary. Too often the missionary becomes the church planter, and the worshiping community has the appearance of the church the missionary represents.

For example, a Tamil missionary going to a Bengali community may do evangelism, disciple a community, and plant a church. The church may use the Bengali language, but it might look like a church that resembles a Tamil community. If the Bengali people are going to join this community in large numbers and experience total transformation, the church must radiate and embrace its cultural forms and styles so the people assume ownership and can celebrate Christ in their own form. Only if we allow such contextualization can God bring forth the necessary individual and community transformation as they study, understand, and apply God's Word to their lives, values, and practices.

When the missionary becomes the church planter and not the facilitator of a church-planting movement, he will attract individuals who are deviants from the local culture and are, most likely, more comfortable with the missionary's culture. Thus, they lose the ability to establish a true church-planting movement with the capacity to allow God to bring forth the necessary community transformation and to have intimacy with Christ.

A NON-FORMAL PROGRAM FOR CROSS-CULTURAL LEADERS

We asked the question, "How should we train Indian cross-cultural leaders and teams?" When we looked at the North American missionary training programs, we saw formal training conducted over a period of two to three years. In addition to a year or more of study in Bible and theology, students learn cultural anthropology, social structures, contextualization, and cross-cultural communication. These schools expect their graduates to leave with a sound foundation in Bible and theology and the basic skills necessary to live and work cross-culturally, but they leave the challenges of ministry to a post-graduate mission experience.

We looked at these formal programs and asked how we might design a better program for Indian learners. The formal academic process did not provide trainees sufficient opportunity to understand the new concepts. We decided that the training should include some practical experience and mentoring. We sought and found a way that students could learn the complex concepts of culture, social structures, and contextualization experientially.

Most of the people who responded to the call of missions at HBI were mature and had done some ministry or vocation. Therefore we decided to implement the training through the non-formal method, focusing on adult learning. Following a model parallel to HBI's Missionary Training Institute program, we first exposed them to cultural studies and then sent them to the field to practice what they had learned. It made the learning process progressive and interactive. The phases of this training program are explained in detail below.

PHASE 1. LIVING CROSS-CULTURALLY

The first phase, taught over three months, builds foundational knowledge and skills to prepare students for a short-term cross-cultural internship. In regular classroom sessions we teach foundational information on cultural anthropology and social structures. Students learn the basic tools of field research, preparing them to gather information, make observations, and prepare a report on culture and social structure. They must use these tools in the field phase of their internship and present a report when they return. We also introduce them to the library research process, requiring them to gather information and write a description of the people group they will live among and study during their field internship. We also teach survival skills, to enable the team to cope with difficult situations. They learn to cook with firewood, fix a flat on a bicycle, diagnose an illness, treat dehydration, plant a family garden, and preserve fresh produce by canning.

Very early on, we expose students to the concept of culture shock. Even though this idea makes no sense to them until they have the experience, we have learned that they need advance warning. The very first team we sent to Bihar in North India had a severe culture shock experience for which we had not prepared them. They arrived in Bihar in a very cold winter, clothed for sunny south India, and carrying a newborn baby. The local contact person appeared very indifferent, making them wait in the freezing cold. When he finally decided to be hospitable, he seemed very rude. No one spoke their language which increased their isolation and helplessness. They reacted first with anger and then with insecurity and fear that they would not survive the winter. The only reason they did not return was the fear of shame and defeat. They decided to tough it out, knowing they could return home in three months. From the experience of this team we learned to equip students to prepare for culture shock.

After three months of classroom work, they form teams of four or five (two couples and a single) and go to a selected location to do a field study on an assigned unreached people group. The trainees may not connect with other linguistic and cultural groups in that area. Their assignment is to apply the knowledge and research skills they have learned and gather data on the targeted people group.

The field internship experience lasts for three months. During that time the students must complete a cultural study, and from that data identify ways of bridging into the community. From their observation and interaction with the people, they must reflect on how gospel witness and a church community might uplift the community. The critical test of their effectiveness is whether or not these people invite them back. If the people love them, they have learned the essentials of building relationships and they will thrive as cross-cultural missionaries.

When they return to HBI, they must submit a written report that includes their cultural analysis and ministry recommendations on the unreached people group. Each team must demonstrate in their report their understanding of the social structure, the decision-making process, the religious beliefs, the social needs, and economic conditions of the people group. The report must include a detailed map of the village, and a description of village activities and social groups in it. As teams listen to each other, they learn from each of the presentations and contribute to each other's learning. The report is an indicator to the instructor of how much they have learned from the first part of the training.

In the first four years of this program, we found that the trainees learned these complex concepts well. They appreciated the training, and were ready to interact with the mentor. They understood cross-cultural communication theory and realized its significance to understand the people and find a way to communicate the message contextually. They knew that God alone reaches the people group, but they must become effective instruments. They gave up the desire to go ahead of the Lord in seeking to evangelize the people.

The cross-cultural internship enables the family to cope with and not fear the unknown. They experience many difficult situations and see the hand of the Lord protect them in every circumstance. Most of the trainees return with greater confidence to fulfill their call. At the end of the three-month experience, they choose either to commit to the task or look for other kinds of ministry.

PHASE 2. MINISTERING CROSS-CULTURALLY

We begin the second phase of the training by focusing on the call and role of a cross-cultural missionary. Sometimes these candidates are not clear about the implications of the decision they have made to serve cross-culturally. If this is not settled, later when they have worked hard without results or have experienced suffering or persecution, they will be strongly tempted to give up. After making very clear the nature and function of their role, and before they advance to the next two-year assignment, we ask them to recommit to their call to cross-cultural missions.

Once they have renewed their commitment, we reinforce the vision of facilitating an indigenous church-planting movement. Sometimes candidates think the mission is to start and pastor a church. We make it very clear that a missionary should never become the pastor of a new church plant among an unreached people group. Following the vision of the mission, the team will serve as a catalyst to get the movement started. From the beginning the missionaries must understand that they need to identify gifts in new believers and equip them to do the ministry of the church.

The team must understand the goal—evangelism and making disciples to develop a church-planting movement among the unreached population. They must accept responsibility to make disciples of new believers and then equip them to witness to and make disciples of others in the people group. When the new disciples in that people group take leadership and ownership of the task, the effort of the team will result in an indigenous church. They will know they are successful when they have mobilized the new church to reach its own community and then other unreached peoples.

To equip them to understand the people group better, to contextualize the gospel message, and to indigenize the church, we teach them advanced concepts in cultural anthropology, social structure, contextualization, and cross-cultural communication. Through these concepts we expect them to learn to accept and appreciate the culture of the people and not to violate the cultural norms. We seek to prevent the alienation of new believers from their community, or the introduction of practices that will not be indigenous and locally sustainable.

To enhance their ability to live in what often are isolated communities, they learn basic medicine to treat themselves and others where there is no doctor. They also learn the value of building bridges through serving the social, educational, and economic concerns of the people, and we expose them to a variety of ways in which they might offer such service.

The debriefing sessions with other teams returning from six months of ministry provide one of our most important techniques for teaching and learning. Candidates listen and learn from the experience of others on the field. Through these stories and discussions all the participants develop vision and gain strategic insights on how to love and witness to the unreached.

Finally they practice skills for team-building so that they develop synergy and work as a team. Most Indians are interdependent and they understand working in teams. In order to ensure good team relationships, however, we develop team-building skills and service. During their training they also network with local churches and cell groups who adopt them and commit to pray for and stay connected with them. The support of the local church becomes a great encouragement to the team.

DEBRIEFING: IN-SERVICE MINISTRY TRAINING

Once a team has completed Phase 2 of the pre-ministry training, we send them out to the selected people group, and the team finds a strategic location where they live and begin their ministry. For the next two years they return to Chennai once every six months to report on their progress to missions department staff and to debrief with others. Debriefing once in six months is essential for these new missionaries. Living in a different culture is lonely. They do not fit in the community. As outsiders they are suspect. As learners they often are overcome with fear. Debriefing provides both a break and reassurance. Missionaries learn many lessons from each other and provide mutual encouragement. They also help one another in the creative process of building bridges for gospel witness.

Listening to one another has become one of our most powerful training techniques. When they can get out of the ministry environment, discuss with others objectively, and make decisions with the counsel of many, it reduces the risk of making cultural blunders and provides wisdom for effective ministry decisions. Teams report their progress and others provide objective assessment of what they report. Too often missionaries are subjective about difficulties they experience in building relationships, and they are not sure what their experiences mean. As they share their feelings and experiences, the group and the mentor help them process their experience and learn from it.

At one of the debriefing sessions a team shared how the people in their ministry community refused to allow them into their homes. The team described how they would stop at a house, call or knock, and the inhabitants would step outside to visit with them. The team interpreted this practice as rude and rejection of them as persons. Later in the session they reported that many men in this village worked in construction, but stealing was the most common way to enhance one's income. As soon as they shared this information, one of their peers suggested that perhaps these people excluded outsiders from their home to protect themselves from becoming the target of thieves. Another encouraged them to break the pattern by inviting locals to their home. When they returned to their town of ministry, they tried this strategy. For a while the local people refused to enter their house. But when they invited children to come in for help with schoolwork, they accepted. This broke the pattern! Soon adults came to consult with the missionaries about their children, providing a ministry bridge into the community.

Loneliness and discouragement often surface in the debriefing sessions. Many need affirmation about their efforts. Others, anxious to share their faith, feel uncertain about the right time and place. One team working in the state of Rajasthan was so discouraged they wanted to leave and start in another location. People from the community had rejected them and some had vandalized their house. When the session ended that day, the director of missions, in a private meeting with them, asked them to stop all ministry activity, focus on praying, and ask God to open the door. They returned to Rajasthan and followed his instructions.

God opened the door for them in a wonderful way. At Christmastime, one of the missionaries bought a star and hung it in the front of their home. To their surprise the children in the community came and asked what the star represented, so they shared the story of Jesus. These children went home and shared the story of the star with their family. Soon other families wanted to hear the story, and asked the missionaries to celebrate the occasion. One of the boys said, "I want to put a cross next to the star," and he made a cross, which the missionaries put up next to the star. As a result of this star, many in the community heard the whole message of the gospel. Since this event the doors opened, and three leaders in the town requested baptism. Another young man indicated a desire to join them in the ministry. Out of this beginning they have taught these new believers and sent them out to disciple the rest of the community.

Debriefing is a time for us to resolve conflicts missionaries have about decisions on cultural issues. Many times missionaries deal with cultural conflicts. The debriefing is a safe place to discuss the matter and help them find resolution. On one occasion a missionary reported how people in their ministry community accused him of living with a woman who was not his wife. In that community all married women adorn their arms with bangles. Since the missionary's wife did not wear bangles, they concluded that she was not his wife. He moaned to his colleagues, "I have lost my credibility. If I do not follow the custom I will not gain acceptance!" For this couple, wearing bangles compromised their Christian values. They shared this conflict at the debriefing and asked for advice. The dialog with peers provided helpful reassurance—this was a matter of culture and not against Scripture. When they returned to the community, they asked the people to help them get bangles for his wife. After the women adorned the missionary's wife with bangles in a public ceremony, the criticism stopped, and the missionaries felt released.

Another couple struggled with a similar conflict. Women in this community placed a dot on their forehead to symbolize their status as married women. The missionary husband understood the dot as a symbol of Hindu religion, and a practice prohibited by traditional Christians in India. The missionary, desiring to be God's instrument to invite these people to Christ, was torn between his desires and traditional convictions. The group discussed this very challenging issue at their debriefing session, and sought guidance and wisdom from God. The men discussed it privately with their spouses before reaching a final decision. While not an easy decision, they all agreed that they should accept this cultural practice—missionary wives would wear the dot to identify with and bridge into community.

Bridge-building to reach people with the gospel provides an ongoing focus for these debriefing sessions. As gifted teachers and well-trained educators, Jameer and his wife sought a bridge by serving as missionary teachers in a churchless community. They asked God to open the door to adults through their work with children. Responding to the leading of the Holy Spirit, they visited the homes of children from their school class. The children were so excited to see the teachers, which in turn impressed the parents. Jameer and his wife had instant access and credibility. By helping children become the best students, they found an open door for witness to the parents.

Our missionaries have discovered a variety of ways to bridge into communities where, as outsiders, people naturally exclude them. Acts of compassion, such as helping families find medical assistance, often open doors. One missionary visited and helped a sick person at the hospital until the patient was discharged and returned home. Because of this compassion, the patient's family shared their gratitude with the entire village, resulting in widespread acceptance of the team. Another team shared that playing volleyball and cricket opened the way to build good relationships with the youth of an unreached village. By helping the youth organize volleyball teams, providing training to improve skills, and coordinating tournaments, the team earned the trust and thanks of community leaders.

Each of the debriefing sessions proved to be different but progressive in the training of candidates and missionaries. Every six months these teams help one another solve problems, grow in faith and confidence in the Lord, and develop creative responses to ministry challenges. We rejoice as we see them learn new languages, adapt to unusual cultural practices, and become effective servants of the Lord Jesus Christ in these unreached communities.

CHALLENGES OF CONTEXTUAL CHURCH PLANTING

Since 1995 we have given serious attention to the special challenges of training cross-cultural missionaries to facilitate new church-planting movements among unreached peoples. Often missionaries successfully evangelize people in an unreached group, but fail to train and empower indigenous leadership or to contextualize the church. Fearing the immaturity of new believers, or the dangers of syncretism, they retain leadership and control of the process and inhibit the birth of an indigenous movement. In the rest of this chapter I will describe some of our efforts to birth indigenous movements, and some principles that we have adopted to build a contextualized church-planting movement.

We have learned that building relationships takes significant time, and the investment of people and resources. Until we achieve trust and acceptance, people have little interest in our message. The missionary must recognize and find ways to transcend the barriers to be accepted as an insider. We teach candidates that building strong relationships establishes a foundation for a healthy indigenous church-planting movement. For example, in 2001, an earthquake devastated a district called Bhuj in the state of Gujarat. We sent a cross-cultural team to help the victims. As the leaders spent time serving the community, they looked for ways to serve the real needs of the victims. The team observed that many schools were destroyed in the quake and people were afraid to send their children to school. Team leaders proposed that HBI offer to run a child development center in the community, which we agreed to support. On the first day more than 50 children attended the center and since then it has grown into a pre-school program. The child development center has served as a bridge to gain more permanent acceptance of our team into the community.

We have also insisted on the importance of learning the language, culture, and worldview of a people group. While English and Hindi may be used in many parts of India, people respond best when they hear the message in their own language. Further, it is important to use a contextual method to communicate effectively. Too often missionaries are in a hurry to stand on the street and preach Christ, thinking the people will understand the message. We emphasize the necessity of building the bridge, establishing oneself in the community, and building credibility before we expect the people to listen to the message.

Another challenge is knowing when to encourage people to make decisions for Christ. We train candidates not to call for decisions until the community asks, "What then must we do to be saved?" When the message and method of communication are indigenized, the decision-making process will become contextual to the people. McGavran (1970) long ago argued that in communities where decisions require collective consensus, the whole group needs to make the decision for Christ at the same time. The missionary must be patient and wait till the community asks the question of what they should do to become followers of Christ.

One of our teams learned this in a very practical way while visiting in one of the villages of their tribal group. That day an old man from the village approached one of the team members and told her about a woman in the village who the doctor said would live for only three days. The old man asked, "Will Jesus help this woman?" She assured the old man that Jesus was able to do anything, and she visited the woman and prayed for her. Several weeks later when the team returned to the village, the village headman told them that the woman had not died, and asked the missionary to pray for her again. Seeing this opportunity, the team returned each week and encouraged the woman's family to join them for prayer. For the next eighteen months they met weekly for prayer to this Jesus, and many people came. Then one day these people asked the team, "What should we do to become followers of Christ?" On that day 38 adults and a group of children made decisions to follow Christ, and a new church was born.

MAKING DISCIPLES CROSS-CULTURALLY

Many missionaries and pastors consider their responsibility ended when a person makes a decision to follow Christ. We have emphasized to our candidates that a decision does not make a disciple of Christ. To produce indigenous churches and a church-planting movement, missionaries must make disciples. Teaching new believers to follow Jesus is always hard work, but it is especially challenging in people groups where they do not have the Bible in their own language. India has more than 400 tribal groups without Scriptures.

The varying commitment of individuals also complicates the picture. New converts do not grow with the same level of understanding or obedience. When people decide in a group, many will follow the leader, making a decision without understanding. It is necessary, therefore, to discern the depth of individual or group commitments, and to nurture those who will provide leadership and support in the discipling of others.

One of the INEF mission teams experienced these special challenges, working among the Hakkibikies, an unreached people group in the state of Karnataka. Over a period of 15 months the missionary team built a bridge into the community by interacting with the leader of the village. A group of 100 people made a decision to follow Christ after seeing the Jesus film. However, these new believers could not read, and had no Scriptures or other material available in their language. As a consequence many did not grow in their faith.

The Hakkibikies are nomadic people who travel great distances to sell their products. On one of their marketing trips, the leader of the village asked his daughter to visit a Hindu temple to worship the god Shiva. His daughter said to him, "I worship Christ and am not willing to bow down to any other god." Very angry at her response, the father forced her to worship but could not change her mind. Because she refused to deny Christ, he canceled the trip and took the whole group home. He sent his daughter to a monastery to restore her faith in the god Shiva. Further, he asked the believers not to attend the church and he chased the missionary couple out of the village. In the months that followed the Holy Spirit strengthened the faith of many who refused to deny Christ. Forty adults and children, although they were persecuted, stood firm in their faith in Christ. Others followed the village leader and returned to their old religious practices.

In this situation the missionary came back to HBI, searching for ways to strengthen these persecuted Christians. The director

of HBI's missions program, seeing this special need to disciple
these 40 believers, invited them to come to Chennai for a month's
training. Aided by resources available at HBI, the missionary began a discipling program. Using the Jesus film, which had been
translated into Kannada, the missionary showed it every day until
they memorized the text of the film. They also discussed the film
daily as a foundation to help them understand their decision to
follow Jesus. Second, he organized reading classes in Hindi, and
in thirty days they learned to read. This provided a way for them
to access the Hindi version of the Bible and to grow in their faith
in the Lord. Third, he asked them to memorize key verses in the
Hindi Bible in order to understand their faith and be strengthened
in God's Word. The missionary explained the meaning of these
verses in the Hakkibiki language. At the end of the thirty days
they returned to their village, God's light in the midst of darkness.
While the missionary had to support them from a location some
distance from the village, the people remained faithful and lived
for the Lord.

The Hakkibiki story illustrates that making disciples of new
believers should not be delayed. Missionaries must find ways to
help new believers grow in their knowledge of the Word of God
and share their faith with others. We learned from this situation
how to use the Jesus film and other audio-visual tools when the
people are non-literate. If the community is literate, the missionary should prepare materials in advance in the language of the
community to disciple new believers.

We need to give highest priority to making Scripture available
in the language of new believers. When materials are not in the
heart language of the people, they will misunderstand the truth.
The missionary who speaks the local language must translate
Scripture and other materials, or find others to join the team to
do the translation work. A church-planting movement is possible
only when the people have the Word in a language they understand. Unless the people of the community study the Word and
understand the truth, they will not see the need for others to receive the Gospel.

DEVELOPING INDIGENOUS LEADERSHIP FOR THE CHURCH

After the thirty-day discipleship training program we described for the Hakkibikies, the very next step is developing leaders in the church. We cannot wait for more materials or training. If the church is going to be a Great Commission church, the very next step is to teach people to share their faith with others and make disciples, using what they have learned. If they have memorized the text of the Jesus film, then they can recite it for others. If they have participated in discussions of these texts, they can invite others into similar discussions. If they have memorized Scripture in Hindi, they can translate that Scripture into Hakkibiki and teach it to others. The role of the missionary is to encourage them to do these things, and pray with them that God will bring forth fruit from their faithfulness.

If the missionary is faithful to encourage these new disciples to share their faith, God will quickly reveal the spiritual gifts of these new disciples. The role of the missionary then is to encourage and equip disciples to use those gifts in service to the body of Christ. Some will have the gift of evangelism, others of prayer, others of teaching, and so on. The missionary who empowers these new disciples to exercise their gifts and minister to others will release these leaders for the ministries of the church.

Whether a new church is a church of the people or the missionary depends on its leadership. If the missionary preaches and teaches, he has failed to equip and empower others. When new disciples do the preaching, teaching, evangelism, and prayer ministries, the community has taken ownership for the church. If the missionary leads the music and songs, she has failed to equip others to develop music and songs expressing their own understanding of God and His relationship to them. The goal is to empower new disciples to define the vision and mission of their local church.

The missionary also must encourage the new believers from the community to develop indigenous materials to disciple others. When these new disciples prepare songs, Bible studies, prayer, and evangelistic outreaches, the material will be more contextually relevant to the community. As we equip the believers and they gain confidence to express what they learn from the Word and the work of the Holy Spirit in their lives, they will become salt and light among their people. The sooner the missionary makes the effort to encourage new believers to do this, the quicker the Holy Spirit will bring transformation to the people and culture.

When new disciples lead new churches, and these churches plant other new churches, the missionary has successfully carried out the first phase of his or her responsibility to reach an unreached people. The second phase is to provide apostolic-type support and encouragement for a church-planting movement. As new indigenous leaders plant churches, they will experience opposition, internal conflict, and other attacks of Satan to derail their work. They will need encouragement and support to continue the development of training and materials to disciple their people. The missionary can play the "John Knox" role, calling leaders together for prayer, helping them do basic research to determine need and develop strategy, and together seek God's vision for this new church. They also need support to develop indigenous leadership training—contextual training that will reproduce leaders for the movement. Even in this role, the missionary should pray for God to raise up other indigenous "John Knoxers" who will provide apostolic vision and leadership for church planting.

SHERWOOD'S REFLECTIONS ON LEADERSHIP TRAINING

After more than twenty years of teaching in formal missionary training programs in the United States, I (Sherwood) marvel at the way Bobby and the team at HBI have adapted the essential content for equipping cross-cultural missionaries to the Indian context. Their most important innovation is the blending of formal and non-formal teaching and learning strategies for missionary candidates.

Phase 1 includes classroom and library work, a three-month field internship among unreached people, written reporting, and debriefing. Phase 2 begins with classroom and library work and then moves to actual field ministry for six months, with written reporting and debriefing. The debriefing strategy used over three years of missionary training and practice captures exceptionally well Kolb's (1984) notion of learning as knowledge gained through a cycle of experience, reflection, abstraction, and experimentation. They have also learned that more mature, well-educated Christian couples make better candidates for cross-cultural ministry. A stronger educational background is essential to grasp the substantive cultural, social, and theological insights foundational to effective contextualization among unreached peoples.

The HBI program has several unique aspects that have wider application for training cross-cultural missionaries and developing indigenous leaders among new converts from an unreached people group:

1. Employing the first six months of theory and practice in the field internship to evaluate and screen missionary candidates is one of the most thorough candidate processes I have experienced. As candidates and staff together invest in six months of training (Phase 1—three months of each), they rigorously test a couple's readiness for cross-cultural ministry. If the teams thrive in this experience so that they are invited to return to the internship field community, they are accepted as missionary candidates, and continue their training. If they do not thrive, they have invested only six months before being redirected to other ministry. This screening is beneficial for both candidates and the mission.

2. Regular debriefing sessions over three years provide a powerful tool for peer- and mentor-based learning. These sessions facilitate reflection, abstraction, and experimentation in ministry that leads to new learning and more effective practice of ministry. These sessions also provide a context for continuing spiritual formation of candidates and mutual prayer support for ministry.

3. Working from Donald McGavran's *Bridges of God*, HBI's cross-cultural ministry training emphasizes finding bridges into unreached communities and contextualizing the message

and ministry (Phase 1 and following). Candidates recognize from the very beginning the unique challenges of cross-cultural church planting and experiment with different kinds of bridges and different ways of contextualizing the message. Because this is so pervasive, all the INEF cross-cultural missionaries work to implement these strategies.

4. Making disciples, equipping leaders, and *never* pastoring a church provide the essential training components for creating a church-planting movement. Bobby and the training staff emphasize what I have termed "power-giving leadership" (Lingenfelter 2005). To facilitate a church-planting movement, equipping leaders, and empowering them to do the work must happen at the very beginning. For most missionaries this means releasing control of preaching, teaching, evangelism, and prayer ministries at a time when they are anxious about the readiness of the indigenous leaders, and afraid about theological or other error. They forget that Jesus sent out the twelve (Matthew 10) and the seventy-two (Luke 10), and entrusted them to the supervision of the Holy Spirit. The HBI non-formal training for church planters and cross-cultural missionaries requires new believers, new disciples, and new leaders to begin teaching others immediately what they have learned. Using John Knox as a role model, they teach missionaries to serve as apostolic facilitators of vision and catalysts for mobilizing others to plant churches.

5. The story of the Hakkibikies powerfully illustrates the terribly difficult challenges of church planting among tribal people who are both non-literate and without Scripture. Having the Hakkibikies memorize the Jesus film, the only Scripture in a known local language, was a stroke of genius. First, it capitalized upon the habits and strengths of non-literates for memorizing things they hear. Second, using the only scriptural material available, they helped people reflect on the stories they had memorized, and discuss the implications of those stories for following Jesus in their villages and tribal context. To disciple these new believers, they applied the

elements of the adult learning cycle—experiencing the film many times, memorizing the narrative, and reflecting on what it means, drawing parallels to their village life, and then experimenting in their quest to follow Jesus. While this does not substitute for making much larger portions of Scripture available in their language, the Hakkibikies grasped the essence of the Jesus story, and what it meant to follow Him.

CHAPTER 4. RESEARCH AND REFLECTION QUESTIONS:

Research Exercise: Access on the Internet the website of a mission organization that is engaged in equipping men and women for cross-cultural church planting. Some examples include: Assemblies of God World Missions; Grace Brethren International Missions; International Mission Board (Southern Baptist); RCA World Mission; WEC International. Search the website for information about its missionary training program.

Reflection:

1. How does the training of cross-cultural missionaries in this mission compare with the training at HBI? What are the significant similarities and differences?
2. What are the strengths and weaknesses of each?

CHAPTER FIVE

EQUIPPING LOCAL CHURCHES FOR CHURCH PLANTING

As you enter the front gate of Hindustan Bible Institute in Chennai, New Calvary Church sits at the center of this urban campus. This congregation is made up of people from the surrounding urban context and families who are part of the ministry of HBI. This is a vibrant community of Christians who have the full range of traditional church services and ministries. For many years New Calvary Church had a more traditional vision of ministry.

In this chapter we explore the question "Is multiplication church planting something we do 'out there' or does church planting begin at home?" After reflecting on leadership for a missional church, Bobby first describes how he began to engage his local congregation and then how to equip pastors in other established churches to train and mobilize their people to share their faith, make disciples, and plant new churches.

—Sherwood Lingenfelter

In 2003, a group of city pastors in Chennai attended an HBI workshop designed to equip them to write purpose and vision statements for their churches. One of the pastors suggested that his purpose was to prepare the bride of Christ so that when Christ comes they will be ready for Him. He said, "I have 75 persons in our church and almost all of them are ready; therefore my task is complete."

Tragically, too many churches and pastors have this limited and self-centered view of ministry. God has anointed His church to serve as His most powerful instrument to gather worshipers from every tribe, kindred, language, and nation of the world. Pastors fail to glorify God when they do not enable every member to fulfill his or her ministry of witness. If the church is to be what God intended, it must function with all its skills, abilities, and resources. When a leader limits the church to his ability and control, the leader and the church both miss the mission of God. When the leader fails to equip the church for God's purpose and mission, the church becomes self-centered—a social, religious club.

A typical Indian pastor receives a call for the ministry, which he interprets to be reaching his community through one church. Caught up in this task, he fails to see that the mission of the church is not just adding members and ministering to them, but more importantly, to disciple them to be God's greatest instruments for the mission of God and His church. Many pastors think their responsibility ends with their weekly preaching and service to members. When he acquires enough resources to operate the church, the pastor stops evangelism and focuses on preaching. His early evangelistic thrust yields to the routine of church meetings, and dynamic growth is arrested. The church may gain a popular reputation and people may come to listen to a great preacher, but while the pastor tries to grow the church through his preaching, members are spectators and the community has no significant outreach. Often a pastor stays until he gets tired of hearing himself or managing the church.

Most traditional churches are content to live in a maintenance mode. As a consequence, the vast human resources of the church are untapped for the kingdom. People live with a false understanding that being a Christian means coming to church every Sunday, paying their tithes regularly, and listening to the preacher.

The Gifts of Leadership for a Missional Church

The Apostle Paul in the book of Ephesians makes reference to five types of leaders the Lord gave the church. "It was he who gave some to be apostles, some to be prophets, some to be evangelists, and some to be pastors and teachers, to prepare God's people for works of service so that the body of Christ may be built up until we all reach unity in the faith and in the knowledge of the Son of God and become mature, attaining to the whole measure of the fullness of Christ" (Eph 4:11–13).

After nearly 1,500 years of Christendom and the contextualization of the church in the West, theologians and church leaders interpreted this text so as to limit leadership roles to priest/pastor, bishop, and teacher. In the Roman Catholic tradition in the West, and then in the Reformation traditions, pastor/priest and theologian/scholar served the critical roles of guiding each new generation of believers within a predominantly Christian culture. The church did not need apostles or evangelists, because the whole population had been baptized at birth. The theologians and monastic orders took the prophetic role, calling the church back to its biblical foundations and its people and leaders to live transformed lives in their cultural context. Christendom struggled constantly against becoming so contextualized to the "empire" that the transforming power of the church was lost. The Reformation movement in the West called the church to revival and renewal, but did not transform its sense of mission or its understanding of leadership. Calvin, Luther, Zwingli, and other Reformation leaders did not understand Matthew 28:16-20 as a call to mission, or to a church-planting movement. They had no theology of mission!

When God gave William Carey a vision for India through his reading of Matthew 28:16-20 and raised up missionaries from Protestant churches in Europe and America during the colonial era, they came to India with a model of church rooted in the Christendom of Europe. The pastor/teacher shepherds the church, and these pastors are trained in theological schools where they learn Greek and Hebrew and skills for preaching and teaching to their congregations. This is the model William Carey and other early missionaries brought to India, and the one that for generations molded the preparation of Indian church leaders.

With the advent of mission, this understanding of leadership and leadership training proved woefully inadequate. With the explosion of the church at the end of the 20th century and entering into the 21st, we must develop a new contextualization of Ephesians 4 for the emerging church in India. Cueing from Paul's outline in Ephesians 4, in pages that follow I take a first step toward defining types of leaders necessary to build a missional church and equip its people for the mission of God. To make disciples of every people group in India, and bring transformation to the people and cultures of India, the church must develop leadership for such a task.

The Pastor. Indian churches need committed, competent, and mature pastor-leaders who love and mentor their people. Indian Christians struggle with their marriages, endure suffering in their workplaces, and often live on the economic margins of society. A pastor must come alongside these people in their suffering, provide counseling and encouragement, and guide them to discern God's mission and purpose for their lives.

An effective pastor must study the Word of God and know how to interpret it in order to provide wise counsel to others. He must have a deep personal commitment to Christ, and a disciplined spiritual life. He must be able to teach and counsel out of a deep understanding of the Word of God and its application to his people in their social and cultural context. He is the kind of shepherd Jesus spoke of in the parable of the lost sheep (Luke 15:3-7) who pursued the one sheep that went astray, and celebrated with his friends when he brought it back home.

Perhaps most important, however, the pastor must understand the urgency to equip his people to participate with him in ministry. Rather than create dependency, he must mentor individuals in the congregation to be about the work of the kingdom. He should help people recognize their gifts, point out open doors for ministry, and watch over and foster the progress of believers seeking to follow the Lord. For God's work in India, the pastor must have a vision for the unreached in his town and beyond, and mobilize his people to fulfill God's mission for His church.

The Apostle. As I think about this role in the context of India, the example of the Apostle Paul is most helpful. God sent him to reach the unreached towns and cities of Turkey and Greece. He preached Christ in town after town, planted new churches, and equipped others like Timothy and Titus to make disciples, plant new churches in different cities, and train local church leaders to pastor and make disciples. He functioned as an evangelist, a cross-cultural missionary, a church planter, a mentor to young leaders, and a trainer, but he did not pastor a church. He equipped others at Corinth, Ephesus, Galatia, and Philippi to serve as pastors and teachers.

In the context of India the apostle-type person must be a visionary leader who brings evangelists, pastors, and missionaries together to envision God's purpose and mission for the church, and then develop strategy together to accomplish that vision. The apostle may have administrative gifts of the kind that grasps the complexities of a vision, and discerns who God is calling and the gifts that are needed to accomplish it. He must be disciplined to build others, manage the vision, and focus on development of the people God had called to do the work. He must release the work to other gifted men and women of God, equipping and empowering them to carry out their ministry responsibilities.

How do we identify and train those God has called and gifted for apostolic ministry? The apostle does not cling to the role of *pastor*. He is not content to shepherd a flock. He is compelled to be about God's bigger vision for the church. He loves to do evangelism and preach Christ, but desires even more to train *others* to be evangelists, pastors, and teachers. After 15 years of spreading the vision of saturation church planting and training pastors to make disciples through planting churches, we began to realize that some of these leaders had apostolic gifting. They might have begun as evangelists and planted churches, but along the way they realized the importance and significance of empowering others to fulfill the Great Commission.

In our leadership training programs we find trainees who respond differently to the curriculum. Pastors and teachers will often focus on biblical knowledge, and be concerned about details of interpretation and theological debate. The apostle will be frustrated by these arguments (I Corinthians 1:10-12; 2:1-2), and will be compelled to get on with the vision of reaching the lost, planting new churches, and equipping new leaders. Evangelists and apostles are best trained in the context of ministry; pastors and teachers love to learn in the classroom context. In the non-formal and informal training contexts, we need to look for those who thrive when they are equipping others to do the work, and mentor them to see whether God has gifted them as apostles. Apostles must have solid biblical preparation and sound doctrine if they are to facilitate the vision of the church-planting movement. But they will be frustrated with the theological debates, find the academic fine points tiresome, and be restless to get on with the movement.

The Teacher. Teachers are essential for the mission of making disciples among the peoples of India. I grew up being taught that all pastors have to be teachers, but I question this point of view. God gives the church teachers that may not have the gift or ability to pastor, and some pastors will never be teachers. At HBI we have had a number of teachers come from America on short-term ministry trips who use their giftedness to teach but would never consider themselves as pastors, nor are they pastoring a church. If we take an objective look at our congregations, we will see individuals who have the gift of teaching, but they have not been released. Many of them warm benches when they should be identified, equipped for the ministry, and released to serve the church and its ministries.

Teachers for the church in India must love to study the Word of God and have a grasp both of the big picture and the details of the Word. These individuals must have the gift of teaching the Word of God and know how to make it relevant for their language and people group. For people to grow as disciples of Jesus, they need teachers who will help them to apply the truths of Scripture to daily living in their tribal, village, or urban context.

Formal education is the obvious method to train teachers and has worked for centuries. However, the special challenges of social dislocation and contextualization require research and mentoring. Often teachers in seminaries have not been equipped to contextualize their knowledge and apply it to ministry. We must equip teachers to contextualize knowledge, to make it personal, so they know, are, and do in their ministry relationships.

The Evangelist. The western model of the preaching evangelist, holding street or tent meeting campaigns, has its amusing distortions in India. A western missionary colleague tells the story of coming to a Bible school in North India where 100 Sikh students were enrolled in an evangelism class. As the missionary walked around the campus, he found Sikh students under every tree practicing preaching. Holding the Bible in one hand, and thumping the air with the other, each turbaned student shouted out his message in English, as another student stood beside him to interpret the message in the local language. While this kind of preaching happens all over India, we do not believe this is the best means of reaching the nation for Christ.

The first requirement for an evangelist is a compassion for the lost that compels him to take the good news. Matthew writes that "Jesus went through all the towns and villages, teaching in their synagogues, preaching the good news of the kingdom and healing every disease and sickness. When he saw the crowds, he had compassion on them, because they were harassed and helpless, like sheep without a shepherd. Then he said to his disciples, 'The harvest is plentiful, but the workers are few. Ask the Lord of the harvest, therefore, to send out workers into his harvest field'" (Matthew 9:35-58). I believe that every local church should have a team of evangelists who are moved with compassion for the people around them and are actively engaged in praying for the sick, ministering to those in need, and proclaiming the good news of the kingdom. This work is not "campaign work;" it is the daily work of the church.

Evangelism is a process of helping individuals and communities to be reconciled to God. The people in the villages and towns have many different problems and pressures, some of which hinder them from hearing the message and others that, through the power of God, may lead them to faith. Most people in India who respond to Christ do so because they have first experienced the power of God in their lives. That power most often comes through prayer—prayer for healing, or for deliverance from some oppression, or finding a job, or gaining entrance to the university. When people pray in the name of Jesus and experience God's answer, they are then eager to know who Jesus is and to become disciples.

The role of an Indian evangelist is to bring the good news of Jesus to the villages and towns, and to invite people to pray in Jesus' name for forgiveness and healing. We have found in the on-site training at HBI that after people have heard in a public way about Jesus, a small team of evangelists visiting people in their homes to pray have an open door to tell people more about Jesus. When God demonstrates His presence and responds to their prayer, people ask, "What should we do to be saved?"

God gives to some men and women the special gift of being an evangelist. They cannot be silent, but are compelled to share the gospel wherever they go. Our challenge is to train them to use their gift in such a way that people see their compassion and are drawn to Jesus Christ. Some are gifted speakers, so we train them to prepare contextual evangelistic messages for public preaching in the towns to which they are sent. Others excel in personal evangelism, so we train them to listen and learn how God is at work in a family or community, and then lead them to prayer and faith in Jesus Christ. Both must understand the message of the gospel and master various ways to communicate the message. They must also learn that different types of people will respond at different times and in different ways.

We have found that those gifted as evangelists are not necessarily gifted to make disciples of new believers. God uses the evangelists to make Jesus Christ known to the seeker. Once the seekers have accepted Jesus as Lord, they need someone to come alongside them and help them to become disciples. This is why evangelism based in a local church is so important. Evangelists bring people to Christ, and others with the gift of teaching help them learn what Jesus taught and how to live as His disciples.

The Prophet. What is a prophet? One who predicts some future work of God, or one who discerns patterns of disobedience in a community, or one who preaches against the evils of the political and religious establishments? In the Hebrew Scriptures the prophets primarily warned the leaders of Israel and occasionally other nations about the pending judgment of God because of their disobedience and idolatry. God used the prophets to call leaders and people to repentance, and to warn them of the consequences of refusing to hear God. What role did Paul envision a prophet playing in the body of Christ? Has God given prophets to minister to our churches today? How may the leadership role of prophet be contextualized to the churches in India today?

Among the evangelical churches in India we understand prophets as those whom God has given the church to keep it from compromise with the world and sin. They see issues as black or white, right or wrong. They do not have the notion of "gray areas" in their dictionary. They give very careful attention to detail, and judge those who compromise the integrity of the church. They are forthright in their opinion and firm in their beliefs. They often serve as gatekeepers, helping the body to be faithful to the teaching and values of God's Word.

In New Calvary Church the chairman of the elder board is a prophet. When we are faced with issues where we might be ready to compromise a biblical or cultural value, he challenges us to stay between the lines. He discerns the boundaries of our commitment to God and His Word, and insists that we stay within the boundaries. I do not think I can do without him. In love he carries out his function as the leader of the church and has saved us many a time from losing the focus. But more importantly, he leads us to uphold our values, maintain our vision, stay with our purpose, and properly select the strategies consistent with our understanding of the Word of God.

Pentecostal churches in India have a different understanding of this gift. In these congregations God raises up men and women who give a "word of prophecy" for edification, exhortation, and consolation to the congregation or to other believers (I Corinthians 14:3). These "words of prophecy" often speak to people or the congregation about how God intends to minister through the person or group for His glory. God may speak about a future time of suffering, or a time of blessing in ministry. God may warn a person or a congregation about a temptation or time of testing. In the Pentecostal context, the "words of prophecy" are less about boundaries and integrity of ministry, and more about God's promise for ministry or preparation for trial.

If the body, whether evangelical or Pentecostal, is to be a light in the midst of darkness in India, we need the gift of the prophet leader in the church. We need to value these people and encourage them to develop their gift in submission to the Word and Spirit of God, and exercise their gift as part of the body of Christ. As we understand the Scriptures, false prophets have always been a problem for God's people. So we need to train people with this gift always to test their insights against the Word of God, to offer them in humility as part of the body of Christ, and to avoid the sin of judgment and condemnation when their words of discernment may be ignored or rejected.

NEW CALVARY CHURCH AND MOBILIZING URBAN CHURCH LEADERS

Just as you cannot develop a surgeon or a carpenter without training him on the job, it is hard to develop good church ministry leaders without giving them hands-on training. My family and I worship and serve in New Calvary Church located on the HBI campus, where I am a teacher and administrator. The church is led by a team of elders rather than by a traditional senior pastor. As a leader in this congregation, I finally accepted responsibility to find faithful people to whom we could entrust the vision and ministry and teach them how to lead. Once I committed to equip these people, they were eager to learn and take responsibility. Today, these leaders have built a cell ministry, children's ministry, youth ministry, a worship ministry, women's ministry, teens ministry, short-term mission team ministry, local evangelism, home visiting, prayer ministry, and have trained others to continue the work.

They are doing a great job of multiplying leaders for our local church and I am free to serve the church in other ways.

The training at New Calvary Church uses a non-formal methodology for highly educated, competent leaders with secular occupations, godly men and women who lacked skills to facilitate their giftedness in the body of Christ. I intentionally selected individuals well established in their professions to serve as teachers for our church. Each of these individuals had shown interest, so I invited them to consider the challenge of being the regular teachers for the church, and offered to equip them for this ministry. After they prayed, seeking God's direction, five accepted the invitation to undergo training.

Over a period of twelve weeks, I taught them inductive Bible study methods and how to prepare lessons by identifying the central theme of a passage, developing a proposition statement, supporting the proposition with key ideas from the passage, and then building upon each idea. They learned to introduce their message and conclude with application. Through practice preaching sessions, they learned to evaluate the content of a message, and its introduction and conclusion. Then each person took the opportunity to actually preach, first in the evening services and later in the morning services as they gained confidence and skill.

My goal for this program was to increase the number of leaders and enhance the body life within the local church. By shifting the focus from one leader to multiple leaders within the congregation, we sought to encourage other members to identify their giftedness and become equipped to serve. We are a cell church and we equip cell leaders and assistant leaders. Often the ministry leader for developing cells throughout the church will call upon one of the teachers to help in the training process because of their skills and giftedness as a teacher. In addition to this cell ministry, they also preach and teach in our church plants.

At the time of this writing, we meet as a small group and discuss the planning of the teaching ministry for a year at a time. We evaluate each other and ask how we can improve what we are doing. They have grown in skill and effectiveness as teachers and preachers. Often I preach in the first service so they can watch me as they learn. One of the emerging leaders speaks in the second service. Another speaks in the evening and a third at a new church plant. Since I often travel for six weeks at a time, they have many opportunities. We now no longer need to invite outside speakers to fill the pulpit in my absence.

The non-formal method of training is an ongoing, continuous process that sharpens and builds the skills of individuals for ministry among the body of Christ. We now have a second group of six teacher trainees, one of whom is only eleven years old. One day this eleven-year-old asked if I would train him to preach. I agreed, and was surprised at how one so young can understand Scripture and interpret the text. The Lord reminded me that the Holy Spirit is at work, empowering even the young to do His work. Identifying and developing individuals to use their gifts does not have to be limited to an age or gender. God will and does use those who are willing to obey Him. We need to realize the work is the Lord's and He is gifting the body. It is the responsibility of those who are entrusted to lead the church to equip the saints and build them for the ministry of the church and its mission.

DISCERNING LEADERSHIP GIFTS

The major challenge any pastor experiences in building leaders within the church is in making incorrect choices with reference to gifting, and then facing the difficulty of repositioning that person to serve in a ministry different from that for which he was trained. For example, a pastor may assume that a person has the giftedness to be a teacher, based upon an aptitude for studying the Word of God, only to learn in the practice of teaching that the person lacks the ability to learn how to communicate the content of the message effectively. The leader must learn how to discern who indeed has the gifts of teaching or preaching, and to test those judgments in practice before spending months in training. When a pastor makes a mistake, he must have the courage to acknowledge the mistake and gracefully interact with the trainee to redirect him or her to another area of service.

Another struggle is identifying the right people to launch new ministries. Often an apostolic leader finds a person responding to the vision for a new ministry, and may expect that individual to launch and implement the new initiative successfully. On several occasions, I had to learn it is not enough to stimulate vision, because I could not equip the individual to carry out the task. Many have the enthusiasm and excitement, but they have never walked the path before. In order to carry out a new initiative successfully, some must be part of a team with a leader, or must have a mentor who will guide them through each step to facilitate the ministry. I experienced this, both in facilitating the cell ministry in the church and in prayer mobilization. On both initiatives I assumed that an individual with the vision could lead the ministry, but in both cases they failed at the outset. When I took the responsibility, mobilized the church, and equipped the individual to take responsibility simultaneously, the efforts took root and began to bear much fruit.

Identifying, equipping, and enabling people to use their gifts and abilities will empower the church to fulfill its mission. We must break out of the "professional pastor" box, develop the leaders in our congregations, and have the courage to release them to train others. Yet, the leader with a vision must take responsibility for the task, identify others in the church with the gifts and commitment for the task, and equip them for the ministry. When they are equipped, empowered, and enabled, the ministry will take off. The leader then is free to initiate other ministry functions and train others to facilitate and run the same. I saw this happen several times in the development of our local church.

Finally, we need to teach emerging leaders how to discern gifts of ministry among the people on their teams, equip them, and empower them to serve. The first step is to help them understand that leadership requires both the facilitation of ministry and building a team. I find that I must encourage my leaders to train other people to take on parts of the task; they do not naturally think to do this. As they equip and train others, they must also open opportunities for them to serve, and evaluate their effectiveness. When they have learned to coach and mentor others, and thus empower another generation of leaders, they have caught the vision for mobilizing church leaders to fulfill the Great Commission.

EQUIPPING LEADERS IN THE LOCAL CHURCH FOR MISSION

The goal to plant a church in every village or a church for every 1,000 people in India demands hundreds of thousands of workers. The existing training centers in India cannot produce the number of church planters and pastors required to fulfill the task. To do this through formal education would require thousands of training centers and a very large number of graduates every year to meet the need. The answer is not more educational institutions, but rather to mobilize thousands of leaders in local churches and release them to serve the church and its mission under the apostolic leadership of a pastor.

Through the ministries of HBI and INEC, the Lord taught us that everyone must play his part for the church to function effectively and fulfill its mission. In our dual roles as both church and training institutions, we expanded our focus to include developing leaders in the local church. We approached this objective through two structures. First, through informal seminars (Church Mobilization Pastors Training) for pastors throughout India to help them recognize the people resources in their churches and to learn how to equip them. Second, we offered at HBI an evening college and special seminars for the people of local churches in our region to assist the pastor to better equip his task force in serving the apostolic vision of that local church.

Both programs emphasized hands-on practical ministry along with information and character development. In the INEC context, we actually trained our pastors during the on-site segment in a seminar "Called to Shepherd." This material begins with an overview of God's Word and some basic doctrines from Scripture. Teachers train individuals to study the Bible, prepare a sermon, and learn techniques for delivering a sermon. Finally they learn the basic content of the gospel and how to share their faith.

The seminar empowers pastors to train leaders within local churches. Using the same material over a period of eight weeks, the pastor asks his local leaders to state the purpose of each book in the Bible, the key verse and a short outline, so as they read the Bible they begin to understand God's Word. He also teaches Bible study skills and how to do inductive and deductive Bible studies. He mentors each person, creating opportunities for them to conduct a Bible study with others in the congregation. Similarly the pastor provides opportunity and coaches these emerging leaders to preach a sermon. Particularly in rural environments where people are scattered, it is helpful to develop many who can preach and teach. The pastor passes on learned skills of communicating and proclaiming the Word of God.

At the same time, the pastor teaches them about the purpose and methods of evangelism. Day after day and week after week, as part of his ministry, they do street preaching, personal evangelism, and house visitation. As they observe him, they learn and practice the techniques and skills of ministry, and they experience the power of the gospel, while learning to depend upon God.

INEC has an active program of continuing education for these rural pastors. At the regional training centers staff conduct ongoing training for pastors on Bible and doctrinal issues, practical seminars such as running a Sunday school program in a local church, and building vision for the development of the ministry through the local church in their region.

INEC has a more formal program to train local leaders in an urban context. Students enroll for a two-year course, coming to HBI three times a week for six quarters until they complete the program and earn a degree. Some of these leaders are in the ministry, some serving as pastors. They have developed practical skills largely from their relationship with a mentoring pastor.

I must confess that we struggled to achieve our expectations for this church mobilization program. Initially the pastors felt insecure, worrying that new leaders might replace them or push them out of their leadership positions. Once they took the risk and began to train some of their people, they reported significant impact for the development of their churches. Other reluctant colleagues gradually accepted the idea and today many more have followed. We now introduce this local leadership training in the very early stages of a church planter's training, so that this strategy has become a significant part of the INEC movement.

BUILDING GREAT COMMISSION CHURCHES

In the early 1990s, the leadership of INEC recognized the need to challenge the leaders in our movement to consider the task of going across our cultural boundaries and reaching people who are culturally, socially, economically, and linguistically different from us. The leaders affirmed this goal intellectually, but it was not until 1998 that we saw active commitment. At that time we invited Larry Ressor from Global Focus to help us equip our national pastors to transform their congregations into Great Commission churches. During his challenges to the INEC missionaries, the Kuvi missionaries caught the vision. Within a short time they sent out cross-cultural missionaries to reach a group called Dongria Kond in the neighboring district of Koraput. Today these Kuvi missionaries have developed a church movement among the Kond.

The transformation of local churches to become Great Commission churches is not a simple task. Over the years Larry taught us to develop model churches in which pastor and leaders in the church together envisioned and mobilized the congregation to take the gospel of Jesus Christ to unreached people groups. Out of this context, and a growing passion of its leaders, New Calvary Church in Chennai chose to become a model church. Sensing the need to support missionaries, the church leaders promoted the vision and concept of "faith-promise giving." We taught our people to look at the world through the compassionate eyes of Jesus, and challenged them to give financially and to be personally committed and involved. As a result they prayed, gave, sent, and went. We first committed to give 50 percent of all we received in offering to missions. But God led us to do more. We chose to enhance our giving with "faith promise" and released 100 percent of these offerings to missions.

Last year, a team of youth, professionals, women, and senior citizens visited our missionary, Nehru, who is working among the Irulas on the border of Tamil Nadu and Kerala states. The older adults served as mentors to the younger church members, and the young people were immensely touched by the lives and sacrifices of the missionary. At our missions conference banquet service we interviewed several of them. One young man, Sammy, said, "I learned that missionary work is hard to do, as communicating to the people and knowing about their families is very tough." Philip said, "In the mission field we should be able to go anywhere and share the gospel with anybody." Jiju said, "I learned there are very poor people living under poverty level and though they were poor, they were willing to be hospitable and gave a warm welcome to us." Prabhu said, "I learned that missionaries love God and go to the unreached and share the gospel in the midst of suffering. They are God's helpers." Along with this team, there was also a medical doctor, and she said, "I want to live among them."

By personalizing the task of mission, these commitments transformed our people and their involvement. When we invited our missionaries from the field to speak, the people saw and heard how God worked through their lives, and how they sacrificed to reach the lost. The people in cell groups began to write and pray for the missionaries every week. When the missionaries came into town, the cell families invited them to speak and treated them as honored guests. By the end of 2004, the church supported 30 national missionaries, 28 of whom are working in India and two others outside of India.

By faith, New Calvary Church people found that God provides resources to fulfill the vision of the church. They have seen God provide out of what seemed meager resources. In that process we became a model church to other pastors and congregations, demonstrating that by faith, God can mobilize a local church to take the gospel to other nations.

Mission must be the heartbeat of every church. Every church member must have an opportunity to experience it, understand it, and be equipped for the task. I believe it is essential that national movements begin to catch a vision for the unreached peoples and challenge their people not only to give but also to go. My passion is for every church to use every opportunity to give their people the vision to understand the mission of God and to equip them to serve as God's greatest instruments in fulfilling the Great Commission.

SHERWOOD'S REFLECTIONS ON LEADERSHIP TRAINING

The most powerful lesson from this chapter is that local churches are fertile ground to produce emerging leaders. Yet the fact of history is that local churches that do produce leaders are the exception rather than the rule. In the brief history of the INEC, Bobby and his colleagues have discovered that they must be very intentional about breaking this pattern. Cultural expectations about leaders and leadership, status rivalry among people, emotional and economic insecurity, and an inherent human propensity to control rather than empower others all work against the vision for multiplying leaders in the church. I (Sherwood) will conclude the chapter by highlighting some of the issues that extend beyond India to leadership emergence across cultural and national boundaries.

1. **The critical importance of vision.** Individual leaders all have a vision of some kind. The opening story in the chapter describes a vision of a congregation prepared to meet Christ when He comes. So the question is what vision, and whose vision, is motivating the leader? Bobby highlights the importance of a biblical theology of mission and equipping pastors to understand the church as a mission-focused community. When the mission of God is not clearly understood, and when pastors do not see their responsibility for this mission, the church succumbs to a personal or cultural vision that distorts and diminishes its effectiveness as the body of Christ. But when they have a clear grasp of the mission and purpose of God, their vision aligns with God's purpose, and they may be trained to participate with and empower others to accomplish that purpose.

2. **The necessity of practical training to break the habits of culture.** From the very beginning of the non-formal training, HBI

challenged and equipped these missionary recruits to plant multiple churches. Yet the idea of training others and releasing control of ministry to them, is utterly foreign to most people and cultures. As soon as a young evangelist calls together a little flock, his first inclination is to define them as sheep that belong to him, rather than to Christ. When sheep belong to me, they become my wealth, and the source of my social standing in the community. Over the fifteen years described in this book, HBI has continually fought against this "my flock" inertia. The on-site training, the challenge to equip thirty "new leaders," the discipling program, and Church Mobilization Training all have at heart the issue of empowering others to take up leadership for the mission of God. This is counter-cultural and counter-emotional—leaders expect to control and to oversee, but they rarely expect to release ministry and equip others to do their work.

3. **The importance of creating new opportunities to serve.** Bobby has shown how a vision to reach people for Christ produced many new opportunities for leadership in New Calvary Church in Chennai. More importantly, he described how he created opportunities for teaching and preaching for all five of the new emerging teachers in that congregation. If a trainee has no opportunity to practice and to grow, the leader will not emerge. Weaver (2004), doing research on five churches in Hungary that had many emerging leaders, noted that these "structures of opportunity" were essential to leadership emergence. The most effective Hungarian pastors, producing emerging leaders in their congregations, created many new ministry opportunities by their vision and compassion for the lost in their communities.

4. **Experience is an essential component of the training.** Bobby illustrates throughout the chapter that training and experience must be linked. Training teachers must be linked to ongoing practice teaching, with peer and mentor feedback to help people grow in their effectiveness. This is critical in the local church context. Bobby noted that when he empowered without training and practice, these individuals failed to become leaders.

5. **Training without mentoring by the pastor or another leader usually doesn't succeed.** This was true at all levels of HBI mobilization training. Pastors did not know how to plant second and third churches without leader or peer mentoring. While they knew they should make disciples, their effectiveness was limited without mentoring and feedback. When gifted people finished the training to teach, they still were not effective without ongoing peer and master-teacher mentoring. To train new leaders and empower them for ministry, they must have mentors, be mentored, and learn how to mentor others.

But the most important contributions of this chapter for me come from Bobby's reflections on the types of leaders needed for a church-planting movement. As I have served on the Board of Directors of Grace Brethren International Missions, Tom Julien and Dave Guiles have educated me over the years on the critical importance of apostolic leadership for church-planting movements. Guiles has talked about the importance of finding men who have "apostolic wiring" to lead a movement. Reflecting on our efforts to plant churches in Europe and Latin America, we realized that over many decades we had recruited "preaching pastors" to serve as missionaries. These men had faithfully planted one church, and then served as pastor to those people for one or two decades. Very few went on to plant a second church, and most were not effective in mobilizing others in the congregation to be evangelists or to make disciples of new believers.

Guiles concluded that we recruited the wrong people to launch a church-planting movement. In this Guiles and Gupta agree—apostolic leadership is absolutely essential to launch and sustain a church-planting movement. These apostolic foundation layers bring people together for prayer, challenge others with vision, discern how to equip and empower members in the body, and then release them for ministry. They are catalytic leaders, and they are not content to pastor a church. They must be about setting new foundations upon which others build the church.

Bobby has recognized that many pastors, even if they do not have "apostolic wiring," can learn to equip and mobilize their people for Great Commission work. He has demonstrated this through the on-site training for church planting at HBI, and now again in the informal Church Mobilization Pastor's Training. In the non-formal on-site training, men who had planted one church learned how to plant a second, and many went on to plant multiple churches. By giving pastors a new purpose and vision for their church, and equipping them to train and release their people for ministry, a good pastor can become the leader of a small church-planting movement. And when more pastors equip lay people to serve as evangelists, teachers, prophets, and pastors, the Spirit of God works through the church to make hundreds and thousands the disciples of the Lord Jesus Christ.

Alan Weaver's study in Hungary highlights two additional factors that are not emphasized in this chapter: the critical need for emotional support among emerging leaders and the economic factor of one's livelihood. Bobby notes the struggle and insecurity that INEC pastors felt about their own leadership position and the risk they perceived about equipping others. These emotions effectively paralyzed them out of fear that someone more capable could replace them. Weaver (2004) notes similar emotions among emerging leaders, who often have experienced rejection and feel inadequate to assume a ministry role. The most successful Hungarian pastors understood these emotional blocks in these emerging leaders, and through prayer, encouragement, and mentoring helped them gain a new sense of worth in Christ and confidence in the power of the Holy Spirit to work through them for ministry. The point here is that we must address the fears, insecurity, and feelings about risk within pastors and emerging leaders. Unless this is a component of our preparation and mentoring, emotional factors may undermine the training process.

Finally, we cannot underestimate the importance of basic livelihood in the capacity of the church to mobilize its people for leadership. Bobby has presented a wonderful case study of New Calvary Church in Chennai that illustrates this well. The people selected for training as teachers all earned good middle-class incomes in careers apart from their ministry. They assumed new ministries in the church while continuing to earn a good living in another career. This model is then a viable model for urban churches, but perhaps less so for rural churches. We already know from the INEF movement that without a stipend of approximately 50 percent of the cost of living in a ministry context, these leaders probably could not have supported their families while carrying on the ministry. We may reasonably expect them to plant five more churches, and train five new leaders. But how will those new leaders survive if they are as poor as the INEF missionary? In his study in Hungary, Weaver found that emerging leaders usually had jobs apart from their church ministry, and while they were eager to continue to grow in their ministry effectiveness, the greatest limiting factor was time available apart from earning a living. These economic challenges must be given more serious consideration in leadership training.

CHAPTER 5. RESEARCH AND REFLECTION QUESTIONS:

Research Exercise: Find the website for Mission Alive on the Internet, an organization formed by missiologist Gailyn Van Rheenen. Examine its curriculum and strategies for planting churches in the urban United States.

Reflection:
1. What are the similarities and differences between the program and processes of Mission Alive and the HBI/INEC initiatives for mobilizing local church leaders for church planting?
2. How do Gupta and Van Rheenen differ in their efforts to implement the "diversity of gifts" from Ephesians into their equipping strategies?
3. To what extent do you see each ministry adapting to its specific Indian or American cultural contexts?

PART II

THE BIRTH OF A
NATIONAL CHURCH-PLANTING
MOVEMENT

CHAPTER SIX

UNDERSTANDING THE TASK

Part II of this book begins with the story of how God brought together a small gathering of 56 Indian church and mission leaders in 1987 to consider the challenge of reaching the whole nation of India for Christ. From this humble beginning, the Holy Spirit, already at work among the people in the villages and towns of India, challenged these men to put aside their parochial interests and unite together around a vision of a "church for every 1,000 people" in India. Over a period of seven years these and other leaders wrestled with the questions: What does it take to launch a national church-planting movement? How long does it take for churches and leaders to catch the vision? What are the critical steps for developing strategy and equipping leaders to do the work? How do the churches of India respond to the movement of the Holy Spirit and mobilize to reap from fields white for harvest?

Bobby Gupta served as catalyst for this 1987 meeting, and Hindustan Bible Institute provided administrative support for the movement that emerged from it. The story of Hindustan Bible Institute and the Indian National Evangelical Fellowship from 1985-2004 is a small part of this much larger movement of the Holy Spirit in India. Bobby Gupta is the first one to say, "This is the work of God, and our task is to be faithful and obedient servants of the Lord Jesus Christ."

—Sherwood Lingenfelter

Is it possible that most movements do not see how a task can be accomplished because they do not see the vastness of the task and what completion would actually look like? That is what happened to us from 1975 to 1985 at Hindustan Bible Institute. We were like men cutting a road through the forest without a clear perspective on the vastness of the task and the path we should follow to reach our destination. As we labored in the forest, overshadowed by its thickness, we failed to see the big picture. Satisfied with some small success, we failed to ask how to obey God to evangelize our generation.

To implement a strategy to complete any task, the workers must begin with the end in mind. They must see the big picture, understand the total scope of the task, and discern the best strategy to accomplish the vision. In those early years, while we struggled to learn how to make disciples and plant churches, God changed our heart, vision, and strategy for discipling the whole nation.

In this chapter I will share with you the story of how the Lord opened my eyes and moved my colleagues at HBI and me to join with other leaders in India to embrace the challenge to disciple a whole nation. This story describes how God brought together leaders across India to develop a national strategy to mobilize the whole church, and then how the Holy Spirit empowered God's people to plant more than 250,000 new churches in India.

FAILURE PROMPTS US TO LISTEN TO GOD

Between 1979 and 1983 HBI planted 10 churches, which we secunded to existing denominations in South India. Our great excitement and encouragement turned to gloom when we learned that only three of the ten churches survived. As we prayed, we sensed we had orphaned these churches and neglected our responsibility to nurture and mature the churches as newborn communities of faith.

Sometimes we get caught up in the task, stop listening to the Holy Spirit, and begin doing our own thing. Paul says, "...Forgetting what is behind and straining toward what is ahead, I press on toward the goal to win the prize..." (Philippians 3:13-14). I heard the Holy Spirit saying, "Do not get caught up with success or failures and become overwhelmed, as you did in the past. Remember I have called you for something you are yet to achieve. Forget those things that have passed; keep your eyes on my call for you and move forward. Keep the big picture before you!"

As I tried to look ahead, my spirit suggested a vision to plant 1,000 churches in a period of 10 years. This seemed like a goal we could achieve! With a good effort we should be able to accomplish the vision! Then I shared the vision with some of my friends. A pastor from a Methodist church told me, "Bobby do you know that we, the Methodist church in India, have been in existence for over a hundred years and our church movement has not planted 100 churches? You must be crazy to think you will be able to plant 1,000 churches in ten years!"

After this strong negative reaction, I was embarrassed! Feeling like a fool to make such a statement, I really got angry with God. I was certain that the Holy Spirit had prompted me to envision 1,000 churches and if He had not done this, I would not have become the subject of public ridicule.

In my private debate with the Lord, God humbled me when the Holy Spirit said, "Bobby you are not going to plant a single church. You see, I am going to build my church. You are only going to be my instrument." After hearing this from the Lord, I was soon back on the road sharing this vision and inviting people to join me in this work.

DISCOVERING GOD'S VISION

No sooner was I back on the road sharing the vision for 1,000 churches, than God began to help me see the bigger picture. Suddenly, I realized my strategy would never fulfill the vision God had placed in my heart. India's people inhabit more than 600,000 villages, and I heard the Holy Spirit ask, "What will 1,000 churches do to reach the nation of India?"

I did not want to think about those numbers. Many people already thought I was crazy to think we could plant 1,000 churches in ten years. At first I said, "I am not going to discuss this, please

find someone else." Then I begged the Lord to leave me alone because my task was large enough. I reminded the Lord that people
were already laughing at me—they might throw me into a mental
hospital and declare me insane.

In spite of all my excuses, the Holy Spirit patiently prodded
me about my vision. Finally, I decided to negotiate with the Lord.
Remembering that HBI had graduated more than 1,000 men and
women, I imagined that we could invite them to join us in the vision and ask each to each plant 100 churches, so that we would
have 100,000 churches. This seemed much closer to the need and I
hoped the Holy Spirit would be satisfied.

I believed the Lord had accepted my idea of 100,000 churches
until I found myself sharing the vision in Cornerstone Bible
Church, San Jose, CA. At that time Dwight Smith was the pastor,
a veteran missionary, and founder of Saturation Church Planting
International (SCPI). Jim Montgomery, founder of DAWN (Discipling A Whole Nation), was also a member of this church. After
I shared my vision to see 1,000 people mobilized to plant 100,000
churches, the congregation gave me a standing ovation. Many
shook my hand at the door, and promised to help. Some volun-
teered to help bring the 1,000 alumni together, so they might hear
and catch the vision.

However, Jim Montgomery walked up to me at the end of the
service and said "Bobby what will 100,000 churches do for the
discipling of the nation?" Montgomery believed that the goal of
discipling a whole nation was accomplished only when there was
a church for every 1,000 people. It did not occur to me that the
Lord wanted me to see the whole picture. I replied to Jim, "I know
it will not meet the need, but your goal is too high, people will not
get involved." He said, "Bobby if you begin with the wrong end in
mind you will never reach the nation." With a gracious laugh, he
acknowledged my problem, but told me he was willing to make a
fool of himself if I would arrange a meeting of the national leaders of the churches in India. He offered to come and challenge the
church leaders with a vision to saturate the nation with churches
and see if India was ready for a DAWN movement. To convince me

that he was serious, Jim offered to cover all the expenses if I would arrange the meeting. I said, "If you pay, I will arrange."

To my surprise, arranging a meeting of church leaders was very difficult. I found that I was not well-connected to church leaders, and could not convince 100 leaders to come together for a meeting with Jim. Nevertheless, I pressed many acquaintances and friends and God brought 56 significant leaders together at HBI in Madras (Chennai) on March 13-14, 1987. At this consultation on national strategy, our purpose was to listen to what the Lord might say to us about His mission to disciple the nation.[1]

BEGINNING WITH THE END IN MIND

When Jim came to India in March 1987, eight participants presented papers sharing various strategies to reach India. Some had impressive plans, but most of them did not include planting churches as part of their plan. Jim then patiently shared his understanding of the Great Commission and examples of what God was doing in other countries. He suggested we did not have a realistic means to know when the task was done. He asked us to break up into small groups and answer the question: "What will India look like when we have fulfilled the Great Commission in India?" In these small groups we talked and prayed. At the end of two days, we agreed to a goal that was both visible and measurable: To plant a church in every village and every colony of every town and city by 2000 (S. D. Ponraj 1988(1): 1).

The end of this meeting proved a great moment for all of us! We could finally see clearly a vision of the completed task. God met us at the consultation and birthed in the hearts of many the beginning of a number of church-planting movements. We finally could see the big picture in a way that made sense to us.

One of the most important affirmations of the delegates was the "need for uniting efforts to fulfil [sic] the great commission by develop [sic] a national strategy while maintaining identity." They recognized their common purpose for a task so great they could not afford to duplicate efforts. Further, "with 96 percent of our country yet to be reached and responsive pockets opening to the

Gospel we need united and organized efforts to gather the harvest" (S. D. Ponraj 1988(1):4).

At the conclusion of the meeting we appointed a 12-member continuing committee to deliberate how to accomplish the vision (See Table 6.1). Two days after the consultation the continuing committee gathered and asked, "What does it mean to see a church in every village and colony of every town and city of our nation so every 1,000 people in every people group would have a church?" The answer was evangelism that led to planting about one million churches. We agreed that the task was so large that no one organization could fulfill the mission.

To disciple the whole nation, we, the leaders, had to challenge the whole church to take the whole gospel to the whole nation. We believed that the mission of God was to establish vibrant Christ-centered communities of people, living transformed lives that radiated the person of Christ, so that people seeing them would turn to the true and living God. Such communities are committed to the Great Commission—making disciples in every people group by giving every person an opportunity, to hear, understand, respond, and be reconciled to God.

TABLE 6.1
COMMITTEE ON NATIONAL STRATEGY, 1988
(S. D. PONRAJ 1988(1): 5)

Role	Member	State Represented
Chairman	Rev. Vararuchi F. Dalavai	Andhra Pradesh
Convener	Rev. Paul R. Gupta	Tamil Nadu
Secretary	Rev. E. Sunder Raj	Tamil Nadu
Members	Rev. Dr. John Richard	New Delhi (N. India)
	Dr. M.A. Thomas	Rajasthan (N. India)
	Prof. B. E. Vijayam	Andhra Pradesh
	Mr. Ebenezer Sunder Raj	Tamil Nadu
	Rev. S. D. Ponraj	Bihar (N. India)
	Dr. S. Yohan	Karnataka
	Rev. A. Vasantharaj	Tamil Nadu
	Mr. K.C. Thomas	Kerala
	Mr. D. Kumaraswamy	Tamil Nadu

BUILDING A STRATEGY TO ACCOMPLISH THE VISION (REGIONAL CONSULTATIONS)

The task force of leaders, appointed to implement the vision, began by asking, "What should we do to transfer and accomplish the vision?" We organized the first regional consultation in February 1988 in Hyderabad, to communicate more broadly the vision, and to develop a national strategy. We also invited all the original participants to attend a second consultation on national strategy to be held in Chennai at HBI on 12 March, 1988. Leaders from nine additional organizations attended, and presented papers focused on national strategy, needs for data and research, starting smaller churches, and the role of leaders in evangelism and church planting. The discussions affirmed the major themes of the first consultation, yet some delegates proposed revising the goal as follows: *By the enabling power of the Holy Spirit, we will attempt to plant a church in every village and colony of town and city by the turn of the century* (1988) (S. D. Ponraj 1988(2): 4).

This proposal, accepted by the delegates, reflected the realization of many of the enormity of the task, and their concerns about dependence upon the Holy Spirit.

Out of these consultations, the committee agreed to objectives and activities for the Council on National Service (CONS, see Table 6.2). As our first priority we sought to clearly communicate the vision with the whole church, all mission movements and parachurch organizations. Toward that end, the committee decided to publish the findings of the consultation and the recommendation of the committee in as many journals as possible. Individual participants committed to share the vision from every pulpit to which they had access during the next three years. We also drafted and planned vision seminars, to which we would invite leaders in different parts of the nation. Finally we agreed to organize the "Congress on Church Development" in 1990.

Encouraged by the response we received from the leaders across India, we planned regional consultations in Mohammedabad,[2] Karnataka, Maharashtra, and Uttar Pradesh. In the third regional consultation in Karnataka in October 1988, Rev. Vararuchi

F. Dalavai, Chairman of CONS, gave an address that set forth the vision of a church for every village and colony, and challenged the delegates to pray and work together to reach this goal. Delegates to this consultation committed to organize mini-consultations in their local areas, and to organize prayer cells to pray regularly for CONS and for a national strategy.

Following Karnataka a contagious excitement about church planting spread like a wildfire—all over the nation people began to speak about evangelizing India and planting churches. Leaders who received the news bulletin wrote letters requesting that someone from CONS visit their organization to share the vision. Others told how God spoke to them to begin church planting in their local area (S. D. Ponraj 1988(4):4).

In the December 1988 news bulletin, *National Strategy*, I wrote the lead article setting forth the objectives for a national congress on church development, and inviting readers to make plans to come to Hyderabad in August 1990. Following the outline of the CONS objectives, I shared our excitement over the response of leaders who

TABLE 6.2
AIMS, OBJECTIVES AND ACTIVITIES OF CONS 1988
(S. D. PONRAJ 1988(2): 7)

CONS emphasizes **church planting** among the unreached.
CONS advocates a **National Strategy** for church planting in every village and every colony of town and city by the turn of the century.
CONS promotes **cooperation** of all churches, Christian organizations, and mission agencies toward a united effort for reaching our **goal** of church planting in India.
CONS conducts **consultations** of like-minded Christians, both leaders and grassroots workers, to formulate their own plans and thus work for a common national strategy for our nation.
CONS helps local churches and organizations by conducting **seminars** to train lay leaders and church planters.
CONS cooperates with other Christian organizations in **research** and **survey** of unreached people groups of India.
CONS communicates its **vision** through national and regional **consultations** and through its **publications**.
CONS plans to gather all like-minded and committed Indian Christian leaders and grassroots workers for an All-India **congress on Church Development in 1990**.
CONS encourages churches/organizations/missions to start **prayer cells** and to pray for the speedy evangelization of our nation.

attended the regional consultations. Seeing God at work in these leaders, we were encouraged to invite other representatives from across India to gather at Hyderabad for prayer, and then to focus on the development of goals and strategies to reaching the unreached in India (S. D. Ponraj 1988(4):1-2). In the June 1990 news bulletin Rev. Vararuchi F. Dalavai, Chairman of CONS, reviewed the history of CONS, and the vision and goal for the congress.

> *India, with 840 million people, has about 6,00,000* villages and 4,00,000 colonies. But Christian witness is only in about 1,00,000 villages and colonies. The remaining 9,00,000 villages and colonies of India are unreached and they are our harvest fields. The churches, denominations, missions, and organizations should take up this challenge and come forward to plant churches in all these villages and colonies. …*
>
> *We have to evaluate our past performance and set new goals and work out new plans for reaching India. …*
>
> *We need to have collective concern; we need to move forward with complimentary spirit with our co-workers and not with competitive spirit. Let us put our labels, organizations, and interests behind the cross of Christ and project the crucified and resurrected Christ to the nation. Let us unite for the kingdom of God (S. D. Ponraj 1990(3):2).*

We planned a five-day congress for prayer, envisioning the task, and bringing participants together for united action over the next decade toward our goal of a church for every village and colony in India by AD 2000.

GREAT HOPE, SMALL ASPIRATIONS— THE 1990 CONGRESS ON CHURCH DEVELOPMENT

The congress on church development at Hyderabad, in Andhra Pradesh, August 14-18, 1990, brought leaders from every state of

---

*In India six hundred thousand is written as 6,00,000.

the nation. We invited 500 people, prepared for 750, and were overwhelmed by the 1,250 people who came. The program included worship, Bible study, and addresses by Indian and international speakers on vision, mission, and strategy. Each afternoon the participants gathered in smaller groups for workshops and discussion of the major issues. We concluded each day with smaller group meetings for prayer and strategic reflection.[3]

Members of the committee had worked very hard to prepare strategic resources for the congress. The manual included five church development case studies to illustrate for the participants how some were engaged in church planting among the unreached. Twenty workshop leaders had prepared materials for participants on diverse evangelistic strategies, training, and mobilization opportunities. Perhaps most important were the carefully planned steps for follow-up and a statistical summary and prayer points for each state in India.

On the final day of the conference, Dr. John Richard presented to the delegates "The Hyderabad Declaration on Church Development," a document prepared by the committee to affirm the vision for a church for every village and colony in the towns and cities of India and to summarize the shared biblical and missional convictions of the participants. The declaration emphasizes the common commitment of the participants to the nation of India as loyal citizens with respect for its religious diversity, yet at the same time with an understanding of its poverty, corruption, and injustice that are antithetical to God's purpose for the nation.

The declaration celebrates the growth in the number of Indian missionaries from 148 in 1963 to nearly 5,000 in 1990, and the establishing of the church of Jesus Christ in areas where the gospel had not been preached. The longest section of the declaration sets forth responsibilities to mobilize, teach, and train men and women in the existing churches to pray, work together, and to engage in the mission of proclamation and church planting.

Some of the distinctive aspects of these responsibilities include assisting the poor to generate income, contextualizing both the message and theological education, conducting systematic research and strategic planning, and preparing themselves spiritually and emotionally for suffering and persecution. Richard challenged the delegates to embrace the declaration, to share it with their churches and co-workers, and to make a specific commitment to the number of churches the Lord has led them to plant in the next decade (CONS India 1990).

I followed Dr. Richard, giving the closing message, and challenging participants to mobilize their task force to fulfill the mission. While the attendance greatly exceeded our goal of 750 participants, the commitments to envision new churches fell far short of our hopes. We expected attendees to commit to a goal of at least 500,000 churches, but to our shock they numbered only 22,000, growing in a few weeks to 27,000 projected new churches.

We asked, "What happened? Why such a poor response?" As we reflected on the congress, God opened our eyes to the complexity of our nation and our limitations for communicating this vision and strategy to 1,250 people from 24 different states that speak so many different languages. A nationalistic pride had blinded our eyes. We had decided to communicate the message in the national language of India, but the majority of the people at the conference did not understand Hindi. The majority of attendees knew neither English nor Hindi. No wonder we had such a low church-planting commitment.

MOBILIZING LEADERS TO ENVISION 500,000 NEW CHURCHES

God humbled us to take a step back and reconsider our communication strategies. As we prayed and discussed, we agreed to take the message to the various states in the different languages of the nation, so they understood the vision and might join the whole church in fulfilling the Great Commission. For the next five years we refocused our efforts and shared the vision and strategy with Christian leaders in as many languages as possible. Expanding the CONS committee to include a member from each state in India in 1991, we worked with these contact persons to organize conferences in each state or in various regions of a state (See Figure 6.1).

FIGURE 6.1
THE COUNCIL ON NATIONAL SERVICE MOVEMENT

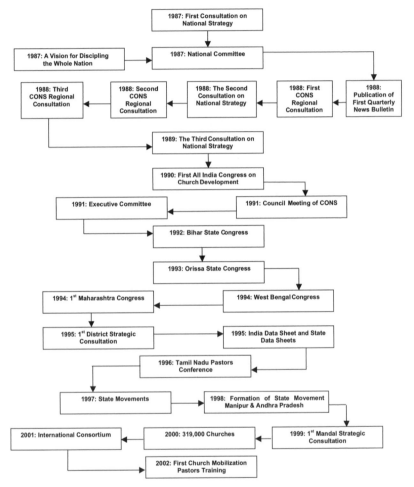

With the financial support of Dr. Gene Davis, a veterinarian from the United States, the first state conference was held in Bihar in 1993. Rev. Vararuchi F. Dalavai, now also coordinator for AD 2000 in India, challenged the participants to "plan and set their own goals toward" the CONS vision of a "church in every village and colony of every town" by AD 2000. By the end of this conference, 21 churches and missions had set goals to plant 1,500 churches in Bihar by AD 2000 and beyond (S.D. Ponraj 1993(4):5).

By 1994 CONS had developed a full calendar of conferences in several of the states in India (See Table 6.3), funded by local and international contributions with Gene Davis again providing significant support. The conference at West Bengal raised some very significant issues for the movement. In the 1991 census the state of West Bengal had a population of 65 million people and 41,000 villages. To meet the goal of a church for every village and colony, church and mission leaders would need to mobilize to plant 40,000 churches. For the 200 delegates of this congress from eight different districts in the state, this was a daunting task. After very stimulating plenary sessions and workshops, the delegates "set a goal to plant 2,500 churches" (S.D. Ponraj 1995(7):). While this was a very admirable, and even daunting commitment for these church leaders, the number fell far short of the need to achieve the vision and national strategy.

TABLE 6.3
STATE AND REGIONAL CONSULTATIONS IN 1994

Date of Consultation	Place and Topic of the Consultation
30 April – 1 May, 1994	Madhya Pradesh – Saturation Church Planting
24-26 May, 1994	Orissa –State Conference on Church Development
28-30 June, 1994	Tamil Nadu – Consultation on Church Planting
4-6 July, 1994	Vidarbha, Maharashtra – Congress on Church Planting
27-29 September, 1994	Kandesh, Maharashtra – Congress On Saturation
15-18 October, 1994	Church Planting
	West Bengal – Conference on Church Development

By 1995, after communicating the vision in multiple languages and helping the church and parachurch movements to understand the vision and strategy, and with the financial support and encouragement of DAWN Ministries in the United States, the Council on National Service (CONS) decided to call for the Second All India Congress on Church Development from 9 to 12 January, 1995, on the campus of Hindustan Bible Institute in Chennai, Tamil Nadu. For this congress 1,367 registered as delegates and 3,500 participated from every state of India.

Habakkuk 1:5 set the theme of the conference: "Look at the nations and watch—and be utterly amazed. For I am going to do something in your days that you would not believe, even if you were told" (CONS India, 1995). Following a devotional time with Neil Anderson, I challenged the delegates to consider a Saturation Church-planting Strategy to disciple the nation of India. I began by emphasizing our dependence upon God, and the need to pray and ask God to help us plant a church in every village and colony of every town and city of our nation. Second, I pointed out that we need to follow Christ as builders, becoming strategic in our approach, setting goals, developing a plan, and creating methodology. Third, we need to base our strategy on accurate information (pp. 3-2, 3-3).

A key innovation of this congress was the availability of significant research data on the states and even districts of India. The conference manual included 56 pages of strategic information that profiled populations, languages, religion, and the status of churches in every state in India (pp. 8-1-56). The data also included brief descriptions of the population and number of Christians in each district of every state in India. I went on to emphasize the importance of partnerships, working together with mission and church organizations, recognizing that no one organization can complete God's mission alone. Finally, I called delegates to develop training programs to mobilize leaders, and to work cooperatively to develop and share resources and evaluate our effectiveness toward completion of God's task (pp. 3-1-11).

Immediately following my address, Tony Samuel of the research team took two hours to introduce the research data to the delegates to help them understand how to use it to begin to think strategically about their states. Then in the afternoon the delegates met in groups by state to reflect on the challenge and to think and plan for a strategy of saturation church planting in their respective states.[4]

Some significant changes had occurred since the first congress. In the Quarterly Bulletin following the congress, the editor reports:

> The most strategic information that emerged from the congress:
> * *India is responsive and is on the threshold of a great revival.*

- *2,00,000 [sic] churches exist throughout the nation.*
- *All 514 districts in India have the presence of Christ.*
- *Northern and rural India are still unreached with the Gospel.*
- *Only 10 percent of rural India have churches.*
- *80 percent of all Christians come from Socio-Ethnic communities that make up only 22 percent of the nation's population.*
- *90 percent of the workers are aiming at the 22 percent and 10 percent are working among the remaining 78 percent of the nation's population.*
- *Only 35,000 Christian workers are discipling the whole country.*
- *For the church to reach her goal of discipling the country, the 8,00,000 new churches must be established among the unreached people groups in villages and colonies by equipping and mobilizing at least 1,20,000 workers to serve as the task force to disciple the nation (S.D. Ponraj 1995(5):2).*

Before the commencement of the congress people from all over the country sent in their goals for church planting, which totaled just under 500,000 churches. By the end of the congress churches and mission societies committed to mobilizing 60,000 new workers to plant more than 500,000 churches. Praise the Lord!

FRACTURES IN THE MOVEMENT

After seven years of hard work, the Council on National Service could celebrate the goodness of God in leading the churches in India to catch the vision for completing the task. Whereas once one million new churches to complete the Great Commission seemed impossible, by 1995 the Spirit of God had moved among us in a powerful way, bringing new vision and commitment. In 1987 when we began, none of us could even imagine planting 100,000 new churches. By 1995 the Lord had moved in the churches of India to plant 50,000 new churches (Johnstone 1991), and to commit to 500,000 more. While the Council on National Service could take no credit for planting a single church, we believed that God had used us to spread God's vision for the nation of India, and God's people had responded.

The testimonies of many individuals encouraged us:

> *I was in the ministry for 27 years. I wanted to plant many churches, but my superiors denied that plan, because they said church planting costs money, which we don't have. So as a result the vision to plant more churches was very small in me. In this conference I feel [sic] ashamed after 27 years and was in tears that I wasted my years. I realized that the local church has to take the responsibility. Only here I realized how important statistics are. Now I have decided to do something in my local church, start many other churches, and will then go to my superior and tell him, this is what I did. Pray for me. Praise the Lord (Pastor from Tamil Nadu).*

> *This vision I heard at this conference has helped me a lot, that there will be thousands and thousands of people in India to establish churches. I have made a decision to spend more time in prayer, and stop running. But I remind you that you should count the number of churches started by women, you will be surprised. We women have a place in all this! (Sister from Andhra Pradesh) (S.D. Ponraj 1995(5):3).*

At the very time when we saw the fruits of our unity and commitment, the national movement began to fracture. While the list of Council members for the 1995 Congress had representatives from every state, the executive and planning committee for the conference came exclusively from South India, and largely from Madras where the conference was held. The language diversity in India has always been a factor, and while English dominates public life in the south, north Indians use Hindi as the language of public discourse. The emergence of the AD 2000 movement in India as a separate committee and network had positive impact for mobilization of grassroots leaders, but it stretched the capacity of a small group of national leaders to plan and participate in state and national consultations. In 1995 Rev. Vararuchi F. Dalavai resigned as chairman of CONS to lead the AD 2000 initiatives in India. Immediately following the Second All India Congress on Church Development in 1995, several leaders from North India decided to break away from CONS and form their own networks.

The unity that we had forged in the first congress was always fragile. Indian Christianity has a long history of leaders and organizations pursuing their own agendas and working in competition with other Christians. For a time the CONS committee had worked with the hope and prayer for both a national strategy and a national unity for the mission of God in India. The very success of CONS appears to have sown the seeds of its fragmentation.

Since the formation of CONS, Hindustan Bible Institute had provided staff and office support for the movement. To financially sustain the movement I had sought funding from various partners in America and Europe and those funds had been channeled through the legal and financial offices of HBI. DAWN Ministries and HBI International made the 1995 Congress possible with about 10 percent of the funding contributed locally. The Lord provided the funds, and while we celebrated DAWN's commitment to match our fund-raising efforts, those funds and the accountability for them became a source of contention among state leaders. When we could not agree on the structures of accountability, that disagreement seemed to fuel other reasons for pursuing separate paths. Yet in hindsight, God continued to work in all of us to accomplish His mission in India.[5]

SHERWOOD'S REFLECTIONS ON LEADERSHIP TRAINING

In this chapter Bobby reveals some of the big-picture lessons that make this story so compelling for all of us who take seriously God's mission for His church. Two critical factors should be obvious: the centrality of vision and the absolute necessity of sound research to provide a foundation for strategic action.

1. Building vision enables potential leaders to break habits and take risks. Bobby's conclusion—we must begin with a clear picture of the end goal—is the most compelling piece of this story. As he tells his story, we see how he is prisoner of his social context, and how the expectations and criticism of others crush his desire to do greater things for God. His people and culture make him feel foolish, and they discourage him from taking risks for God. People everywhere subject their leaders to this type of pressure and criticism, so that most take the safe route, and work within the limits of public expectations. The most powerful insight in this story is how Jim Montgomery and then CONS used informal gatherings of leaders to focus on critical questions and build vision for change. Once these national and district leaders caught the vision, they felt empowered to break old expectations and habits of ministry and lead their people to do great things for God.

2. Research provides an essential knowledge base for action. From the very beginning all the participants had difficulty imagining that India could ever have a church for every 1,000 people. The first All India Congress illustrates clearly this pessimism and reluctance to engage what is obviously an impossible task. The modest changes in the vision statement reflect the underlying skepticism about the dream. By the second All India Congress in 1995, a small team of researchers has brought clarity to the problem. As the consultation of West Bengal illustrates, the numbers are not comforting, but 40,000 churches are clearly more possible than one million. More importantly, the researchers discover that Christians are present in every state and district of the nation. This fact provides a door for the district strategy, which is the subject of the next chapter.

3. Building strategy to achieve a vision takes much more time, finances, and hard work. Three years of committee work—networking, praying, preaching, and five regional consultations—laid the groundwork for the Hyderabad Declaration at the 1990

All India Congress. The declaration set forth an agenda for mobilization, training, and a national strategy for saturation church planting. Yet the response of those attending fell far short of the expectations of the organizing committee. Some dropped out, others joined, and over the next five years the steering committee continued to organize regional and state consultations to spread the vision and develop strategy for a church-planting movement. Fund-raising was a critical part of this work, and without international financial partners the movement would have languished. By the second All India Congress in 1995, the committee rejoiced in God's answer to their prayers, as the delegates attending committed to plant 500,000 churches across India.

Finally, these conferences had an amazing impact on Protestant Christian leaders in India, building unity around a new vision of the mission and purpose of God. Protestant Christianity is famous for its factionalism and isolation that cripples the mission of the church. While church leaders of mainline denominations in India had earlier bridged some of these theological and ecclesiological differences through mergers into the Church of North India and the Church of South India, the Pentecostal, Baptist, and other independent movements generally refused to cooperate on any matter. By 1995 representatives of every state and from most of the Protestant denominations and movements in India had gathered to envision together the task of discipling a whole nation. God wrought a miracle of unity around mission that led to their collective commitments to plant 500,000 new churches. While this unity was short-lived, soon fracturing into several church-planting mobilization networks, I believe it is still the most important lesson from these seven years! Discipling a whole nation requires the whole church to unite together in prayer and submission to God. This becomes clearer in the chapter that follows, when leaders begin to work together to implement the vision.

CHAPTER 6. RESEARCH AND REFLECTION QUESTIONS:

Research Exercise: Find on the Internet the website for DAWN International, (www.dawnministries.org at this writing), an organization formed by Jim Montgomery, referenced in this chapter.

1. How does the DAWN vision compare to the vision described in this chapter?

2. Can you find a similar story about the movement of the Holy Spirit for church planting on another continent and nation?

Reflection:

3. How has the DAWN movement been used by the Holy Spirit to foster church-planting movements?

4. What similarities and differences do you see between India and other nations impacted by DAWN?

END NOTES

[1] These 56 leaders represented national movements like the Evangelical Fellowship of India, India Mission Association, Evangelical Fellowship of Asia; church leaders from the Church of South India, Evangelical Church of India and the Indian National Evangelical Fellowship; mission leaders such as the head of Evangelical Team India, Indian Evangelical Mission, Friends Missionary Prayer Band, Church Growth Movement; leaders from theological institutions such as Madras Bible Seminary, Bharat Bible Institute, Hindustan Bible Institute and Emmanuel Bible Institute; and international leaders from the Southern Baptist Mission board, Partners International, Bible Centered mission and a host of parachurch movements and many others represented the gathering at the consultation (S. D. Ponraj 1988(2): 2).

[2] In July 1988 in the second regional consultation in Mohammedabad, Gujarat, 65 participants attended representing diverse church and mission organizations. In a keynote address, "Operation Reach India," I emphasized the importance of vision, planning, and proper training of leaders for reaching India. Rev. Ted Sudhaker taught the essential biblical principles for planting small churches, and Rev. V.F. Dalavai challenged participants with the need for organized prayer that regularly brings together pastors in a region to seek the Lord for His church. At the closing session the participants responded spontaneously to Rev. E. Sunder Raj's challenge "to dedicate themselves to reach India for Christ with coordinated efforts" (S. D. Ponraj 1988(3):4).

[3] I gave the inaugural message, setting forth the goals of the congress. Rev. Tissa Weerasinga and Jim Montgomery of DAWN led us in worship and Bible study each morning. Dwight Smith of United World Mission gave daily plenary addresses on Partnerships in Mission. Dr. Samuel Kamaleson addressed the conference on the Church in Mission, followed by a series of strategy studies by Weerasingha, Montgomery, Dr. John Richard, Dr. Chris Marantika from Indonesia, and Dr. K. P. Yohannan. We finished each morning with a time of intercessory prayer. Rev. Luis Bush, Chairman of the "AD2000 and Beyond" movement, challenged us in the evenings with messages on God's mission for the church (S. W. Chandhrasekhar 1990:ii).

[4] In the second and third days of the congress leaders from the state congresses in Maharashtra, West Bengal, Bihar, and Tamil Nadu shared the results of their vision and strategic planning conferences. Martin Alphonse, Ramesh Richard, and Samuel Kamaleson gave inspiring and practical messages on evangelism and church planting, and S. D. Ponraj gave an address on the "People Movement Approach in Mission" on the final day of the conference.

[5] The North India networks that facilitated the vision process include the North India Harvest network led by Dr. Raju Abraham, the Madhya Pradesh Network led by Dr. Victor Choudhri, the Bihar Network led by Dr. S.D. Ponraj, and the Punjab Network led by Dr. Alex Abraham.

CHAPTER SEVEN

REFOCUSING STRATEGY— MOBILIZING DISTRICT LEADERS

The goal of one million churches seems insurmountable in any church, mission, and national context. How do we begin to think strategically about achieving such an impossible goal? How can we convince Christians who have never cooperated to begin to pray and think strategically together about reaching their districts for Christ? Who will provide the leadership to create vision, and energize local Christians to reach out to hundreds of unreached people groups? How does one financially support a movement so diverse and scattered over such a vast population and geographical region?

The challenges inherent in this vision seemed insurmountable to the leaders and participants in this growing movement. However, through some basic research on the distribution of Christians and churches in India, God provided the key—focusing on the districts in each state of India, and mobilizing the Christians already there.

—Sherwood Lingenfelter

In preparation for the second All India congress, God enabled us to see the prophetic message He wanted us to share at the congress. For the first time we understood from the research on the distribution and state of the church in India that God had established Christian churches in every district of the nation. Second, we understood that the outcast Sudras constituted the largest segment of unreached people. From this data, God gave us the message for the participants. But we still did not have a clear picture of the strategy needed to mobilize the leaders and churches of India to complete the task. For seven years we had worked hard organizing national and state congresses, and challenging church and mission leaders in each state to catch the vision for their state, and partner together for a mission of saturation church planting. While the response of participants in the second All India Congress encouraged us, the collective commitments of participants reached only halfway to the goal of a million new churches.

During and after the congress, Tony Samuel (Hilton), National Coordinator of CONS research at Hindustan Bible Institute, observed that the scale of the task in each state was so enormous that participants, although willing and hopeful, could not imagine how to achieve the goal. Using the state of Uttar Pradesh to illustrate, Samuel noted that with its population of 139 million people, it is half the size of the United States, and larger than all but six nations in the world. To have a church for every 1,000 people would require 139,113 churches. If every Christian leader planted five churches, it would take 27,823 church planters to complete the task. For the small number of leaders from Uttar Pradesh at the second All India Congress, this seemed indeed an impossible task! (P.S. Shalem Raju 1995(6):3).

As the staff at HBI brainstormed together about this problem, Samuel (Hilton) did further data analysis that demonstrated to us that by focusing on the districts of each state in India, we could break down the problem into much more manageable pieces. First, we must seize the opportunity to mobilize the Christians in each district to disciple the district with a strategy of saturation church planting. Second, we must reach out to those almost untouched with the message of Christ, and particularly the Sudras.

As a result of the congress and the significant research of Tony Samuel (Hilton), God led leaders and churches to refocus their efforts from nation and state to districts, developing church-planting movements for every district of the nation. Researchers gathered information on the villages, cities, and towns in every district, including the population and distribution of Christians in each district, so churches could mobilize the believers in those centers to develop a movement. In such a large nation as India, breaking the task down into 521 district movements proved very helpful. We realized, on an average, every district had two million people that included Christians. We then examined which of the villages had the largest number of Christians to see how they could be mobilized to disciple their district. CONS research and mobilization staff helped to identify leaders in each district and assisted them to develop a vision to plant 2,000 churches in each of these districts. Many people found this local vision exciting and within their reach! They also discovered how they could work together to see it becoming a reality. When the people of God organize to do the work of God, they find God at work ahead of them.

DEVELOPING THE STRATEGY AT THE DISTRICT LEVEL

CONS staff at HBI organized the first district consultation (DSC), April 18-20, 1995, in the district of Adilabad in the state of Andhra Pradesh with the local support of Paul Wiig of Outreach Map of India. We had 25 contacts who had attended the congress from that region. We asked, and they agreed, to help us hold a consultation for the district and to invite others to attend. To our surprise 60 delegates—pastors, evangelists, and Christian workers from 13 missions and church movements—gathered at the town of Mancheriyal for the consultation (P. S. Shalem Raju 1995(6):8).

Following Jim Montgomery's strategy, we asked, "What will Adilabad look like when we have fulfilled the Great Commission in this district?" For the first time they began to think of the larger vision. Tony Samuel Hilton "provided the details of the Harvest Fields of this District to the Taluk (a cluster of villages), Block, and Village level with demographic details, literate levels, and percentages. This is the first time for the Adilabad church to hear and see information of this nature. … Then the Consultation spent time in intercessory prayers for each village" (p. 8).

We shared the vision of saturating the district with a church in every village and colony of every town and city, a church for every 1,000 people and every people group. Using research data from the District Profile (see Figure 7:1), we showed them that with 2,082,479 people in the district, one church for every 1,000 people would require 2,082 churches. When we asked how they might possibly achieve this, all affirmed that the goal was impossible to do independently, but jointly they could fulfill the mission. All 60 delegates agreed that, if they were willing to share the task in two major phases, they could achieve the goal. As a first step they agreed if each of the approximately 100 Christian workers in the District would recruit and train three church planters from among the 10,800 Christians worshiping in churches in the district, this would develop a mission force equal to the task. Once they had trained these people, each leader, including the delegates, would be challenged to plant five churches, which would achieve the goal. At the end of the consultation, the delegates agreed to gather regularly for prayer for their district and for the workers needed to plant churches to reach the district for Christ.

With the support of a challenge grant from a Christian foundation, we raised funding to facilitate research and district consultations

TABLE 7.1
SATURATION CHURCH PLANTING CONSULTATIONS IN ANDHRA PRADESH, 1995

District:	Date:	Local Convener:
1. Adilibad	April 18-20, 1995	Mr. Paul Wiig
2. Twin Cities	June 26-28, 1995	Mr. S. J. Peter
3. Karimnagar	July 27-29, 1995	Mr. M. Joseph
4. West Godavary	August 3-5, 1995	Pastor Ch. Samuel
5. Medsak	August 17-20, 1995	Pastor Steeven G'Kumar
6. Srikakulam	September 8-10, 1995	Rev. P. Abraham
7. Krishna	October 13-15, 1995	Rev. M. J. Rajkumar
8. Chittoor	October 20-22, 1995	Bro. Simon Caesar
9. East Godavary	November 3-6, 1995	Bro. Babu Rao
10. Vizianagaram	November 10-11, 1995	Rev. P. Theophilus
11. Rangareddi	November 23-25, 1995	Pastor D. Shanthi Kumar
12. Nalgonda	December 15-17, 1995	Mr. A.D.K.V. Prasad
		Mr. P. David

(P. S. Shalem Raju 1995(7):2)

in selected states of India. From April to December 1995 Rev. P. S. Shalem Raju, CONS training co-coordinator, facilitated twelve district strategy consultations for Saturation Church Planting in the state of Andhra Pradesh (see Table 7.1). At the same time Tony Samuel Hilton mobilized a team of researchers to research the entire state of Tamil Nadu in time for a World Vision-sponsored Pastor's Conference, January 22-26, 1996, in Madras (P. S. Shalem Raju 1995(7):2-3).

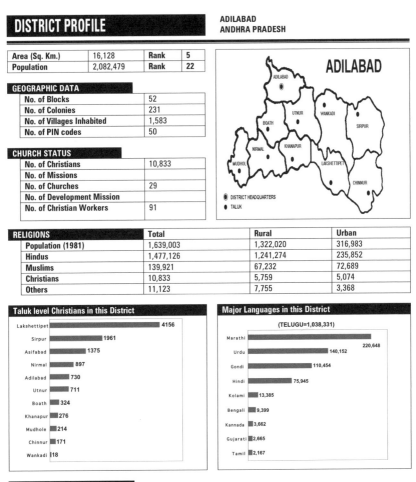

FIGURE 7.1
DISTRICT PROFILE, ADILABAD (GUPTA AND HILTON, 1995:111)

The momentum for Saturation Church Planting spread like fire.[1] In each location leaders from diverse denominations came together to pray and seek the will of God for His mission in their districts. Out of these consultations leaders caught a new vision for evangelism and church planting.

As we shared the vision in district after district, state after state (Gupta and Hilton 1995, 1996, 1997, 1998), we saw thousands of people committed to fulfill the Great Commission. City, state, and national leaders came eager and ready to help. Often unnoticed, these hard working grassroots leaders were already involved in planting churches, but had very little training. We soon realized that God had already burdened people all over the nation. We found pastors' prayer fellowships around the country at district and Taluk levels. As God led us to present the vision to these pastors, they caught a new vision for their district and many committed to gather again for prayer for one another and for the mission of God's church.

As they shared their individual stories of God-size events, they realized that God was at work outside of their personal spheres of ministry. They all felt a new zeal to embrace God's mission for their district and they committed their lives to disciple the district together. God confirmed His leading for us, as a national steering team to disciple the whole nation through the development of district movements.

UNDERSTANDING THE ELEMENTS OF A DISTRICT STRATEGY

In the course of sharing the vision with local church leaders of each district, we found that God always raised up a number of workers to serve. Equipped at various levels, with skills appropriate to the context where they live, these people took the vision and mobilized to bring Christ to unreached villages and people groups. We challenged each church to take responsibility to plant five new churches in the district. After several years of consultations to mobilize district pastors and churches (Table 7.2), Christians across India caught a vision to release and sup-

TABLE 7:2
CONS DISTRICT STRATEGIC CONSULTATIONS, 1995-97

State	Number Consultations
1. Andhra Pradesh	22
2. Bihar	2
3. Delhi	1
4. Himachal Pradesh	1
5. Karnataka	6
6. Madhya Pradesh	4
7. Maharashtra	10
8. Orissa	5
9. Pondichery	2
10. Punjab	1
11. Tamil Nadu	22
12. Uttar Pradesh	6
13. West Bengal	19

(P. S. Shalem Raju 1997(1):3-5).

port their people to go to the unreached peoples in the nation. Through these district consultations, God called out leaders who would play a key part in the planting of new churches in the district. Two types of leaders emerged, Christian professionals and grassroots evangelists. The grassroots evangelists led people to Christ, but most of them did not see the significance of the church. Mostly rural people, they worked independently, although some had small congregations. Some were connected to different church or mission movements, but most were unsupervised and did whatever they wanted. While they often struggled financially, they faithfully did the work of an evangelist.

The professionals had a recognized place in the community. Some of these leaders worked for the government, others as school principals, and others in jobs that allowed them to have influence in the community. Because they earned decent salaries, they usually did not need resources to make things happen. They saw themselves as God's instruments to serve the church and to encourage the pastor and workers. I believe the Lord especially brought them to help and encourage the grassroots workers.

Samuel Ebenezer, a correspondent of Jude school and the president of Jude Educational Trust in Shadol district in Chattishgar, is one such leader. He met Dr. Lamech Inbaraj, the national co-ordinator of CONS in 1999, and learned about the vision of

CONS. Fascinated by the vision with a burden for his district, he invited both Dr. Inbaraj and Mr. Jeyakumar, one of the training coordinators of CONS, to Shadol to conduct a district strategic consultation. Prior to the consultation, he shared the vision of CONS with pastors working in Shadol district and asked them to pray for the discipling of their district. Samuel Ebenezer then gathered 65 pastors for a consultation of the Shadol district in the year 2000. During the consultation they together set a goal to plant 89 churches and develop 125 leaders in the next two years. Ebenezer is leading the pastors' fellowship that meets once a month for prayer and planning to achieve the goal.

SEEKING "JOHN KNOX" DISTRICT LEADERSHIP

We soon realized that the work of discipling a district required much more than providing a vision. Between 1995 and 1999 we learned that we needed the "John Knox" in the district who would say "give me the district or I die." We needed a leader so committed that he would take responsibility to develop and build a church-planting movement. Further, each leader needed an apostolic team to serve as the caretakers of the vision, to equip and motivate the church planters, and to network with the national movement. Without such leaders, the initial enthusiasm of local leaders gradually faded, with only a few carrying on the initial vision. The following case study illustrates the significant role of such a leader.

CASE STUDY: TRICHY DISTRICT, TAMIL NADU

Pastor Rajasekhar of Apostolic Fellowship Tabernacle in Trichy district of Tamil Nadu attended the district strategic consultation conducted by CONS in 1999. There Rajasekhar heard for the first time the vision to plant churches in every village and colony of every town and city of his district. The Trichy district of Tamil Nadu has a population of 4,100,000 and thus required a minimum of 4,100 churches to achieve the vision. In 1998 Trichy had only 282 churches and 273 pastors. Further, Rajasekhar pastored a small church with 70 members. Challenged by the vision, he prayed to the Lord to help him plant a minimum of five churches.

As Pastor Rajasekhar prayed for Trichy, he discussed with the CONS Tamil Nadu state coordinator, Mohan Cornelius, how the district might be discipled. Cornelius asked Rajasekhar to continue to pray and to mobilize other pastors and lay leaders in Trichy to pray for the discipling of the district. Rajasekhar, determined to see his district discipled, started to mobilize prayer in his local church and became the John Knox of Trichy. After much prayer, he initiated a pastors' fellowship, shared the vision, and today 80 pastors gather every month to pray for the district and to discuss how to multiply churches in Trichy.

When the national office conducted a follow-up meeting at Trichy in the year 2001, Rajasekhar reported that in two years God enabled him personally to plant four churches and develop 11 leaders. Further, the pastors' fellowship had been faithfully meeting to pray, and during that same period, God worked through them to plant 105 new churches and disciple 92 additional leaders in Trichy district. Praise God!

Pastor Rajasekhar illustrates the passion and commitment needed in a leader who can translate a vision into the reality of committed prayer and the hard work of church planting. This type of leadership is apostolic, focused on vision, spiritual leadership, and equipping and empowering others to serve. The typical "John Knox" mobilizes pastors and lay leaders to pray for God to raise up leaders and churches in the district. Every district experienced spiritual opposition and attacks from the wicked one. This process of mobilizing people to pray turned them to God and created new bonds among believers in the district. As people grasped the vision, God led many new workers to join the task force. Young evangelists soon asked for more training: "How can we do effective evangelism? How do we plant churches? How do we make disciples?" Many said, "We do not know how to study our Bible and preach effectively. Can you help us?"

As the demand to equip the task force grew, the trainers could not meet the demand. We needed what we called trainers of trainers, skilled people indigenous to a region who understood the local people and were able to impart evangelistic and church-planting skills. In order to equip them effectively and empower them to equip others, we needed teaching and study materials in the local languages of the people.

THE FORMATION OF STATE MOVEMENTS

By 1997 the effectiveness of the district strategy was evident to all of us in CONS.[2] Praising God for the movement of the Holy Spirit among the churches, we began to think together about how to implement the district strategy in every state of the nation of India. In the Comprehensive Status Report of 1995-1997, *CONS News Tracks* articulated goals to mobilize existing churches and leaders for this task.

> 9. *To guide the church, mission societies and para-church organizations to develop State, Regional, and National Partnerships for mutual encouragement in prayer, fellowship and sharing of resources.*
> 10. *To establish a working community in every state represented at the Congress 1995 who will carry the vision of discipling the state through the strategy of saturation church planting (P. S. Raju 1997 4 (1): 3).*

To assist and enable church leaders for this mission, the CONS staff in Chennai organized a program of research and publication to support these goals.[3]

One of the strengths of CONS leadership was their continuing effort to assess their effectiveness and measure annually their progress toward the goal of a church for every 1,000 people in India. In an article in *CONS News Tracks* (Raju 1997 (4), pp.6-7) the editor, Shalem Raju, asks, "Why is church planting not taking place in spite of serious overseas contributions to the effort?" The article concludes that

1. Past and present churches are reluctant to share the resources of leadership;
2. Leaders lack experience in church planting and setting time-bound goals;

3. Leaders in historic and emerging churches do not understand how to empower grassroots men and women to make disciples, train others, and raise financial support;

4. Discipling activity is methods/manual-oriented rather than mentor-oriented; Bible school training typically replicated western formal schooling.

The national CONS team recognized that for saturation church planting to take root, the momentum of the movement had to shift to state leadership and local training of leaders to catch the vision, to commit to planting new churches, and to equip grassroots leaders to proclaim the gospel and plant new churches. Toward that end they identified state coordinators and facilitated the formation of state committees for Maharashtra, Andhra Pradesh, and Tamil Nadu, and they identified a state coordinator for Gujarat.

During this same period they organized and staffed training through five Schools of Evangelism in three states and four languages.[4]

SHERWOOD'S REFLECTIONS ON LEADERSHIP TRAINING

The District Strategy provided a critical breakthrough for these Indian leaders. By shifting from nation and state to district, CONS leaders demonstrated that an enormous task could be addressed on a scale that local leaders could imagine possible. Moving from the impossible to the possible nurtured the spiritual fires of faith and hope among local Christian leaders. Gathered together in a local city, CONS staff inspired them with God's mission for the church, and then, using good research, helped them grasp the possibility of equipping leaders to evangelize their district and plant churches for every village, colony, and town for every 1,000 people. Some very specific applications may be drawn from their discoveries and insights.

1. Defining achievable goals is critical to the mobilization of leaders. The District Strategy converted the scope of the task from a goal of impossible magnitude (one million new churches) to a goal approachable and possible (four hundred new leaders, each planting five new churches) for existing churches and leaders.

2. Prayer networking leads to learning and cooperative engagement. One of the most powerful forms of informal learning comes from peer networking. Table 7.2 documents how CONS organized district consultations that launched these prayer networks. When the prayer networks continued, the leaders gathered, told their stories of God at work, and prayed for one another. These stories of God's work and of people's responses are the most important part of peer learning. Through this interaction they shared knowledge and challenges as they sought to implement the vision. These same networks became the sources of requests for other forms of informal training.

3. Christian professionals are key leadership resource persons. Financially able, and gifted with skills of communication, organization, and management, they may assist movement leaders and pastors to encourage and train others. Further, their engagement in ministry models for church planters the recruitment and empowerment of "non-clergy" in the mission work of the church.

4. Apostolic leaders, the "John Knox" types, mentor others to greater effectiveness. Bobby made the specific point that the district strategy worked best when a "John Knox" stepped up to inspire and mentor others. Like the Apostle Paul in Acts, these leaders lay foundations upon which others can build. In the two case studies presented, these men served as catalysts for the ministry, and filled the training gap inherent in the informal seminar strategy of training. They called pastors together and led them through a process that resulted in shared vision and goals for their district. They then organized monthly fellowship meetings for prayer and planning. In the context of these meetings they built relationships with the other working pastors and evangelists, helped them to encourage one another through sharing and prayer, and guided them in planning and implementation. In effect, the apostolic leader fills the training gap, facilitating peer learning, and

personally mentoring and coaching the slower learners in the group.

Finally, the staff and financial support of Hindustan Bible Institute sustained the momentum of a movement launched in conferences and consultations. Without this institutional leadership, support structure and funding, the district strategy would have collapsed. A team of people had to take responsibility for contacting local leaders, organizing district consultations, and supporting local district leadership with staff and materials to facilitate the initial consultation and follow-up leadership training. HBI provided a coordinating leadership and management center for the CONS movement.

Chapter 7. Research and Reflection Questions:

Research Exercise: Find the websites for the Joshua Project and the Caleb Project on the Internet.

1. What are the distinctive missions of each of these organizations?
2. Where are the least-reached peoples of the world (Joshua Project)?
3. How might you learn how to get involved with Hindu and Muslim outreach (Caleb Project)?

Reflection:

4. How does research contribute to the development of church-planting movements and reaching unreached peoples?
5. How would you mobilize people in your local church to begin to do research and strategic thinking about reaching the unreached?

End Notes

[1] During the same period CONS Orissa State co-coordinator, Rev. D. N. Sahu, completed five district consultations. Rev. Shrikanth B. Pathane, CONS Maharashtra State co-coordinator reported "the Lord has enabled a very strong prayer movement" emerging out of five district consultations in that state, and Rev. Subro Sekhar Sircar, CONS West Bengal State co-coordinator reported a

similar work of the Spirit of God in seven district consultations in West Bengal (P. S. Shalem Raju 1995(7):3).

[2] In the annual review at the end of 1996 CONS leaders reported the completion of District Consultations in 95 districts, involving 5281 leaders; delegates at these consultations had set goals for planting 28,290 churches, and mobilizing 11,384 workers (P. S. Raju 1997 4 (1): 3).

[3] By April 1997 they had prepared and published 13 State Charts illustrating the essential needs for strategic church planting in each district of these states. The Unfinished Task, a book that summarized census data, religious affiliation, languages, literacy, caste, and profiles of church-planting needs for each district in a state, was published for Andhra Pradesh, Tamil Nadu, Maharashtra, and Gujarat (Gupta and Hilton 1995, 1996, 1997a, 1997b). Publications on the states of West Bengal, Rajasthan, Karnataka followed in 1999 (Gupta 1999a,b,c). To support training of leaders they translated the church planters manual into Tamil, and a leadership training Bible study manual, Called to Shepherd, first into Kanada, and later into Telugu, Tamil, Marati, Oriya, Bengali, and Hindi. Researchers began the work of preparing profiles on 837 people groups and entered all data from their research into a computer database.

[4] The results of this intensive effort at mobilization and training included 34 new researchers and district consultation coordinators, 114 new church planters, and mobilization seminars and consultations for 1,703 church leaders (Raju 1997 (4), pp.6-7).

EQUIPPING LEADERS—MOBILIZING LOCAL CHURCHES

The district strategy for India transformed "vision impossible" into a vision within reach of existing churches and mission organizations. But no one had the capacity to train all of these people in the basic skills of church planting. The magnitude of the task required a wholly new approach to leadership training. Through the state and district consultations the vision for church planting spread far beyond the capacity of existing training institutions and resources. Further, the demand for immediate training expanded as rapidly as the vision, and people needed it today, not five or ten years later.

In this chapter Bobby recounts how God provided new resources for training from international partners, and a new method—informal seminars—to meet the immediate needs of pastors and church planters. Through this strategy HBI and other ministries provided "as needed" training on a variety of topics in different languages and in places and at times that best served the needs and interests of the participants.

—Sherwood Lingenfelter

In 1987 the primary task of the Council on National Service was to broadcast the vision to disciple the whole nation. Church, parachurch and mission organizations had to understand the message God was bringing to the church. As the church caught the vision and got involved, CONS leaders heard a cry from pastors all over the country. "How do we plant churches?" This forced council members to address a new need, that of equipping leaders in the local churches to implement the vision.

In the first effort, the district consultations created vision and brought pastors together for prayer. As a network of pastors, they worked to reach the district. But as we facilitated the district consultations, the Lord showed us the power of the local church to do God's work. This led us to develop a second phase of training, mobilizing local churches to own the vision and equipping the pastor to enable the task force from the local church.

After years of working with the informal process, two broad types of training emerged to equip leaders for this national church-planting movement. The first is a series of seminars to train church planters and pastors in the vision and steps to implement a church-planting movement. Without these skills, pastors and lay leaders could not achieve the essential tasks. The second group of seminars are designed to equip the pastors to help their local churches articulate a vision, and then to mobilize and equip lay leaders to do evangelism and church planting.

The needs for informal training have expanded dramatically. In 1987 India had a task force of about 25,000 evangelists and church planters, but in 2004 there were more than 250,000 committed to planting new churches. Most of these workers have little or no training, but have responded to the call of pastors who have caught the vision to plant thousands of churches in their districts. The large majority of these pastors and lay workers will continue to need informal training, or they will become discouraged and may quit.

By 1998 we had gained a new appreciation for the power of God to mobilize His people for his work, and at the same time, our research had demonstrated the enormous challenges before us. As we assessed our progress in 1998 we observed that

80 percent of the Indian Christians come from less than 22 percent of all the ethnic communities of

India…more startling is that 90 percent of all the task
force is concentrated among the 22 percent and less
than 10 percent among the rest of the people groups.
There are 4,635 people groups in India, less than 10
percent have a church. … If we are going to enter into
new people groups, efforts must be made to train… a
task force with the ability to cross cultural boundaries
(Gupta 2001:5-6).

The first and greatest need is to equip thousands of men and women across the nation to focus on discipling these unevangelized peoples.

By this time we had also learned some basic principles that we believe are essential to fulfilling the Great Commission in India in our generation. First, we must work in a "synergetic environment," working together across denominational and mission boundaries to serve the Lord in building His church. No single organization could ever plant churches for every 1,000 people in India. "The synergy we create will hasten the process…and enable us to accomplish this task…. We need to look for networking opportunities, understand the limitation and partner with movements so the highest level of effectiveness is generated in partnership to finish the task" (Gupta 2001:6).

Second, we must "think of new ways of equipping the task force. We cannot live with the luxury of training individuals for 3 to 7 years before sending them to the field" (Gupta 2001:7). We need to develop new paradigms of informal and non-formal training for those already in ministry, and for those new leaders whom God calls and moves to become evangelists and church planters. This training must be available when and where people need it, and it must move them immediately into ministry application. The training must be available in all the major languages of India so that people can be equipped in their mother tongue, and can worship God and give the good news to others in their own languages.

Finally, we understood that the largest pool of untrained leaders were the people in our local congregations, who had been

taught that only ordained pastors do ministry. Our biggest challenge then lay in "the mobilization of the national church to do
the work of evangelism, call its people to surrender for the task of
cross cultural missions, adopt unreached people groups and challenge the people to give for the work of discipling the nation." We
believed that God was leading us to envision and equip local congregations, and to focus upon calling and equipping the emerging
youth generation of India (Gupta 2001:8).

HBI'S DEPARTMENT OF CHURCH MOBILIZATION

From the very beginning of CONS the board of HBI had
committed to support the movement by providing staff, office, ac-
counting, and other technical support for the movement. From the
start HBI's staff produced the newsletter and facilitated the state,
national, and district consultations. By 1999 God made it clear to
us that HBI should have a department of church mobilization with
a full-time director and staff to organize and support the training
of church leaders across India. My job was to raise partners and
funds in the United States and Europe to finance this effort.

The mission of the Church Mobilization Department is to support the Council on National Service (CONS) in its efforts to mobilize and equip the body of Christ in India to complete the Great
Commission. In 2000 we appointed Dr. H. Lamech Inbaraj to lead
this department, to assess the progress of the CONS movement up
to that time, and to coordinate and carry out our mission of mobilization and equipping church leaders.[1] In 2003 the department conducted 31 seminars in 15 districts of five different states to spread the
vision. One pastor testified of the impact of such a vision seminar:

> *I am in the ministry of the Lord for the last 20 years
> but so far I did not know as to what the purpose and
> the vision of a church were and what they should be.
> After 20 years God helped me to see it. The CMPT
> programme has helped me to see the vision in the way
> God would look at the task that needs to be completed*
> — Pr. Paul Joshua, Vellore.

The training programs of the department aim to equip pastors, evangelists, and missionaries with both content and skill to implement and finish the goal of the Great Commission effectively. The training ranges from evangelism to church planting and leadership development. Table 8.1 summarizes the range of programs offered in 2003/04, through which we trained a total of 1,329 pastors and missionaries.

TABLE 8.1
CHURCH MOBILIZATION TRAINING PROGRAMS
APRIL, 2003-MARCH 2004

Name of the Training	No. of Training Classes
Church Mobilization Pastors Training	51
Saturation Church Planting	5
Global Focus	1
Saturation Church Planting (Dwight Smith)	1
Training of Trainers (GGCC – AIMS)	1
Asian School of Evangelism (In Tamil Nadu, Rajasthan, Orrisa, Andhra Pradesh, Gujarat, Maharastra and Bhopal)	7
Urban Consultation	1

(Lamech Inbaraj 2004)

SCHOOLS OF EVANGELISM

Focus on evangelism has been a part of the CONS movement from its inception. Early in the movement we established a partnership with Evangelism Resources to establish Asian Schools of Evangelism that offer a ten-month, two-semester, residential-type training program to equip evangelists to understand and communicate the gospel, and build skills for evangelism and church planting. The Department of Church Mobilization has continued to facilitate the establishment of these schools in various states and districts of India, and it currently provides administrative, academic, and advocacy services to seven schools situated in seven states of India. The following report from Gujarat illustrates the challenges of equipping leaders in diverse parts of the nation.

> *By the immense grace of God and according to the desires of CONS, Gujarat Institute of Evangelism and Church Planting … was started at Fort Songadh in the quarters of the Jungle Cooperative Society Ltd on 1ˢᵗ of August 2000. … The pioneering work … was carried out by Mr. Lamech Inbaraj and Rev. Isaac Soundaraj with the help of the local pastors and INEC coordinators in Gujarat.*
>
> *To start with ten students got enrolled … but in October, 6 students went away for the reason unknown. … To teach and train these boys the local pastors and evangelists came forward who are well qualified theologically and with church-planting experiences. They are from different denominations and working in different organizations. … In the middle of last year … mainline pastors … were prohibited to teach in the school by some forces. But our God is great. With the help of parachurch pastors the school went on smoothly under the guidance of Mr. Premchand Patel. … By the immense grace of God we were able to get the permission from the Bishop of North India for their Pastors and Leaders to teach in our school.*
>
> *The students showed their keen interest to learn deeper truths and equip themselves in serving the Lord. … During the weekends they were made to assist the local pastors and thereby train themselves in the ministerial work. … The Final Examination was taken in May 2001 and four students completed the course successfully (Devanboo 2001:10-11).*

In the Asian School of Evangelism the students engage in practical evangelistic ministries networking with the local churches and assisting leaders of local church-planting initiatives. They also are required to prepare and write a viable creative project for their future ministry. Graduates usually find ministries with regional church or parachurch organizations.[2]

TRAINING PASTORS FOR CHURCH MOBILIZATION

In 2002 we launched a "Church Mobilization Pastor's Training" for 750 pastors in the states of Tamil Nadu, Karnataka, Kerala, and Maharashtra. Using informal and non-formal modular training, our goal is help these pastors develop church-planting movements among unreached peoples and areas through their churches. The training focuses on helping the pastor understand the purpose and mission of the church, to build and cast vision for the congregation, and then to discern who in the congregation has the potential to serve as evangelists, pastors, teachers, and church planters, and equip them to accomplish the task of the Great Commission.

The church mobilization pastors' training (CMPT) begins with a module to help meet this need (see Table 8.2). After working with pastors and leaders of several hundreds of denominations in the last 17 years, we found that only a handful had a well-defined purpose and vision statement for their local churches. Therefore, we developed a two and a half-day module to train the pastors with these skills. At the end of the course they will have prepared a clear purpose and vision statement for their local church, and they will have a draft plan for its implementation.

In Module II (see Table 8.2) we help pastors reflect upon a biblical theology of leadership that focuses on the spiritual giftedness of the members and the five ministry functions in the local church according to Ephesians 4:11. We then teach the participants how to develop leadership and mobilize all of Christ's people in the local church to be part of the mission's work. This module, conducted for three days, has as its foundation material developed by Dwight Smith on Saturation Church Planting.

In subsequent modules we provide materials and equip pastors to train their people in the basic skills of evangelism, discipleship, and church planting. In the final module of the training we expect

TABLE 8.2
TOPICS FOR CHURCH MOBILIZATION
PASTORS TRAINING

Module	Seminar Title	Topics
I	Vision Building & Purpose of the Local Church	a) Writing a purpose statement b) A biblical purpose statement for local church c) Writing a vision statement d) Communicating the purpose and vision statement e) Developing a detailed strategic plan
II	Saturation Church Planting	a) Restoring the local church to its biblical purpose b) How to mobilize the church into the world c) Identifying your circle of accountability d) No Leadership? No Future!
III	Evangelism and Church Planting	a) Theology of Evangelism b) Evangelism and Church Planting c) Barriers to Evangelism d) Process of Conversion e) Identifying and Developing Effective Methods of Evangelism. f) Saturation Church-Planting Strategy g) The Church is God's Instrument to Disciple the Nation h) Reaching the Unreached i) The Cycle of Church Planting.
IV	Equipping the Saints in Making Disciples	Jesus' Model of Discipleship: a) Come and See b) Follow me c) Be with me d) Remain in Me State
V	Growing a Great Commission church	a) The plan of the church for global mission b) Building a missions committee in the local church c) Mobilizing prayer for missions through the local church d) Developing a comprehensive plan to mobilize missions e) Planning & implementing a missions' conference f) Understanding and learning to communicate faith promise g) Mobilizing the church for personal involvement in missions h) Building partnerships to target unreached peoples

these pastors to mobilize prayer in their churches for unreached people groups. The pastors are introduced to important mission concepts, a biblical basis for partnerships to reach the unreached people groups, and how to make harvest connections and church-planting movements. We encourage them to form networks with other pastors and congregations so they can launch out and send missionary teams to reach the unreached.

We believe that some, and perhaps many, of these pastors may have apostolic gifts and thus serve as foundation layers, equipping others to plant and build new churches. The training seeks to develop foundation-laying skills, and to encourage those who are capable to serve as apostolic leaders in their regions. We pray that many who go through this training will move from being pastors to becoming apostles. And for those whose gifts are clearly pastor or teacher, we pray they will also gain a vision for envisioning, empowering, and releasing their people for the work of the Great Commission.

In the CONS effort to mobilize the whole church nationwide and to sustain the multiplication process, we had to develop trainers of trainers for every state. God helped us understand that unless we commit to develop lay and pastoral leaders, the churches will not grow spiritually and numerically, nor will they carry out their responsibility for the Great Commission. Toward that objective, in 2003-04 we supported Church Mobilization Training Centers in five states (see Table 8.3).[3]

Each center functions like a modular school in which 50 participants come together for 15 days over a 12-month period to undergo training in the five modules of CMPT. We encourage participants to function as a close-knit group of people with a common vision to mobilize the body of Christ to reach unreached people groups and to disciple them. We also encourage the participants to form a minimum of five partnerships, consisting of ten pastors in each, that form an alliance to raise enough resources to reach and disciple an unreached people group. As a partnering group they will identify and send a missionary for cross-cultural training for eventual outreach engagements with an unreached people group.

Table 8.3
Church Mobilization Pastor's Training Centers, 2004

States	Centers	No. of People	Modules conducted
Tamil Nadu	Vellore	58	5
	Kancheepuram	56	4
	Cuddalore	48	5
	Chennai	40	5
	Madurai	52	3
Total		254	22
Maharastra	Thane	35	3
	Nagpur	48	3
	Nashik	42	3
	Amaravathi	40	3
	Chandrapur	56	3
Total		221	15
Karnataka	Bangalore	52	5
	KGF	56	5
	Davangere	38	1
Total		146	11
Kerala	Quilon	54	2
Andhra Pradesh	Warrangal	56	1
Total		*104*	3
Total	15	809	51 Programs

Saturation Church-planting Seminars

To equip emerging leaders in the nationwide church-planting movement, the Department of Church Mobilization, working with

CONS state and district leaders, developed an informal curriculum to meet the specific needs articulated by denominational leaders and pastors in the district movements. These seminars changed, depending upon the location and needs of the churches calling for help. Some topics, such as methods of evangelism and church planting, had to be contextualized for particular regions and translated into local languages. The level of training also varied, so that in some places we taught very basic skills, and in others we helped leaders gain advanced skills for training others. By providing this training in context, pastors and lay leaders need pause only for a short time from their work to gain new knowledge and skill.

One area of critical need was training for Saturation Church-planting for leaders of denominational and parachurch organizations. We developed two levels of training, using materials developed by Dwight Smith for Saturation Church Planting International and Richard Lewis of United World Mission. The first level focuses on Philosophical, Exegetical, and Theological expositions of Saturation Church Planting. The second level, the Omega Course of United World Mission, focuses on practice.

From 2001 to 2004 we taught a total of 84 key leaders of denominations and parachurch organizations (See Table 8.4). The participants ranged from CEOs to executive managers, taking seminars in four centers in North India and one in Chennai, South India.

The training program offered five modules (Table 8.5), one every six months. The final module was held in Chennai at HBI where 64 delegates from the other centers came together for the Certification Program and Ceremony. Fifty-two participants completed the five modules, receiving certificates in New Calvary Church from United World Missions Vice-President Dr. Richard Lewis and his team members. The graduates of this program are expected to be master trainers, equipping pastors and leaders of organizations in their home regions, who will in turn train the local church leaders in their districts for evangelism and church planting.

I believe that leadership development is non-negotiable. We have learned in hundreds of district consultations that local pastors are eager to embrace the vision, but they lack basic knowledge

Table 8.4
Saturation Church-planting Centers, 2003/2004

SCP Centers	No. of People Trained	Modules Completed
Jodhpur (Rajasthan)	25	1
Bhopal	13	4
Chennai	23	4
Kolkota	23	4
4 Centers	84	13

(Lamech Inbaraj, 2004)

Table 8.5
Saturation Church-planting Modules

Modules	Thrust
Module I	SCP Vision
Module II	Evangelism and Cell groups
Module III	Discipleship
Module IV	Stewardship
Module V	Multiplication & Mobilization of Churches

(Lamech Inbaraj, 2004)

and skills essential to mobilize their people. We will never fulfill the Great Commission unless we equip leaders for the church and its mission. In the Indian National Evangelical Church association (INEC), evangelists found it easier to plant multiple churches than to grow existing churches. We must intentionally help to equip leaders to plant and build the church to achieve our goal of discipling the whole nation. This has been the central mission of the Church Mobilization Department at HBI.

Based on the need and request of local pastors, we have provided short seminars to thousands of emerging leaders, equipping them to do evangelism, plant churches, study the Bible, prepare a sermon, make disciples, start a cell ministry, and lead a church. From the inception of the movement in 1987 to 2004, the CONS staff at HBI had equipped more than 45,000 emerging leaders in all the various trainings for church planting.

Through this process we have seen God building His church. The pastor who learned to enable leaders in his church saw God at work in fresh and powerful ways. People grew in their walk with God and in their service, and they gave more sacrificially to support the mission of the church. The churches began to target villages where no church existed. Pastors planted new churches and witnessed growth in existing congregations. This created a need for new leaders, people who could teach new converts and shepherd small churches. Most of these leaders emerged as bi-vocational workers who had only local church training.

GOD GREW HIS CHURCH BEYOND OUR IMAGINATION

Between the years 1987 and 2000, the number of churches in India grew at an unprecedented rate. The story touches every denomination and mission movement.

In January 1998, the Evangelical Church in India inaugurated its 1,000th church building. I wanted to know … how many more churches did they have without a building? The answer was astounding; there were 1,200 more churches ready for buildings. … In addition…Emmanuel Ministries in Kota, Rajasthan, has work stretching all over the nation, they have planted over 1,800 churches with a membership of over 85,000. The Indian National Evangelical Fellowship, the church-planting wing of HBI set a goal in 1987 to plant 1,000 churches. INEF not only reached its goal but planted a total of 1,154 churches with a membership of 40,950. The New Life Assemblies of God Church in Chennai is the largest church in the nation but the exciting phenomena that is taking place in this church is the growth of the cell movement. Today, they report that God has helped them start over 1,000 cell groups in the city. As a denomination they have over 3,600 churches all over the country with a membership of 350,000.

> *Maranatha ministries in India have planted 245*
> *churches with a membership of 11,000. The Gospel for*
> *Asia has planted 2,500 churches over the nation, and*
> *Prince of Peace ministries has planted 200 churches*
> *with a membership of 4,500 (Gupta 2001:4).*

We rejoice in how God has motivated churches and mission organizations in ways that we had hoped and prayed for from the very first gathering of CONS in 1987.

By way of illustration, in our very first district consultation at Adilibad, Paul Wiig of Outreach Map served as a key facilitator for prayer, research, and mobilization of leaders in that district. Outreach Map started its ministries from that consultation with a Portable Bible School, providing two months of training for 55 young people from Evangelism Resources. Accepting the challenge to reach the unreached, Outreach Map then sent out a pioneer team of these trainees, mentored by a senior pastor, to strategic centers where there were no churches. They planted churches in Adilibad, and then in two other districts of the states of Maharastra and Madhya Pradesh (Wiig 2004).

Convinced by this experience that they needed more in-depth training for pioneer church planters, Wiig constructed the Fishers of Men training center, and with funding and curricular help from Evangelism Resources, began the Asian School of Evangelism. Over a period of seven years 100 students graduated from this school, and Outreach Map sent many of them to pioneer new church-planting work. The shortcomings of this program was its one year residential requirement, which required dormitory facilities and limited the numbers who could be trained. As a consequence, Wiig adopted from Bible League a modular, field-oriented Church Planters Training, where students come for training every three months for 5-10 days. The curriculum had five major components:

1. Faith that leads to evangelism
2. Goodness that flows from repentance and leads to discipleship

3. Knowledge of foundational truth that leads to membership
4. Self-control in community that leads to leadership
5. Perseverance in worship and service that empowers others to lead.

Through this equipping initiative, Outreach Map trained 175 new leaders who established congregations in more than 300 villages. These church planters received scholarship support for 15 months, after which they became self-supporting (Wiig 2004).

According to the research of Patrick Johnstone (2001), India had 114,766 churches in 1985. By the year 2000, it had grown to 319,024, an incredible growth in a period of just 15 years. It took the church 1,985 years to establish the first 114,000 churches. But after the church leaders gained a vision with the end in focus, and developed strategies to fulfill the mission, God added more than 200,000 additional churches. It is also very interesting that in the last five years of the 20th century, God added the largest number of churches across India. We can trace this directly to the movement of prayer that followed the redirection of CONS focus from the national to

FIGURE 8.1
NUMBER OF CHURCHES IN INDIA FROM 1980 TO 2000

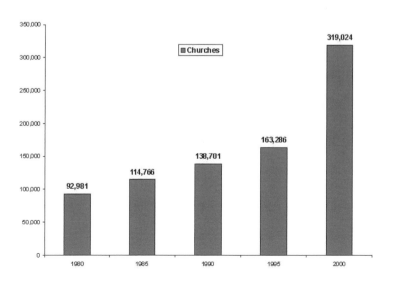

the district level (see Figure 8.1), and the emergence of other prayer and mobilization networks in North India at about the same time.

The greatest growth of the church took place between the years 1995 and 2000. It is my contention that the District Strategy Consultations, led by CONS in South India and the regional and state networks in North India, enabled the church to catch the vision. The efforts of all of these networks contributed to mobilize the church through vision and training for saturation church planting. As church leaders caught the vision and obeyed the Lord, God grew the church at a rate that exceeded all of our imaginations. If the church continues to grow as it has in the last 15 years, by the year 2010 India will have more than a million churches (see Table 8:6).

TABLE 8:6
INDIAN CHURCH GROWTH &
THE AVERAGE ANNUAL GROWTH RATE*

Year	Churches	Members	AAGR - Churches
1980	92,981	13,590,673	
1985	114,766	17,267,321	4.56%
1990	138,701	19,922,296	3.71%
1995	163,286	22,319,711	3.37%
2000	319,024	26,413,139	14.29%

* Church and membership data taken from *Operation World* 2001, Patrick J. St. G. Johnstone.

WHAT DID WE LEARN ABOUT THE MISSION OF GOD?

If we desire to fulfill God's commission to make disciples of the *ethne* ("peoples") of India, we learned that we must begin with a clear picture of the end product. What will India look like when we have finished the task? Once we understood that end, "a church in every village and colony of every town and city…a church for every 1,000 people," then we could begin to work together and build a strategy to do the work of God. Unless the body of Christ is willing to see the larger picture and understand what needs to be done, we will not fulfill the mission of God.

Second, God taught us the significance of the church. The whole body of Christ is a powerful instrument, and when networked together it can do an incredible task. God led us to build from the bottom up, to network many small groups with a tangible vision and strategy. The district strategy brought together pastors of local churches, and helped them grasp a tangible vision for their district. As they began to pray together, God worked in power through them to plant new churches and make thousands of new disciples.

We also learned that each believer has a birthright to participate in fulfilling the Great Commission. We do not need denominations or mission organizations to start churches, nor do we need to fear the increase of denominations. The people and the churches are the Lord's and He is building His church. He will use all—rich or poor, great or small, trained or illiterate—who hear His call and commit to His mission.

Finally, we learned to develop diverse training strategies to meet the very diverse needs of the leaders God called into service. As pastors, grassroots evangelists, and professionals stepped forward to join the task force, they cried out for training in many different aspects of the work. To meet these needs we had to respond with informal seminars directed to very specific people and situations. We could not pull an existing curriculum off the shelf, but had to understand the local dynamics and build up the local leaders, so they could be effective in serving the church and fulfilling the mission.

God also challenged me, and others at HBI, about our focus on quantitative results. If we want to accomplish the vision of Christ, being light and salt to bring transformation, we need both quantity and quality measurements to assess our effectiveness. More than just planting a church in every village, we have come to understand that these churches should represent the values and character of Christ so they bring transformation. If we do not focus on that quality, we will plant churches that will have no impact on society.

SHERWOOD'S REFLECTIONS ON LEADERSHIP TRAINING

In his conclusion above, Bobby has captured the big-picture lessons that make this story so compelling for all of us who take seriously God's mission for His church. At the same time this chapter has introduced the informal leadership training strategy that played such a crucial role in equipping men and women for saturation church planting. I will highlight some of the strengths and weaknesses of informal leadership training strategies.

1. "Asked for" training brings motivated learners. After pastors caught this new vision for their district, and together defined a strategy to achieve it, Bobby related how they suddenly had significant learning needs! "How do we plant churches?" "How do we make disciples?" "What should we teach new believers?" The unanticipated challenges of new ministries create the most powerful motivation for learning. The critical problem for trainers in a movement this large is meeting these demands in a timely way. The CONS team conducted seminars in church planting for 45,000 leaders over a seven-year period. Without the context of vision and district strategy, this scope of interest and training just would not have happened.

2. Movement leaders are best served through "as needed" curriculum and delivery. Bobby makes the point that a compelling mission leaves no time for formal training. The informal seminars (Church Mobilization Pastors Training, Saturation Church Planting) used by CONS delivered training on a variety of topics, at different levels, and in various languages in places and at times that best served the needs and interests of the participants. The inherent flexibility of the informal seminar is both its greatest strength and weakness. In the context of such a large movement, the "as needed" curriculum and delivery can and did serve thousands of emerging leaders. However, because follow-up sessions may not be planned or requested, slower learners may never acquire the skills they need for the task.

The weakness of informal teaching and learning lies predominantly in its ad hoc nature. Because it is learning-on-demand, the students and trainers engage in brief encounters that lack continuity and feedback. The trainer shares as much information on a topic as possible in a very short, intense seminar. However, learners rarely take home more than half of what was taught. When they return to ministry, they still face the challenge of applying what they do remember to everyday life and work. Special adult learner pedagogical strategies can increase the retention of knowledge for learners, and improve their capacity for application, but most seminar trainers have not mastered these techniques. The informal programs also lack the built-in repetition that is possible in formal and non-formal programs.

The marvel of the story told in this chapter is how God used this informal process of consultations and training to transform pastors, professionals, and grassroots evangelists into a mighty task force for a church-planting movement in India. Leaders emerged from every possible sector of the church, and with incredibly diverse educational backgrounds, including no education at all. The informal process helped all of them to frame a shared vision, and then form prayer and ministry networks through which they planted 250,000 churches in less than 15 years. Praise the Lord!

CHAPTER 8. RESEARCH AND REFLECTION QUESTIONS:

Research Exercise: Access International Mission Board (www.imb.org/centralasia) for an overview of the characteristics of church-planting movements.

1. How many of the "10 universal elements" do you see in the India districts?
2. Which of the 10 common factors outlined on the web apply to the district movements described above for the district strategy in India?
3. What is a strategy coordinator and were they present in districts in the India case?

Reflection:

4. How is the India case similar and different from the IMB analysis?
5. Why do some nations have movements and others do not?

END NOTES

[1] In his assessment of the impact of the CONS movement, Dr. Inbaraj (2001:2) reported that by January 2001 CONS had completed about 250 district consultations in 14 states of India. In addition CONS leaders in these states had conducted numerous training seminars on "research, prayer mobilization, accountability, church planting, portable Bible school, School of Evangelism" and even on computer programming. Since its inception in 1987 more than 28,000 leaders had attended at least one CONS consultation or training seminar.

[2] In 2003/04 the Lord enabled twenty-eight committed, qualified, and experienced faculty to train a total of 118 grassroots level church planters and second line organizational leaders in seven states (average of four staff per state) (Inbaraj 2001:2).

[3] The department has successfully completed all five modules for the five centers in Tamil Nadu and two in Karnataka. In 2004 there were 26 partnerships in existence preparing to work with 26 unreached people groups. As a result of the five-module training given to a group of pastors from Cuddalore many have increased their church-planting efforts. About 48 pastors attended regularly all five modules of the CMPT training, and about 50 percent of these pastors have mobilized their people to increase the number of members in local and branch churches. For instance, Pastor Don Bosco had only 120 people in his church when he enrolled for CMPT. Today he has more than 160 attending and has started a branch church as well. There are many such examples in the seven districts where all five modules have been completed (Lamech Inbaraj, 2004).

PART III

CHALLENGES TO ACCOMPLISH
THE VISION

CHAPTER NINE

REGIONAL CONTEXTUALIZED TRAINING

The explosion of the church in India from 1987 to the present has profound implications for leadership training. Who will train pastors for 500,000 churches? To put this in a western educational context, Fuller Theological Seminary, one of the two or three largest seminaries in North America, graduates approximately 250 men and women for pastoral ministries each year. The ethnic and linguistic pluralism of the Indian continent adds greater complexity to the sheer massiveness of the need. What are the languages essential for training? Who will develop contextual materials for students from 400 different language groups? How will these pastors find the travel resources to access training opportunities?

Hindustan Bible Institute, like Fuller, is one of the larger institutions in India seeking to respond to this massive need to equip leaders for the church. In this chapter, Bobby shares the HBI vision for ten regional extensions, and the challenges of providing leadership training for church leaders for the one million new churches envisioned in the movement.

—Sherwood Lingenfelter

By 1998, after ten years of facilitating the vision to see a church in every village and colony of every town and city of India through

Hindustan Bible Institute (HBI), Indian National Evangelical Church (INEC), and Council On National Service (CONS), our ministry extended to all four corners of the nation. As HBI expanded its influence, many individuals expressed their desire to join the HBI training and church-planting movement. We invited them to join our movement and enroll in the Missionary Training Institute.

However, the people who came from states hundreds of miles from Chennai noted the difficulty of traveling such great distances for repeated ten-day cycles of training. Some came two or three times from these great distances, but then dropped out. Seeing a growing attrition of new recruits who gave up because of the travel distance, we became deeply concerned about the loss of potential church planters.

The administrative and mission leadership team of HBI prayed together, asking the Lord what we should do to stem the loss of these good men and women who wanted to be equipped to serve the vision. The Lord humbled us and asked us to take the training to the people. The Holy Spirit directed us to decentralize our training to various regions of the nation. In this chapter I will share with you how the Lord led us to develop centers around the country to increase the effectiveness and establish a movement that is indigenous to the region. This again is one of our growing edges, where we are learning as we go, and have many unanswered questions.

UNDERSTANDING THE NEED FOR
REGIONAL TRAINING CENTERS

The trainees of North Orissa, Central India, North India, West India, and East India experienced various challenges to remaining faithful to the equipping process. They were traveling from 17 different states. Some of them had to travel six days to attend 10 days of training. This was a great sacrifice of time, money, and separation from the family and ministry.

On closer scrutiny the mission's director found numerous other difficulties for these people. Students and their families suffered anxiety and distress, disconnected by such great distances. In some situations terrorists harassed family members while the father studied at HBI. The trainees had to adjust to the food in the South. The local police in the city of Chennai often exploited them because they did not know the language. Sometimes police held a trainee at the police station and made life difficult. After such experiences many individuals did not want to return to the south.

But the greatest disadvantage of bringing them to Chennai was the mono-cultural delivery of the MTI curriculum. The staff taught them as though they were from Chennai, South India. Our trainers did not have cross-cultural training or experience, and thus were not sensitive to the various contexts and could not contextualize the training for students from other regions.

Training a Bengali from the East is different from training a Telugu in Andhra Pradesh. These two people speak different languages. They think out of different cultures and worldviews. To be effective in reaching each of their communities, they need to contextualize skills and Scripture to their local issues. For HBI to help them to serve and mobilize the church effectively, we needed to provide training in or close to the region, and find trainers living in the context who understood the challenges of reaching the people in the targeted area.

South Indian trainers at HBI noticed how North Indian leaders resisted their teaching. While they lived with this during the initial stages, as the northerners gained skills and abilities, their critical responses hurt the cause. We also noticed that we lacked credibility in the northern states. Northern church leaders and trainees saw us as outsiders, lacking familiarity and experience in their contexts. We realized we needed to build acceptance and credibility and to establish a local training presence to serve in these northern states.

God humbled us to accept the call to establish training centers in four of these regions, make the adjustments to incarnate the ministry, and entrust it to other faithful men and women whom the Holy Spirit called to the movement. Developing regional centers forced us out of our cultural box. We asked, "How do we make MTI relevant and contextual and keep it as a non-institutionalized movement?" Our first lesson was that the teacher must teach in the local language of the people. Translation was a poor substitute. We decided to start regional centers and hire the best available trainers.

As the Missionary Training Institute staff sought teachers, they found themselves isolated, lacking the network of people from which to draw. We tried to identify leaders from North India who were willing to come to the South, spend time in training and learning our vision, but we failed. We could not find them at such a great distance. Second, those we thought had potential refused to leave what they were doing and join us without developing a relationship with the movement. So we looked for someone we could equip to work cross-culturally and understand the vision and strategy of a training center.

A LEADER TO BRIDGE NORTH AND SOUTH: BIJU SAJAN

God provides when we give up trying to make it happen or trying to solve the problem. In 1999 the Holy Spirit brought to our mission Biju Sajan, a young man from North India who grew up in several different locations in India, because his father worked for the Indian railways. Biju married a South Indian woman, who grew up in Gujarat, West India, so together they had learned to understand the differences of various Indian regions and had adjusted well.

Biju and his wife, Reenu, first came to teach in the non-formal training program for pastors from the field at HBI. After several years of teaching, Isac, the director of missions program, invited Biju to become the national coordinator of the non-formal training, and God led him to accept this responsibility. Through that experience Biju became acquainted with all the different training programs that HBI had developed for the Indian National Evangelical Church.

When we began to experience the attrition of northern trainees, we asked him if he would serve as director and develop ten different regional training centers for the movement. He protested that he did not understand what we were asking him to do, but he agreed to trust God and try. None of us understood how to do this, but we believed God was calling us to develop regional centers and contextualize the training to the various locations.

To help Biju understand the various types of leaders HBI is training, we assigned him to spend two to three months in each department involved with leadership development in order to understand the vision, strategy, and values of each program, and the purpose of each department. Our goal for the formal program at HBI is to produce theological leaders and urban pastors. In the MTI, On-site, and MBI our vision is to develop rural evangelists, pastors, church planters, lay leaders, and cross-cultural leaders essential to the movement. We showed him how the church mobilization department, in cooperation with the Council On National Service, envisioned, equipped, and enabled pastors to be effective in saturation church planting. Once he understood the various leadership programs, he then had to learn how to contextualize the training to each region.

After a year of thorough study of each program, we sent him to inaugurate and supervise the first center at Bhopal, Madhya Pradesh. While the building was being constructed, Biju focused on understanding the strategies and processes for the training center. Over the first year he organized the center's operations and programs, and began planning to train leaders to carry on its programs. He developed a training manual for the trainees and an operation manual to equip leaders for each of the centers. He began building bridges with community leaders, and he identified potential regional leaders ready to be trained to run this and other new centers. Biju mentored them in the philosophy of training for mobilization church planting, and in the operation of the center.

MENTORING A LEADER FOR ANDHRA PRADESH: JEYAN BABU

Jeyan Babu was a promising young leader. Biju invited him to Bhopal to take the responsibility to lead the Andhra Pradesh regional center. Jeyan and Asha are from Andhra Pradesh and speak the Telugu language. I first met Jeyan at a CONS training in the state of Andhra Pradesh, where he translated my seminar on Saturation Church Planting, a strategy for discipling the nation. I asked him about his plans for ministry and found he was in transition and uncommitted to any organization. I invited him to join our Asian School of Evangelism training. It is a one-year residential training that equips second-level leaders to facilitate a church-planting movement as a strategy for their organizations. Several months later he applied and joined HBI that next year.

While Jeyan and Asha were enrolled in our School of Evangelism course, God gave them a burden to be part of a leadership development team for the nation. As they expressed their desire to be part of this vision, we took them on as interns with the ministries of HBI. As interns, they studied and taught in our non-formal training program and then in our informal training program. After they understood the vision and philosophy of our non-formal and informal trainings, Biju Sajan invited them to Bhopal to run the center. They gained the necessary experience to run a center while the Andhra Pradesh center was under construction.

Sajan first helped them understand how to oversee the various training programs, and gave them basic management training for center operations. He helped them to see the purpose, vision, and multiple strategies to carry out the vision. Second, he equipped them in the overall operation of the center while they taught in the first three months. He then released them in stages to run the Bhopal center under his leadership. Within a year they had learned to conduct and co-ordinate the various training programs, administer the various activities of the center, and manage the center. As a team, Jeyan and Asha provided excellent leadership and management, and today they direct the center in Andhra Pradesh.

THE TRAINING MISSION OF REGIONAL CENTERS

Today HBI has four regional centers—Bhopal, Siliguri, Kamavarapukota in Rajasthan, and Jaipur in Andhra Pradesh—that offer non-formal and informal training for evangelists, church planters, and pastors in those regions. With a great deal of prayer and intentional work, we have developed local leaders to run the programs, and at the same time we have begun a dynamic process of contextualizing the training to the needs of the people and region. It has been our faith goal to have ten centers up and running across India by the year 2005.

The center in Siliguri, West Bengal, is strategically placed, surrounded by Nepal in the Northwest, Bhutan to the Northeast and Bangladesh to the Southeast, Calcutta and Bihar to its South and Southwest. This state and the bordering countries are home to people of Muslim, Buddhist, and Hindu religious groups, as well as many tribal religions. The center's proximity to these nations makes it a strategic location to train nationals from these neighboring countries in our two-week non-formal programs, and still return to their home areas after each training session for three months of practical ministry.

This center equips trainees from West Bengal, Nepal, Bangladesh, Bhutan, and Bihar. The team God provided for this center comes from these different regions, understands these cultures, speaks the languages, and has skills and cross-cultural ministry experience to equip the task force. The team is diverse enough so that trainees who come to this center study in their national or state languages.

In 2003 the Bhopal, Siliguri, Rajasthan, and Andhra Pradesh centers offered the INEC non-formal training program, the HBI formal theological training, and the CONS informal training program (see Table 9.1). Through these centers we continue to expand the INEC church-planting task force and equip local pastors and Christian leaders seeking to enhance their skills for serving in their local churches. Missionaries in the region may apply for extension training through HBI Chennai, and the cross-cultural missionaries in the region may use the center to debrief and to continue training. Each center offers non-formal and informal training for the church-planting movement, and some formal training for those who wish to enroll in a degree program at HBI. Each center can accommodate up to 10 residential students who stay for nine months. The formal training students enroll and pay tuition for evening and/or extension classes, which helps to offset some of the cost of operating the centers.

Table 9.1
Enrollment in Regional Center Programs
2003/04

COURSES		CENTERS	
	Bhopal	Siliguri	K. Kota
Formal Training Program			
S.O. Evangelism/Diploma in Theology	---	5	9
B. Theology (Extension)	12	--	--
B. Theology (Evening College)	8	9	--
M.A. Christian Studies (Evening College)	8	4	--
Non-Formal Training Program			
Missionary Training Institute	53	33	---
Mobile Bible Institute	9	--	---
Couples Training	20	20	---
Informal Training Program			
Saturation Church Planting for Pastors	17	---	---
T-Net Pastors Training for Discipling	---	---	17
TOTAL	127	71	26

At its peak a center may equip three hundred trainees a year through the non-formal and informal methods of training. The non-formal courses may enroll up to 60 trainees every two weeks. These trainees will return every three months for additional training until they have completed the course.

The CONS informal training is designed to equip pastors already serving one or more congregations. Since 1987 many new churches have emerged across the nation. Most of the individuals who planted these churches entered the ministry without any formal or non-formal training. Sensing a call from God, they stepped up to the challenge and seized the opportunity. While God continues to use them, most lack skills to study the Word and lead the church. God enabled us to design informal programs to enhance the ministry of these emerging pastors. One series of topics focuses on study, interpretation, teaching Scripture, and basic skills to pastor the church. The second series guides the pastor to equip and mobilize his people in a Great Commission church. These five-day training seminars are offered periodically or on demand. We also have other organizations who want to offer courses for pastors, such as T-Net's discipling program.

THE IMPACT OF REGIONAL TRAINING

Each center has the potential to serve and equip the whole body of Christ in a region and serve as a resource center to increase church-planting efforts to reach the region for Christ. The center focuses on developing courses contextualized to the trainees and to the ministry and people they intend to reach. While two of the four centers have been running for less than two years at the time of this writing, and a third was just dedicated, we have already seen some significant benefits.

For INEC church planters, the centers have eliminated the interruptions in ministry and have improved the student return rate for the training. Contextualizing the training has enhanced the impact locally without losing the vision of the movement. The centers are beginning to produce a new generation of local leaders and new churches for each region. The local leaders of each center recognize the need to contextualize the training and create ownership for the task.

Through these new centers we have begun to facilitate consultations of regional leaders to understand what God is doing and how the church should respond. On the growing edge, we see centers as a place where pastors may gather at minimal cost to consult with one another on our vision for church planting, and to assess our direction and progress. We also desire to make these centers places of research, gathering and maintaining data on the status of the church, helping church leaders understand what God is doing in the state and region. Our mission is to assist the church to keep its mission and vision focused on finishing the task of establishing a church for every 1,000 people in India.

Decentralization enabled HBI to develop a regional presence for its national vision. Through the centers HBI is positioned to build better relationships with church leaders to serve the region and the nation. We also envision these centers as strategic locations to support cross-cultural mission efforts among the unreached peoples of the region. At the present time researchers at HBI in Chennai have gathered data on efforts to evangelize unreached people groups. We hope to conduct more accurate research through the regional networks, and thereby develop strategy to recruit and field cross-cultural missionaries in the region.

THE GROWING EDGE OF DECENTRALIZED TRAINING

Is God preparing HBI for a coming era? Could the nation of India face a period of disintegration similar to what happened in the Soviet Union and Eastern Europe? The last decade of the 20th century witnessed tribal insurgence and religious conflicts in India, Pakistan, Afghanistan, and Indonesia and ethnic cleansings in the Balkans, Rwanda, and the Congo. Samuel Huntington (1993) in his article "The Clash of Civilizations" proposes a new era of conflict focused upon major religious and cultural loyalties. Could the marks of the next two decades be further fragmentation and smaller, more numerous nation-states?

If we should see uprisings that result in the fracture and rebirth of nations, how can the church prepare? I believe these regional centers can be significant in preparing for the uncertainties of a future we cannot foreknow. I believe the church must plan to fulfill its mission in the most difficult times and circumstances. By working today, while the door is open, to establish indigenous church-planting movements in every state and mega people group of India, we seize the moment that God has given to us. By developing indigenous training centers in many regions, we can now create a training infrastructure and indigenous leadership for each center to meet the future needs of the church, regardless of the political upheaval that may overwhelm us. By developing contextualized, indigenous materials today, we lay a foundation to equip a future generations of church leaders.

In less than 50 years we have witnessed the end of colonialism, the rise of nationalization, and the emergence of globalization. In each of these quantum shifts of political and economic control and power, peoples and civilizations have undergone dramatic changes, and the church has been forced to adapt to each new era. Church leaders must realize that looking back to Jerusalem, or Rome, or Geneva, or Serampore quenches the Spirit of God, and threatens the mission that Christ gave to His church. Our world will continue to change, and we must seriously weigh the trends and develop strategy now. We cannot "do business as usual" and expect to respond dynamically as the peoples, nations, and world change around us.

When we lose relevance to our cultures, and fail to bring the transforming power of the gospel to the people, millions die and go into eternity without Christ. The human and spiritual cost of our failure to adapt and innovate grieves the heart of God. We must keep evaluating our efforts, identify our weaknesses, look at the opportunities, identify our responsibilities and—without compromising our purpose, vision, and values—make the changes that will keep us on the cutting edge of our mission.

Sherwood's Reflections on Leadership Training

Western missionaries and educators have failed to grasp the profound implications for leadership training of linguistic and ethnic pluralism. Working within the artificial unity created first by colonial domination, and then through post-colonial states and national languages, the institutions and programs they created for leadership training have limited access to an educated elite. Bobby has documented how these institutions cannot meet the challenge of leadership training when the Spirit of God moves to bring hundreds of thousands to faith in Jesus Christ. The emerging church leaders often have little education and marginal competence in a state or national language, and their congregations may be completely monolingual in a tribal language. Further, the reliance upon national and trade languages for training and literature excludes millions of new believers from resources essential for nurturing them to become disciples of Jesus Christ. As a consequence, local congregations create theologies and practices that are a blend of their limited knowledge and understanding of the gospel, the strength or weakness of their leaders, and the religious worldview of their pre-Christian communities.

The regional training centers of HBI, founded in response to these challenges in India, have discovered some basic principles that have broader application for training leaders where church-planting movements have begun.

1. Access is a critical issue for people in ministry. If they cannot readily access the training, they will proceed without it. The regional centers demonstrated that, given access, many more people come for and finish their training.

2. The legitimacy of faculty and center leadership is perhaps more important than the curriculum. People learn best from those they deem legitimate and qualified to teach them. Sometimes ethnic and caste differences undermine legitimacy. HBI recruited leaders from each region to serve as faculty for regional centers. When this was not possible, they trained local leaders to become the teachers and administrators. Identity was often as important, or more important than, qualifications to establish the legitimacy of a teacher.

3. Cultural diversity requires serious attention to appropriate languages for instruction and contextualization of content. Finding faculty who were competent in one or more of the languages of church planters became one of the pressing needs of the new centers. Effective teaching over a long term cannot be done through translation. These new teachers must translate, revise, and reshape curriculum materials to equip their student-leaders and serve the populations of ministry. These multi-lingual teachers took responsibility to create contextualized materials and ministries.

4. A church-planting movement requires the full range of training opportunities—informal, non-formal, and formal—so each center provides all of these options. The informal seminars meet critical needs of existing leaders, offering help on strategic issues within their limitations of time and cost. The non-formal programs provide long-term, developmental training for people committed to and deeply engaged in ministry. These are the best options to develop new leaders for a church-planting movement—equipping evangelists, church planters, pastors, and teachers to mature while they work. The formal programs equip

the specialists—Bible translators, curriculum specialists, educators, and theologians. Training cross-cultural missionaries occurs best using a blend of the formal and nonformal methods.

CHAPTER 9. RESEARCH AND REFLECTION QUESTIONS:

Research Exercise: Access the Operation World website (www.gmi.org) and select India.

1. How many of India's languages have translated Scripture available to them?
2. How many languages remain for translation?

Reflection:

3. What are the implications of this fact for evangelism and church planting among the other language groups?
4. What are the implications of your research for training leaders for the task of making disciples of these "nations"?

CHAPTER TEN

DEVELOPING MASTER TRAINERS

Perhaps the greatest challenge of leadership training is recruiting and equipping capable, experienced leaders who can train others. The Indian context with so few trained leaders, very limited economic opportunities, and extensive ethnic and linguistic pluralism makes recruiting faculty impossible. How many disciplines, skills, and languages does a teacher need to master? How do teachers teach a class in which students speak ten or more different languages? How does one contextualize for such diverse cultures? Who will pay those who have the qualifications and giftedness to do this?

Bobby and the team at HBI have defined this challenge at two levels: master trainers and trainers of trainers. The master trainers must have the skill to equip men and women for advanced levels of leadership and leadership training. They need a global and historical understanding of the church and at the same time the capacity to guide and empower local trainers of trainers to produce contextual and indigenous ministries. The trainers of trainers must understand the local context, and learn how to translate the gospel and the church universal into those local communities and cultures. They equip the grassroots leaders who are planting churches to reproduce culturally relevant and biblically authentic disciples of the Lord Jesus Christ. In this chapter we

explore the opportunities and challenges of equipping master trainers
—Sherwood Lingenfelter

In trying to develop leaders for the exploding church-planting movements in India, we have confronted challenges that are unprecedented in the history of the church. We have already seen how God has gifted and called different types of leaders, and that each type must be nurtured to maturity in the service of Christ and His church. We have seen that the pattern of church leadership and the process for equipping leaders that emerged from the Protestant Reformation are inadequate for the emerging churches in India. But the dramatic growth of the church in India adds three very specific challenges.

The first challenge comes from the sheer numbers required to make disciples of those who have responded in the harvest. In fifteen years the number of churches in India has tripled, requiring leaders for more than 200,000 new churches. Thousands of people continue to hear the gospel and accept Jesus as Lord, and more new churches are being added every week and month. Untrained or marginally trained pastors lead most of these churches, and few of them understand anything about the gifts of apostle, prophet, evangelist, pastor, and teacher. They do not even know how to make disciples of the people who worship with them weekly.

The second challenge lies in the more than one hundred languages and cultures represented by these new converts, and by another one hundred mega people groups yet unreached (Daniel Sathiaraj, 2001). In India there are so many language and cultural groups (more than 400), that the church is faced with an impossible task. Where can we possibly find capable and equipped trainers who are ready to train leaders in this multiplicity of languages?

The third challenge is the lack of materials, including Scripture, to equip leaders in their own heart language. In India we have at least 20 different state languages, yet the majority of teaching materials are available only in English. One temptation is to try to translate these English materials into the state languages, but the better strategy is to get the Scriptures to people in these languages and then equip them to develop contextualized materials to train the trainers in their state. While some of the English materials have been produced by Indians seeking to contextualize the training, much has been imported directly from the reformation church context of Europe and America. As such they are inadequate for the need of the movement in India.

At Hindustan Bible Institute we have taken the first steps toward the development of a process to meet this need. We recognized that the problem far exceeds our human and financial resources, but someone has to try to address creatively at least part of this need. To conceptualize the challenge, we began with the linguistic and geographic component. How do we train grassroots apostles, prophets, evangelists, pastors, and teachers located in a single language group of a single district of an Indian state? With our vision to establish ten centers for HBI in strategic areas of India, we agreed that we needed first to equip the master trainers to staff these centers, to develop materials, and to equip leaders to teach others in the districts and among the people groups of India. This second level of trainers we call "trainers of trainers," and these are the people who will actually equip the grassroots apostles, prophets, evangelists, pastors, and teachers.

The master trainers must know English to study with our staff at HBI and be equipped as a master trainer. The master trainer must also speak a state or local language through which he will teach the second generation staff, trainers of trainers. As the master trainers equip these trainers of trainers, they in turn will revise the training and contextualize the information to make it relevant to the grassroots leaders. By multiplying the number of trainers of trainers to serve the church in each state, we hope to multiply the people and places where grassroots leaders may be equipped to serve their local churches.

In India, where each state has a different language, and millions in the population speak languages other than the state language, we often need many master trainers to teach students from the diverse language groups. We decided that we needed a minimum of 25 master trainers in each state, and in some states more. The variables include the size of the state or people group, the rate at which the church is growing in the region, and projections of future growth in specific language groups. The number of denominations in the region and the independent movements added to the complexity.

An additional factor that we added for consideration in this process is the level of maturity of the believer being trained. If candidates come as new believers, lacking any foundation, then master trainers must design or enhance the curriculum to disciple these new believers. Until they have learned what it means to be a disciple, they will not be able to disciple others, and they will not learn the deeper discipline for leading a church.

MASTER TRAINERS

My first exposure to the concept of "master trainers" came through serving as a trainer for Haggai Institute of Leadership Training in Singapore and Hawaii. Haggai Institute, based in Atlanta, Georgia, USA, has been training leaders for nearly 50 years. They have focused on developing national leaders for churches in the two-thirds or majority world. Each person they train as a master trainer contracts with Haggai to return to their countries to train other leaders. Many of these master trainers have caught the vision of Haggai, and after returning to their various countries, have contextualized the training and developed an indigenous leadership training movement in their nations. By developing trainers of trainers they have equipped large numbers of leaders to support the church and mission.

The foundation of our curriculum for master trainers is based upon our non-formal training experience at HBI. Our basic leadership training programs include the two-year Missionary Training Institute to develop evangelists and church planters, and the thirty-day Pre-MTI Basic Christianity for new believers. The master trainers must learn to teach trainers of trainers to run these two programs. To support multiplication church planting they also need to develop skill to supervise on-site mentoring for advanced church planting. Finally, we offer a three-year Mobile Bible Institute program for pastors. This is a complex curriculum, and our Master Trainers need to have mastered the whole curriculum so they can train others to complete any part of it. In addition they need to understand how to train others to contextualize any part of this training for a specific language and people group.

Once the curriculum is developed, we have the task of identifying people who have the background and gift to serve as master trainers. The process of selecting these trainers is very important and comprehensive. The master trainer must have skills of working cross-culturally or must develop those skills in the master-trainer program. The ideal candidate will bring into the program a solid grasp of the culture and language for which he will develop trainers of trainers. To be effective he or she must be able to train the local leaders in their own language and enable them to contextualize the knowledge and skills in order to train others in their own culture. We may find it necessary to first train master trainers in a second language and then support them to translate and contextualize the training into the local language for the next generation.

Haggai Institute will not allow a master trainer to be involved in teaching more than two courses. They want their trainers to be experts in their areas of teaching. Such specialization may be a luxury we cannot afford, but we believe we must work toward that goal to sharpen the effect of our training. Initially our need for master trainers is so great and the diversity of trainees so broad that our trainers need to master a broader range of courses and skills.

Yet too often a trainer is developed with the expectation that one person can be skilled in all areas of training. Practically, we understand that no one person will be able to serve the complete training needs of one community. We will have to equip a team of master trainers to deliver the full curriculum, and none of them should or can be involved in teaching every component. While they need to have a picture of the entire training so they do not overlap each other, it is unrealistic to expect one master trainer or trainer of trainers to train all types of church leaders.

The First Class of Master Trainers

In the initial stage I served with other CONS leaders in testing a program for developing master trainers. Our goal was to identify 25 leaders in each state and equip them in the curriculum. We began with just two states and selected 25 individuals in each state to equip them with the knowledge and skills to train the next generation of trainers. During this experience I found that by mid-course eight of the twenty-five had dropped out for one reason or another. Another five dropped out before the end. Of twelve who completed the training, only seven were able or willing to commit to serve as master trainers for more than one class of trainers of trainers. This demonstrated to us the difficulty of recruiting and keeping qualified people to do this very difficult work.

We also found we could not have a group larger than 25 because we had decided at the beginning to mentor the master trainers, not just pass on information. Over the years we have learned that training master trainers and trainers of trainers has to be done in small groups. We experimented with many training sessions in large groups, but we found in the end the participants were poorly prepared for the task. We could not answer questions or coach people through problems in large classes. To transfer skills, build character, and develop deeper knowledge and understanding, we had to use a slow, interactive process that gave master trainers time to process and implement what they learned.

At one point we tried to teach through translation to develop master trainers for particular language groups, but we found it very difficult to mentor the leaders and provide an effective interactive environment. Though we took them through the training, trying to adjust by enlisting the best student to help the teacher mentor the weaker students, it did not prove successful. We finally concluded that the best candidates for master trainer had cross-cultural experience and had a good working knowledge of English and the language of the trainers of trainers they would be equipping.

TRAINERS OF TRAINERS

In partnership with an equipping movement called "Trainers Network" (T-Net), HBI began a process of developing master trainers to train trainers of trainers for our rapidly multiplying churches (INEF). Going through the learning process, we used translators to train our master trainers who did not know English. We encouraged them to identify local leaders in their regions and to equip them to serve the church to fulfill the mission. These master trainers taught the future trainers of trainers in their mother tongue, or a second language in their local area. Our goal for this program was to mobilize a whole new task force equipped to train men and women to serve as grassroots apostles, prophets, evangelists, pastors, and teachers.

This first class of master trainers has produced fruit for the kingdom. I will cite two examples of how the training helped our missionaries. One graduate of a T-Net discipleship training program in INEF, Pastor K. Philip working in Tuni area in Andhra Pradesh, started to train eight local leaders under his supervision. Since the books had been translated into Telugu, he taught them in their own language. Now these eight local leaders have started and are leading small groups of believers in their areas. Another INEF T-Net graduate, Pastor Mesra Murali, developed sixteen small group leaders in the Krupam area of Andhra Pradesh, using the Telugu language materials. These sixteen leaders are now working in eight new villages and have started eight small groups.

As the result of the master trainers program, in a period of two years church planting by the INEC fellowship grew from 1,463 churches to 2,093 churches and the membership of the INEC churches grew from 66,555 to 93,286. We rejoice in the blessing of the Holy Spirit upon the work of these master trainers and those they have equipped for ministry.

Lacking a financial base to support such a large training task force, we have tried to develop a vision, sell the concept, and pray for trainers who will grow in their commitment to serve the church without looking for personal benefits. In many cases the people being trained are committed to serve the purpose, more so than the organizations that provide their support. Sometimes even if they commit to the task, their mission may not be willing to release them for this work.

THE IMPOSSIBLE TASK AND THE GOD OF THE IMPOSSIBLE

Recently I received a letter from a leader in India who is developing leaders for Evangelism Explosion (EE). I think his statement in this letter will describe the complexity of trying to develop master trainers and trainers of trainers.

> ...We have this training for leaders scheduled in October and thereafter we will be ready to fly (not even run but fly) with it. I will depend on you to send some people from your organization who are working with children, teachers, hostel staff, etc. I did not think that your choice last year was the best, with due credit to Mr. R. He is busy in his own work and I found him too preoccupied with the work on his hand, and did not have time even to think about training children. That is why I am asking you to send people who are directly involved with kids. Once these people are trained, then we can work with them to train as many kids as possible.
>
> We are also busy preparing the material for the training. A huge task of getting the training material prepared in the major languages....

Developing trainers and facilitating them to serve the body of Christ is difficult. We must learn to select leaders who fit the function and ensure they have the commitment and time for the purpose we are inviting them to fulfill. If they do not see their calling for the task we will have invested in equipping them in vain. We also must work on reducing the attrition rate in developing the task force.

With all of this effort, a large task force made up of volunteer master trainers and trainers of trainers is an ideal that is beyond our reach. Men and women must have financial support in order to commit themselves wholly to this task. Our experience at HBI shows us that we need to provide at least 50 percent of the support needs of our evangelists and church planters. Our core faculty, the master trainers, all receive full-time financial support from HBI. We are able to draw some of our best graduates back into the training cycle, and seventy-five of our graduates serve as occasional teachers and mentors in the MTI, On-site, and the Mobile Bible Institute programs. All seventy-five receive a small stipend from HBI. Until the established churches in India and abroad make it a priority to support financially the work of the master trainers and the trainers of trainers, training for grassroots church leaders in India will not be a viable reality.

Developing master trainers is absolutely essential if we hope to make disciples of the great harvest the Lord is giving to the church in India. This is not about church growth or church planting or being the fastest-growing religious community. Unless we develop master trainers and trainers of trainers to equip the grassroots leaders for the church, we will continue to see the church miles wide and only an inch deep. The great cost of our failure will be millions of people who never discover the joy of becoming disciples of Jesus Christ.

Our hope is in the God of the impossible. As we look back over 15 years, God has given us hundreds of evangelists and church planters to carry out His mission, and He has moved thousands of people in America, Europe, and now among thriving churches in India to support these missionaries. And then, exceeding all of our hopes and imagination, God has given us a harvest of thousands of churches and hundreds of thousands of new believers. Therefore, we will not despair! The fields are still white with the harvest, and we are praying for master trainers, trainers of trainers, and a new generation of apostles and pastors who will reach the unreached in India and teach them to become disciples of the Lord Jesus Christ.

SHERWOOD'S REFLECTIONS ON LEADERSHIP TRAINING

The difficulty of finding master trainers, as Bobby describes, is not so much a problem of people, as it is a problem of resources.

Earlier in the book, Bobby has documented how a very modest stipend from HBI has empowered and enabled men and women whom God has gifted for ministry to do the work. But no stipend at all leaves people struggling to survive and effectively removes them from ministry. Philip Jenkins (2002) has remarked that the greatest growth of the church has occurred among the poorest of nations on earth. The implications of this for training leaders cannot be ignored! The economic factor is one of the most crucial issues.

The Western church has great resources, reflected in the mega-churches with multi-million dollar facilities and programs. While most middle-class families would not hesitate to spend four hundred dollars a month on a car payment, two or three hundred dollars on credit card purchases, and another two or three hundred on cell phone, cable television and internet access, they do not comprehend that they could fully support seven Indian missionaries or trainers of trainers with those same dollars. The opportunity and challenge for the western church is to invest in the equipping of leaders in India, Africa, and the poorest nations of Asia. The opportunity is vast, and the needs are critical. The Lord is waiting for the rich to partner with the poor to make disciples of the nations.

This chapter also highlights again the critical need for Scripture and leadership training materials in the vernacular languages of those being reached with the gospel. The India Missions Association, Wycliffe India, and a handful of Indian mission organizations are committed to this task. Further, many gifted men and women in Indian churches have stepped forward, eager for training and ready to serve. The good news is that the churches in India have stepped up to this challenge and have supported many couples, first for the training, and then for the long arduous task of Bible translation. Yet many more are needed, and while many young people are willing, the resources to support them fall short.

Finally, this chapter highlights the complexity of a church-planting movement, and the need for administrators and master trainers to support and sustain it. Without good administrators a movement so vast as that described for India cannot coordinate the training needed for leaders, organize support and materials, manage funds, and operate training centers. In chapter nine Bobby reported how God provided a key administrator, Biju Sajan, who then created the organization and trained the managers to make the regional training centers work. In this chapter Bobby documents the critical need for master trainers and trainers of trainers to equip the emerging leaders in the movement. In essence, this chapter completes the circle, bringing us back to the need for formal education. The administrators must be men and women who have mastered the complex skills of planning, program development, and management of people and resources. The master trainers must have fluency in two or more languages, have a deep understanding of the Scriptures, know what it means and how to contextualize and apply the Word, know how to teach effectively, and must have practiced the ministries they intend to teach. In essence, these highly gifted people must have mastered the practice and theory of ministry, in order to equip others by informal, nonformal, and formal means.

Chapter 10. Research and Reflection Questions:

Research Exercise: In this chapter Bobby has referenced Haggai Institute and T-Net International as resources he has used for developing materials for equipping master trainers in India. Look up these two organizations on the Internet, and review their mission statements, curriculum, and faculty.

Reflection:
1. How do the curricula of Haggai Institute and T-Net International differ? How does this reflect their different mission statements?
2. How do the faculties of Haggai Institute and T-Net differ? How does this reflect their different goals as organizations?
3. What are the potential contributions of each of these organizations to equipping leaders for a church-planting movement like Bobby has described for India?

4. As you reflect on the kinds of people in India who need training and the special leadership needs of these grass-roots and regional leaders, how must Bobby and the team at HBI adapt and change the materials from these organizations for the Indian context?

PARTNERSHIP FOR MISSION IN THE 21ST CENTURY

If the church wills to fulfill the vision of discipling the nations in our generation, it must embrace global partnerships. Millions of new believers have joined the body of Christ, and the Lord Jesus is calling out hundreds of thousands of men and women to work in His harvest.

Mission is no longer a work in "foreign fields." Jesus has extended His church into the uttermost parts of the world. We believe the Holy Spirit is calling nationals and expatriates to join together, employing the skills, abilities, and resources that God has entrusted to us. As we partner together in obedience to Christ, God blesses our work through the synergy of a body that manifests God's love to the world.

In this chapter we (Gupta and Lingenfelter) describe how mission has changed as we begin the 21st Century, and then we explore the new cutting edge— the opportunities and challenges of partnership between national and western churches, educational institutions, missionaries, and mission organizations for the mission of God

—Sherwood Lingenfelter

More than 200 years ago William Carey set out for India, called by God to leave his cobbler's shop and home to share the gospel with people who had never heard. While the British colonial office did everything they could to keep missionaries out of India, Carey persevered as a pioneer missionary. He learned the language, studied the culture, and established relationships with a broad spectrum of people. He saw the poverty and the injustices of both the traditional and the colonial system, and with great compassion he worked to bring physical, social, and spiritual freedom to the people of India.

Carey considered himself a failure as a missionary because he was not an effective teacher or preacher. Instead he translated Scripture into Bengali and produced the first printed form of Scripture in the nation. He founded schools to teach people to read and write, and he started a university for higher education in India. Working to bring social reform for the rights of all people, he used every possible means to share the love of God and the gospel of our Lord Jesus Christ to the people of India (George, 1998).

Often called the father of the modern missionary movement, Carey set a precedent that others who came after him institutionalized. Career missionaries established a mission compound and put down their roots for a lifetime of ministry to the peoples of India. They learned the language, found ways of preaching the gospel, developed relationships with the nationals, and established a church movement rooted in their traditions from home. They found it beneficial to translate Scripture, produce literature, establish schools and hospitals, and bring about social changes that would improve the quality of life for the people.

While these missionaries brought blessing and transformation to the rejected, poor, and uneducated, they transferred their culture of Christianity to these people, and the churches they founded looked and acted very much like those at home in Britain and America. Only in the mid-twentieth century did missionaries learn to appreciate the barriers that Euro-American culture created for the gospel, and begin working to contextualize the message and indigenize the church.

Today many churches and mission groups still understand mission in those terms, and send personnel much as they did in the colonial period. While they train these missionaries to become sensitive to the culture, learn the language, and develop contextual ministries, most often their goal has been to plant their denominational churches in a nation with the view that they have the right way to interpret Scripture and practice church.

Philip Jenkins (2002) and Lamin Sanneh (2003) have documented the emergence of a World Christianity that is no longer bound up with the denominational divides of Europe and America. They show how in sheer numbers and cultural impact, Christianity is now a non-western religion. Asian, Latin, and African Christians now worship in dynamic indigenous churches based upon their own interpretation of the Scriptures that have been translated into their languages. These World Christians, to use Sanneh's term, have developed their own mission and church-planting movements, and with great energy have mobilized to reach the unreached in their nations and beyond.

With the explosion of the church in the Southern Hemisphere, we must ask, does the church of the Lord Jesus Christ still need the western, denominational career missionary? Since this model of service is 200 years old, have we not come to a stage where we need to ask "How does God want us to serve the church in the present context?" Philip Jenkins has shown clearly that European Christendom is past, and moribund, and Andrew Walls (2002:64-65), suggests that God has shifted the momentum of the church to a new center in the Southern Hemisphere. The sheer numbers of Christians outside the West and the dynamic growth of the church and mission force us to ask, "How should we be doing missions today, and what should be the role in missions of the expatriates from the West?"

STRATEGIC PARTNERSHIPS

We (Gupta and Lingenfelter) agree that the western church must seriously re-evaluate its understanding of the role of the western church in world evangelization. After ascertaining what God is doing in the global church, we must rethink how western and world Christians may work together to fulfill the Great Commission in our generation in the most effective way. Almost every nation on earth has a national church, and Jenkins reports that these churches have experienced exponential growth through evangelism and church planting. *The World Christian Encyclopedia* (Barrett, Kurain, and Johnson 2001(1):842-843) reports a parallel growth in missionaries, sent out from these southern churches. Yet, many people groups and geographical areas remain unreached. One of the other factors in the equation is that most of the fastest-growing churches are located within the poorest nations in the emerging global economy.

While there may still be a significant place for the well trained, western, cross-cultural church planter, the growing edge of mission today is strategic partnership, coming alongside the national church and mission task force, and working together to reach the unreached. As we have described in chapter nine, the greatest need in India today is for master trainers for the church-planting movement. But even more critical is the need for Scriptures in the four hundred languages of the unreached and materials for trainers to use to equip grassroots leaders of new churches among these peoples. The national church in India does not yet have the economic or human resources to meet this need. While many Indians have responded to the call of cross-cultural church planting, they lack the training and skills to do Bible translation or to develop training materials. Educated western missionaries, who are willing to serve under national church and mission leaders, can have a profound impact equipping, mentoring, and supporting a national mission force. By working alongside nationals, expatriate missionaries can multiply their impact one hundred fold.

The national church and mission agencies have much to learn from the knowledge of the expatriate missionaries. As we detailed in chapter six, equipping Indians for cross-cultural ministry has proven just as challenging as equipping westerners. Because western missionaries have already struggled for two hundred years with these issues, they have gained knowledge, theoretical and practical skills, and training methods of immense value for training Indian cross-cultural workers and teams. Westerners also have extensive training and experience in the academic and technical aspects of equipping leaders for a wide range of church and service ministries. The expatriate can consult with or serve on a national team in a partnership and add significant value to that team in the work of fulfilling the Great Commission.

The "pioneer missionary" strategy of the colonial past, or the "all-expatriate team" strategy sent out to establish a church-planting movement is not only inefficient and limited in capability to carry out that task, it is arrogant in its exclusion of those in national mission movements whom God has called to serve. If these same agencies and churches actively sought to partner with the emerging national churches and mission movements, they would greatly expand their ministry and impact for the gospel and the kingdom. We firmly believe that every local church in India and America should develop a global strategic plan, and actively seek global partners to implement that plan. By way of example, Oscar Muriu, pastor of Nairobi Chapel in Kenya, has actively sought to mobilize his church for the Great Commission, and to develop partnerships with churches in America, Britain, and India, so together they might plan and partner in God's mission to the lost. By partnering together in this way we fulfill God's purpose for His church, a body endowed with many gifted people, social structures, and financial resources that when deployed together, transform a lost and broken world into the kingdom of God.

SHORT-TERM MISSION PARTNERSHIPS

One way the Lord is enhancing and bringing synergy to fulfill this task is through short-term mission activities. Not many years ago in India and other parts of Asia, nationalism and the denial of missionary visas prompted western agencies and churches to refocus their contributions through short-term teams. Because the traditional missions approach was closed, national churches requested the assistance of short-term team workers. This short-term strategy had the unanticipated consequence of helping the average church member to understand missions in a whole new way.

Early in this process churches and mission agencies designed most short-term mission trips to do projects. But as the paradigm began to mature, these projects enabled the local church to serve the national church and/or the missionary strategically by taking missions to a new level. Strategically implemented projects enable a church to minister to a larger number of people in a very short time. By working alongside the national church, or a local ministry, the national personnel followed up the short-term outreach to accomplish the long-term task of making disciples. Further, short-term ministry became a means of recruiting long-term missionaries and training local church mission leaders who advocate for the vision, strategy and mobilization of the church in fulfilling its mandate.

In recent years several local churches in America and Holland have conducted short-term mission trips in partnership with HBI. In the early 1990s a local church in California sent a pastoral team to help us equip national church planters. After the first trip, the pastor of the church saw how he could mobilize his church to help enhance the ministry of a national movement. For the next teams he chose people based upon an awareness of the gifts, skills, and ministries that would add value to different aspects of our mission.

Over several years he developed a mutual strategy for HBI and his church, sending to us a computer team, a music and drama team, a teaching team, and a children's team. Each of these teams contributed significantly to the ministries of HBI, working alongside our staff to fulfill what had become a mutual vision. The church formed each ministry team based on their skills, giftedness, and abilities, and the pastor and team leader prepared them for the challenge and opportunity to help HBI achieve a new level of effectiveness.

The computer team came, consulted with our school and mission staff, and set up computers in our administrative section and several computers in our follow-up department. They learned that our radio ministry team was almost always six months behind in maintaining their database. On an average they received more than 300 letters each day. By the time they answered the letters, they had no time to maintain the database. The information technology team developed a strategy that helped us restructure the entire follow-up program so that the staff had caught up a year later, and maintained current data. The new database enabled us to track the locations from which people responded and, as a result, identify potential locations to plant churches.

The database also helped us track the various stages of our listeners in the follow-up process. With the tracking system we helped our listeners progress from stage to stage in the discipling process. We could tell when an individual stopped writing. We would then send them a follow-up letter to ask how we could help them keep growing in the knowledge of the Lord. This church team made an incredible contribution to our mission. Today we still are current and strategic in our efforts through this one ministry.

Over ten years this team returned several times and helped us develop an entire Information Technology Department. Within five years HBI developed its local team of IT personnel. The church continues to send a team to work with HBI personnel and they provide guidance, knowledge, build computers, and help build the information technology environment for the mission.

Today HBI has a computer lab for students where they can do research and assignments, and the college library now uses an electronic cataloging system. Year after year, teams have returned and built upon the work of others so that today HBI has a network with 60 computers for our entire staff and they use computer technology for daily operations. Our national IT department has a training wing, which serves HBI and other mission movements that are seeking to equip their staff. HBI did not have the financial or human resources to develop this technology. This church partnership contributed both human and financial resources to enable HBI and INEF to use the latest technology to support the mission and achieve our church-planting vision. At the same time, individuals and teams in the American church discovered a way to use their gifts, abilities, and skills to serve the Lord.

HBI has also invited churches in America to send young people from their churches for a short-term team experience. As we listened to American pastors, they asked if we could help them challenge their youth with a vision for mission. We invited them to send their young people to us, and we arranged for them to share their testimonies and build relationships in local schools. After a time we realized that many children and young people in these schools had expressed an interest in Jesus. We asked, "What are we doing with all these children who responded?" This provoked us to think about how we might invite these young people into the kingdom and teach them to be disciples of Jesus.

The local Christian day schools in Chennai opened their doors, inviting these American teams to do special programs. The school enrolled large numbers of Hindu and Muslim children into these schools, and they welcomed these teams and a weekly follow-up by HBI staff with children who indicated a desire to know more about Christ. Out of this partnership, and our desire to help American churches, we launched a new department at HBI to disciple the emerging generation. We appointed one person in 1995, and by 2003, teams of nationals were at work among many schools reaching the children and youth. Over the years the ministry of discipling these children has opened homes of non-believing parents for prayer and witness. The staff started prayer cells every week with the children, the parents, and the friends of the children.

There is a synergism in these international partnerships that empowers the ministry and leads the partners to support, enhance, and love one another, and thus expand the kingdom of God. The short-term partnerships have expanded our vision and mission, leading us to sponsor weekly clubs in schools, conduct seminars on career opportunities for young people, and host youth camps for evangelism. Through these children and youth ministries, we have bridged into non-Christian families in the community.

PARTNERSHIP FOR THEOLOGICAL EDUCATION

When HBI decided to move to graduate and postgraduate level training, we did not have the faculty or leadership to move forward. We shared our vision and a dream with a Dutch pastor, who in turn challenged one of his pastor friends to help us. This man, a leader in developing educational programs all over the world, had the skills and knowledge to help us develop a graduate program. His church released him, giving him time to help HBI, and the pastor friend found a way to support him and the project. Using the short-term method he came to consult and he enabled us to build the Master of Divinity program.

Two Dutch churches and HBI created a three-way partnership, and by networking with other leaders, they staffed the program until HBI could build national staff and independently run the program. Today the national staff offers the program with national resources. We sometimes invite expatriates to lecture but we do not depend on them to operate. This partnership enabled HBI to achieve a new academic level in equipping national leaders for the church.

Partnership may also be an important strategy for national organizations. In 1999 a private foundation in California and the School of World Mission at Fuller Theological Seminary organized a meeting of presidents of four theological colleges in India to discuss the possibility of forming a consortium to provide doctoral-level training in missions to prepare faculty for these Indian theological schools. Over a period of two years the leaders of these schools formed a board, invited two other institutions to join, formed the Consortium for Missiological Education in India (CIME), hired Dr. Siga Arles as Dean, and enrolled the first class of six students in June of 2002. Fuller, with the support of the foundation, sent faculty to teach selected courses in the program and to work with Indian faculty to mentor these students through a program of doctoral research.

The partners in this venture sought to provide a doctoral program of the quality that a student could obtain abroad, yet without the dislocation that such study creates for the students and their families. Often schools in India have sent faculty abroad for advanced study, only to find they do not return home. After living for four or more years in Britain or America, their children have adapted to western culture, and sometimes refuse to return home. In addition to the family pressures, the research and training they receive abroad is often far removed from the cultural context and ministry demands of India. The members of the consortium designed a program through the assistance of Fuller that would return graduates to staff their colleges.

This model of partnership has potential for leadership training more broadly in India and around the world. Theological colleges seeking to develop national leadership and contextual scholarship in theology and other disciplines may look at similar consortiums to address the shortage of theological leadership in a nation. The colleges in CIME supported their faculty candidates financially, and agreed to share the responsibility of hosting the students and courses at their various colleges. Fuller supplemented the program with some of its best faculty to serve the national movements and enable them to have the best training. Anticipating the success of these doctoral candidates, the partners envision the graduates as doctoral level faculty in missiology, equipped to run a nationally staffed doctoral program within India.

THE IMPACT OF PARTNERSHIPS ON SENDING CHURCHES

As we developed a vision for partnership at HBI, we invited churches to form teams with particular gifts and focus, and send them to work with us to fulfill the Great Commission in India. For most westerners, coming to India means stepping out of their comfort zone and trusting the Lord. Until that time many have not thought that God could use their skills and abilities for His mission purpose. But they accept the challenge and in faith trust God to provide the necessary resources and to use them for His work. As they prepare, pray, and work together, they develop deeper relationships with one another and the Lord. As the day for departure approaches, they see the Lord do some exciting things for the team, a new and powerful experience.

When they get to India they experience culture shock; they cannot believe what they see, smell, feel, and hear. Many look to the Lord and say "Lord I do not know if I can handle this and how you can use me in this context." The first night goes by and about 3:00 a.m. in the morning they wake up because of jet lag. They do not know what to do. They cannot sleep so they take out the Bible and begin reading God's Word. This is not what they do back at home, but because they are anxious, they find great comfort and strength in Scripture and prayer. This becomes a pattern, and they enjoy it, and gain great energy from the Lord. They start to wonder what is happening, and then they realize the power of spending time with the Lord. For the first time God has their full attention and He is able to bring transformation in their lives.

Along with this spiritual experience, they soon see the Holy Spirit using their skills and abilities. Working alongside nationals, they experience for the first time contrasting values and ways of working. This intimacy touches them deeply, challenging many to rethink their priorities. The empowerment from using their gifts helps them experience what it means to serve God. Because they are so dependent on the Lord, they build a new level of relationship with God. The challenge to their value systems has its impact on their priorities for living. They come home a different person with a deeper commitment for the Lord and His church.

My adopted niece is one of those whose life was changed through short-term mission. As a child her family neglected and abused her, until the court placed her in my brother's family for adoption. Although she struggled because of the early abuse, she came to know Christ through the love my brother and his wife showered upon her. As a young adult she chose to come on a short-term team to HBI, where God taught her that there is more to life than making money and living for self. Sometime after the ministry at HBI, she received a birthday gift-package of new clothing from her grandmother. When she opened it, she looked at my brother's wife and said, "Mom, do I need any more clothes?" The answer was obvious, NO! She insisted that her mother return the clothes for cash and send the money to the orphan ministry at HBI. Her experience so transformed her life that she equipped herself to work among abused children and is now serving those who have never experienced God's love.

Churches in partnership with our mission have found they gain much from the partnership. Individuals who come to India return with a greater commitment to their local church, ready to serve at home as they did on the field. In a period of two weeks many develop a new intimacy with God, as they are forced to trust in ways they have not experienced before. Pastors report that their people return home with expanded vision, readiness to serve as leaders, and with a great sense of satisfaction and joy from their service to God and His people in HBI and the Indian churches.

PARTNERSHIP AND CAREER MISSIONARIES

Western-trained missionaries may still choose to do pioneer work, but the emerging national church and mission movements need such qualified people as strategic partners. In India we have thousands of young Christians who are eager evangelists and may be trained to be effective church planters. We also have an emerging group of young missionaries who are ready for the regional demands of cross-cultural evangelism and church planting. What we need are experienced veteran missionaries or trained cross-cultural leaders to partner with national movements and jointly develop strategy to target unreached people groups.

One North American fellowship of churches uses what they call a strategic coordinator approach in which an individual or a team of individuals takes responsibility to lead congregations in focused mission outreach. The coordinators mobilize churches to commit to prayer and they partner together to develop strategy and support for reaching an unreached people group. The development of strategy includes identifying a national church, movement, or individual in the vicinity of the unreached group that shares the vision, and then to send a U.S. missionary to partner with the national church in framing a strategic plan to reach the unreached people group.

The strategic coordinator calls people to prayer and gathers resources to implement the strategy. The prayer and support network may include churches all around the world. As the Holy Spirit leads, members may come to the state or towns where the unreached people live, and pray on site for God to open the eyes of the people. The national partners look for ways of bridging into the community, either by identifying nationals from that context who may be trained or by doing research on how to build bridges into the community. Needless to say this task takes time to build relationships and earn the confidence of the people.

One example of their ministry is the case of a partnership relationship to reach the Bhojpuri people in India. Over a period of two years their national partners developed 600 house groups and trained local leaders to disciple these small house fellowships. Today the project is complete and the church is self-sustaining.

A similar idea I have found in other denominations in the U.S. is the "champion" or advocate for prayer and outreach to an unreached people group. Like the strategic coordinator, they mobilize prayer, identify a partner, and build a strategy that includes U.S. and national personnel to reach the group. One church I have visited promotes a champion for every project in its Great Commission program. The champion networks with a U.S. missionary and a national partner, and from that relationship engages the local U.S. congregation for action. They may send short-term teams for prayer walks and social work, and they may pray regularly for and support the U.S. and national missionaries to reach the unreached people group.

INDEPENDENCE OR INTERDEPENDENCE?

Too often the national church thinks it can fulfill the mission without the expatriate missionary, not realizing that cross-cultural mission is just as challenging for nationals as it is for expatriates. It is not uncommon for a national to go into a cross-cultural setting, struggle to learn the language and culture, and then fail to win acceptance from the unreached people group. Just like many expatriates, many nationals experience rejection, become discouraged, and want to return home, leaving the unreached people unevangelized.

On the other side, expatriates often ignore the national church, to their peril. Many governments are antagonistic to foreigners, especially if they seek to promulgate a religion. Therefore the expatriates often must take a low profile position in that nation. In our view we gain great strength in today's world when we view mission as a joint venture of nationals and expatriates.

When expatriate missionaries network with the national church they may earn the opportunity to use their expertise and play a strategic role in equipping cross-cultural leaders and developing strategic church-planting movements. By serving in this way they may empower nationals, and coach them to avoid many of the mistakes of expatriate missionaries. Through the synergism gained by empowering each other, we can hope to make disciples of the nations. When we become kingdom community, cross-pollinating with each other, we enhance our effort for the single cause of fulfilling the Great Commission in our generation.

We believe the time for the western, professionally trained, "pioneer" missionary has passed. But expatriates have an even greater role to play: equipping and mobilizing thousands in these newly planted churches to be on mission for God. As a trainer, consultant, and facilitator, expatriates may serve the national church to develop a church-planting movement, or to equip that movement with the essential leadership skills and resources to grow mature, dynamic Christians and churches. As expatriate churches and mission organizations adjust their vision and redefine their role to partner with national churches, they may have a greater impact for the kingdom of God than was ever possible through "pioneer" efforts.

The international business community has already made this significant shift in focus. Ford Motor Company serves as a good example in India. During the colonial or nationalization period Ford might have negotiated the development of a Ford plant in India. However under the current paradigm of globalization, they chose to partner with Mahindra, a national automobile manufacturing company. Through the partnership Ford benefited from the knowledge of the national company and employed the existing work force. Combining the name and resources of Mahindra, with the technology and financial resources of Ford benefited both companies. Ford enabled the Mahindra Company to provide safer and better cars, and moved its production capacity to a new level.

The partnership enhanced the economy of the state and nation, uplifting the people and the quality of life.

Ford expanded its market and export within the region. It developed leadership in the region to support the maintenance of the product they produced. India, the second largest nation with a fast growing middle class, enabled Ford to capture the market in the region and develop their economy. This was a win-win situation for both companies.

THE CHALLENGES OF CROSS-CULTURAL PARTNERSHIPS

While we are convinced that partnerships flowing out of the unity of the body of Christ are essential for mission in the 21st century, they are much more difficult for both parties than working alone. The economic, social, cultural, motivational, and emotional differences among the partners are enough to shipwreck any attempt to work together. Add to that mix theological and ecclesiological differences, and partnership becomes nearly impossible. Yet if Ford Motor Company can do it for profit, surely Christians, called by the Holy Spirit, can partner together to fulfill the mission of God. The key to mission partnerships is obedience to the Lord Jesus Christ—loving God with all our hearts and loving our partners as ourselves.

During the past five years I (Sherwood) have been consulting with various mission organizations seeking to partner with national churches or agencies. All these people have been deeply committed to working together to plant churches, train leaders, translate Scripture, and minister to orphans, widows, and the poor. They all love God and have sacrificed in significant ways to work together in these ministries of reconciliation. Yet, they have struggled in their partnering relationships, sometimes so greatly that they can no longer work together. Sometimes they work side-by-side, yet without respect or love for one another. The partnership becomes like a broken marriage, and the ministry slowly dies with these broken relationships. It is not our purpose here to provide a guidebook for creating effective partnerships, but we will offer a few cautionary signposts for those who desire to follow the Holy Spirit in the work of partnering together to train leaders for a church-planting movement.

The first caution: work must never substitute for a deep relationship together that is focused upon the Lord Jesus Christ. In the first flush of partnership, people begin with much prayer, vision, and unity together to do the work of God. Then they tackle the challenges of planning, framing strategy, raising funds, training people, and engaging in the task. Ever so gradually, the business of work replaces the times together of prayer and seeking the direction of the Lord. Worship becomes private, Bible reading and prayer become personal—not corporate—and soon the only links the partners have together are focused upon work. At this point our own private interests rear their ugly heads. If that were not enough, Satan subtly divides us so that we begin to doubt the efficacy of our relationships and the integrity of our partners. Every troubled partnership that I have observed had lost its spiritual heart! People no longer loved one another, nor prayed about persons and ministry together. They refused to confess sins to one another, and rejected pleas to forgive one another when hurt in some activity of ministry. They had fallen into fundamental disobedience to the Lord Jesus Christ on these very basic principles of relationship.

The second caution: the partner with money will be tempted to use the control of money to dominate the partner who does not have money. The most common quarrels in partnership focus upon the control, use, and accountability of money. Most funding partners have strong expectations about how "their money" must be used and accounted for. When nationals fail to live up to their expectations, the funding partner may lose trust, become critical, or even sever the relationship. The funding partner then uses the power that comes from the control of money to dominate the receiving partner. Neither partner, in the excitement of launching a church-planting movement, thinks about discussing at length their assumptions and expectations about money. Rarely do they take time to pray together about the funding and their mutual responsibilities to the Lord to use God's resources for God's work. And rarely do they pray together about the regular use of funds in ministry. Funding partners give conditionally, forgetting that the money is the Lord's—not theirs. Supported partners feel inferior, because they are indebted to the funding partner and not to God. Neither partner takes time to read Scripture about money together or alone, and to pray together asking the Holy Spirit to guide them in its use for kingdom work.

The third caution: differences about organizational culture may become more important than mission. Churches and mission organizations always have assumptions about organizational culture that guide their internal relationships and engagements in ministry. Usually people find Scripture to support these assumptions and practices, so that their social community becomes an extension of their theological and spiritual commitments. Because they have over-learned their culture to the point where they act out of habit and emotion, rather then conscious reflection, they cannot discern when their habits become a "plank" in their eye (Matt. 7:3, NKJV). These habits lead to quarrels and misunderstandings over organization and process that end in broken relationships and tragic failures in partnerships. Because people know and use their organizational cultures routinely, they find it extremely difficult to explain to others how they do things, nor do they find the need to do so. But when people clash with one another in the practice of ministry because they have played very different organizational games, these matters become critical. Also, as we have noted above, when the spiritual basis of relationship has been replaced by work, then structure becomes more important than persons, control more important than mission, and both partnership and ministry are lost.

The fourth caution: the urgency of the task may replace the critical priority for relationships, and when relationships are broken, God refuses to bless the work. Christians called to mission often become so passionate about the task that they lose sight of the God who has called them. Stories abound in the history of missions about passionate servants of God, so consumed by the tasks of evangelism, leadership training, feeding the poor, or translating the Scriptures, that they have trampled on their families, run over their fellow workers, and left a trail of broken and abused people in the wake of a completed task. Often they do not comprehend what they have done until they look back at the wreckage. The Scriptures are very clear on this matter. "Dear friends, let us love one another, for love comes from God. Everyone who loves has been born of God and knows God. Whoever does not love does not know God, because God is love" (1 John 4:7-8). We must never give the task priority over loving God, our co-workers, and the people to whom God has called us to serve.

The most effective way to address these threats is to view partnership as an opportunity for power-giving leadership! Shuster (1987) notes how most human beings seek power to find their self-identity. Believing they will discover meaning by controlling the outcomes of life, they willfully seek to control people and events around them and thereby assure their own significance. Jesus calls us to a different way: "If anyone would come after me, he must deny himself and take up his cross daily and follow me" (Luke 9:23). The practical application of this text in partnership is to give away the power we have to others. By empowering national brothers and sisters to do the work of the gospel, by esteeming them better than ourselves (Phil 2:3), by adapting our organizations to the people and the work, by making spiritual relationships the heart of everything we do, we follow Jesus and thereby earn the privilege of teaching others to follow Him. Peter sums this up so well, "Above all, love each other deeply, because love covers over a multitude of sins" (1 Peter 4:8).

EMBRACING THE GLOBAL PARTNERSHIP MODEL

The church of the Lord Jesus Christ is a body, joined and knit together for the work of the kingdom. When we work together, our Lord is pleased. Our objective is to finish the task entrusted to the whole church. Our mind should be set on obedience to our Lord and working together with His people to accomplish God's mission in the world. Our calling is not about control, nor developing an identity, nor about making a name for ourselves. We must recognize that God is at work and we are all His instruments. We must unite God's people and resources and work together toward fulfilling the mission of discipling the nations.

Partnership is not about nationals or expatriates in competition, or one or the other taking control. It is about allowing God to work through us and learning that evangelism, church planting, and leadership training is about serving Him. We all need each other. We all can and must contribute to each other. When we realize that the work is God's, and that we are one body of believers, obedient in our love for one another, then we will see God finish the task.

From the perspective of India, we need global partners. We cannot meet this great challenge alone. We welcome these new cross-cultural missionaries who seek to serve the national church. We know that we will have the greatest impact when we work together and empower each other to fulfill the mission of the church. Let us not try to do it alone but let us work together for the completion of the task in our generation.

CHAPTER 11. RESEARCH AND REFLECTION QUESTIONS:

Research Exercise: Access on the Internet the website of a mission organization that is engaged in church planting and leadership training. Some examples include: Assemblies of God World Missions, Grace Brethren International Missions, International Mission Board (Southern Baptist), RCA World Mission, WEC International.

Review the information provided about their mission statement, their ministry plans, their leadership-training programs, and the stories they tell about their ministries. From this information, evaluate the place this western agency gives to partnership.

Reflection:
1. How effective is the ministry in developing local and national partnering relationships that advance the planting of new churches and equipping master trainers and local leaders?

2. How are partnerships structured among the local, national, and expatriate churches and mission organizations? To what extent are these structures contributing to leadership training and church mobilization?

3. How does this mission explain its commitments to manage the control of resources in the partnering relationship and the contest for power? What evidence do you find for power-giving leadership?

CHAPTER TWELVE

TRAINING LEADERS FOR A CHURCH-PLANTING MOVEMENT

In 1987 after the first consultation on national strategy, I asked members of the Council On National Service (CONS) committee, "Can we fulfill the vision of planting a church in every village and colony of every town and city of our nation by the year 2000?" We all confessed the task was too large for us to achieve by the end of the year 2000. Nevertheless, trusting the Lord, we set a goal to envision and mobilize the church for the task. In this book we have told the story of one small part of that national church-planting movement, centered on Hindustan Bible Institute and the mission of the Indian National Evangelical Fellowship.

The church in India must assess and reflect on the things that have happened in the last fifteen years to reposition herself for the remaining task. We must not forget the major lessons we have learned in this spiritual battle. We must evaluate our successes, struggles, and failures and make necessary changes to seize the days of opportunity that are ahead. In this concluding chapter of the book, we (Gupta and Lingenfelter) reflect on the lessons we have learned about mission, church planting, and training leaders for this task. And finally, we revisit the mission of the global church, and review some of the challenges we must face together as we seek to fulfill the mission of God in the 21ˢᵗ Century.

—Bobby Gupta

The most important lesson we learned from the HBI/INEF story is that mission is not about a school, a denomination, or individuals, but the mission and the power belong to God. Church and mission leaders serve as God's instruments, and God, through the work of the Lord Jesus Christ, and in the power of the Holy Spirit, fulfills that mission. A leader's greatest challenge is to listen to the Holy Spirit and follow God's leading. Often over the last twenty years I was tempted and tried to take control of the training and the mission. Every time I strengthened my grip, I found our mission spinning its wheels, but going nowhere. But every time I released control, and allowed God to lead, we made progress.

As we wrote this book our greatest encouragement came from recounting the stories of God at work, filling His people and through them achieving His mission. While we had work to do at HBI, our most important commitment was to let God work in and through us, equipping and empowering God's people. We learned that we had many ideas and plans for ministry, but if God was not the source, we wasted our time, energy, and effort. God had always gone ahead of us, touching people, opening hearts, and calling out future leaders. We learned to look for the people God had touched, encourage them to follow God's leading, and assist them with training and support to do the work of God. Our most important lesson was learning to listen and then to do the work of God as the Holy Spirit taught us.

LESSONS ABOUT GOD'S MISSION

1. Mission is more than proclamation; it is about making disciples! Jesus clearly commanded that we should make disciples among all the peoples of the earth. We have yet to master the implementation of that vision. We began by describing disciple making as "planting churches" and the mission leaders of INEF and HBI planted more than two thousand churches. But over a decade we found that these churches had limited impact on their local communities. What does it take to bring transformation to a body of believers and to a local community? If the process of discipleship does not result in transformation, then how can the church bring light in the midst of darkness? Jesus asked His disciples to make disciples and teach them to observe all things He had commanded them. We learned that teaching leaders to obey the commands of the Lord Jesus Christ had to be our focus.

While we remain deeply committed to planting churches, we now understand that making disciples means nurturing godly men and women who are constantly in the process of transformation in character and action in community. We are seeking to build an awareness of how God's calling "out of darkness into his marvelous light" means serving the world in the name of the Lord Jesus Christ, and becoming a kingdom people, transformed into His likeness with ever-increasing glory.

2. The unique challenges of mission require thinking with God "outside the box." We have been amazed at how often we fall back into institutional thinking. We discover new ways to serve the mission of God, and when this brings success, we assume that is the right way. We stop listening to God, and rely on our past practice to fulfill the mission.

God led us to lay the foundations of the church in many cities, towns, and villages in India. Yet we often stopped with the foundations and never got around to completing the buildings. Blinded by our success, we have failed to equip leaders to build to the next level. While we sit back to enjoy our success, the world is changing. New technologies are transforming the next generation in India. We must listen to God, and ask ourselves, "Are we locked in a traditional paradigm? Have we created our own little box of success? Or, are we seeking to discern how God is at work today, and then reframing our movements and work to serve God, and equipping the church to do the same?"

We must stay on God's cutting edge of mission. The emerging generation of leaders will face challenges that differ from ours. They need our help to look forward, learning from the past, but creating new ways to follow the Lord in mission. These changes may require new forms of service, perhaps as tent makers, or development workers, or information specialists, called to serve the Lord through a local church to fulfill the Great Commission. We need to challenge local church leaders to listen to the Lord, seek His leadership, and mobilize their members in a contemporary context. And because we have international connections, we may serve by building networks of teams that are multinational and multicultural, that work together in a state of interdependence to form mission task forces. Clearly we must look at new and innovative ways of fulfilling the mission of God in the context of the 21st century.

3. The church is God's most powerful instrument in fulfilling His mission. God wants His church to work together to accomplish His vision. When CONS realized the task was to plant one million churches, we knew no one organization could accomplish the task. God led us to mobilize the whole church in the nation, with each part participating in the multiplication and growth of churches. When the whole church caught the vision and the people prayed and worked to fulfill the mission of the church, God did great things, tripling the number of churches and calling out millions who were lost and without hope. The church must see itself as God's instrument and never lose sight of this reality.

The church in India and throughout the world must unite as a body for the mission of God and resist the temptation to lord or rule over one another. At the beginning of the movement in India in 1987, many leaders could not imagine working together. Yet through district consultations focused on prayer, we surrendered many treasured differences to join the Lord's mission to make disciples of the peoples of our nation. The church globally must come to grips with the importance of "one body," that we all belong to Christ, and have been charged with the same mission and agenda. We must learn to serve one another and work to meet the need in the most contextual way, yielding our parochialisms to the headship of Christ. If we fail to see the significance of this dynamic, we will bind the hands and hearts of God's people, and redirect their skills, abilities, and resources from the mission of God to the seductions of materialism and the media of an emerging global culture.

Some in the body of Christ have separated themselves from national movements, such as India, out of fear of fostering dependency in national churches. While colonialism often did lead to cultures of dependency, separation is not of God! The church is the Lord's, and the God of the Bible made the church interdependent, connected in all of its parts (1 Corinthians 12). If we obey Jesus' command to make disciples of the nations, it will take the whole church, united under the lordship of Jesus Christ, to reach the whole world. We must work together and find partners nationally and internationally to fulfill the mission of God. Resources belong to God and not to the church. He is the source of all resources and we are dependent on the Lord. We must focus on the fulfillment of the mission and ask how we can work together and accomplish it in our generation.

4. The local church and pastor are the front line of leadership training. Every pastor and church must take the responsibility to equip members to lead by making disciples of others. The professionally-led church is a distortion of God's plan and purpose. We return to the pattern of the church in Acts, where apostles, evangelists, prophets, pastors, and teachers made disciples and empowered people in local churches to shepherd and disciple others. God gave gifts of leadership in the people He calls to the church; pastors must learn to identify, equip, and release them to serve the body interdependently in fulfilling the needs of the church.

Leaders with advanced theological training provide a very important resource to the church, but such training is not essential to a rapidly growing church. These leaders fit most readily in an urban context and in roles of ecclesiastical leadership where they lead and train other leaders. Theological training institutions may better serve the larger body by adopting different methods to equip pastors to train others in their congregations to lead. Schools must not expect all leaders to come to them. Rather, they must go to the people, understand their need, and develop training that will serve the development of leadership in the region and in the context of the church and local culture.

The strength of the church—its ability to serve its people and fulfill its mission—is directly proportionate to its success at developing leaders for ministry to its people. Every seminary and Bible institute must train its pastors to equip leaders at the local church level. Without this multiplication of leaders, the church will remain a superficial community of people who lack understanding and obedience to the teachings of Jesus, and who have no understanding of how to engage their communities with the transforming power of the gospel.

5. We must develop leaders in the context of their own cultures to meet the need of thousands of new churches. Theological colleges in India prepare pastors for an urban elite, but the large majority of people without Christ and churches live in rural contexts. When we press evangelists and church planters into theological seminaries, we give them academic skills and make them so unlike their culture, they may no longer function in their own context. To serve effectively in the mission to make disciples, we must equip leaders in the context of their own culture, first guiding them to become disciples, and then teaching them to make disciples of those who are lost.

Today the church is growing at an unprecedented rate. Many new converts have joined the evangelistic task force without a single day of training. They profess Christ as Lord, but have not learned what it means to follow Him, and have no one to teach them. Many have a great desire to learn, but cannot gain access to leaders or schools that might train them. We must find ways to disciple and equip hundreds of thousands in ways that are functional and contextual to the culture and challenges of the people. In countries like India where more than 90 percent of the people groups have yet to be reached, this is the most pressing issue of our time! Where the harvest is great, we must pray and work to equip leaders properly to disciple the people. Without properly equipped leaders, we risk misleading thousands who respond to the message of Christ.

Lessons about Training Leaders for a Church-Planting Movement

The story of this book has focused on how HBI sought to recapture its vision and renew its educational mission for equipping Indian leaders to reach India for Christ. In that story we have reported the mistakes in our history, what we learned from those mistakes, and our efforts to correct and redirect our training to fulfill the mission of making disciples of the peoples of India. As we look back, God has blessed us with an amazing group of men and women missionaries who have planted more than two thousand three hundred churches. We have sought to equip them, first to become disciples of the Lord Jesus Christ, and then to take that good news back to their villages, towns, and districts, and do the work of evangelism and church planting. We will summarize briefly some of the key lessons we have learned about training leaders for a church-planting movement.

1. It's not the curriculum. When the subject of training leaders comes up in a conversation of church or mission leaders, many move quickly to the issue of knowledge content and curriculum. In our work on this book I (Sherwood) pushed Bobby to include at least outlines of curriculum to show the readers the "creative" work of HBI. Bobby has made it very clear that there is nothing new in the curriculum. These Indian church planters study the basics of the Bible, theology, and the disciplines for spiritual life and ministry. Perhaps the only innovation in the curriculum is one that westerners would find boring, and that is its repetition to serve the need of oral and non-academic learners.

This is not to say that knowledge of Scripture, skills at biblical interpretation, and an ability to think theologically about issues that face the church have no importance. Indeed, the team at HBI found this a critical need in the early 90s and founded the Mobile Bible Institute to equip their leaders in these areas. The most important insight is the placement of this training after four years of ministry, and delivery on location in the context of daily life and ministry. Whereas in most seminary training programs students learn this material before they enter ministry, these INEF church planters enrolled after planting their third church.

2. It's about mobilizing and equipping people. The new paradigm that guides HBI is not really "new." It is, in fact, a blend of the ancient and biblical "master/disciple" relationship, classroom in-struction, peer mentoring, and three-month periods of immersion in the hard work of ministry. To extend the analogy of "builder," used by Paul in 1 Corinthians 3:10, in this new paradigm, the train-ees spend eight weeks a year in seminars that teach basic principles for laying foundations and building the local body. They spend forty-four weeks a year on the construction site, doing evangelism, leading those who respond to Christ, and bringing new believers together to pray, to worship, to study, and to do what Jesus taught. The emphasis is first on mobilizing and second on equipping so that these leaders are often teaching those who will listen to what they learned in their last two-week seminar.

In the first six months of the training they lived in their home-towns, and did the work! They led people to Christ, brought them together for fellowship and prayer, and taught these people what they had learned about God and about becoming a follower of Je-sus Christ. At the end of ten weeks of practical work, they returned to HBI for two weeks of reflection, prayer, mentoring, and further training for the next 10 weeks of hard work.

The mentoring relationships (master/disciple, or peer mentors) had the greatest impact when these new builders encountered problems, lost direction, or depleted their resources. The on-site training for the multiplication of churches provided powerful mentoring experiences, and greatly expanded the resources of a church planter to enable him to move beyond his single church ministry.

3. It's about character and commitment. The most powerful innovation in the new paradigm is the admissions program. At the very beginning of this movement, the leaders at HBI recognized the problem of recruiting the wrong people! After the crisis mo-ment in 1987 when we discovered that none of our graduates was going into ministry, we decided to search for people who had a passion from God for the mission. We believed that if they had been called by God to serve as evangelists and church planters, then we could equip them! These church planters were often new believers who had a deep passion to tell others about Jesus. Many had limited education, and one was illiterate. Many of these people would *never* be admitted to a formal education program, but they responded to God's call and eagerly sought training for ministry.

The MTI program was designed to test the calling of church planters. First, we provided a stipend (Rs 700) that met only 50 percent of their need. In this way, we tried not to attract people seeking a reasonable income. Then, after the first two weeks of training, we sent them home with specific assignments for evangelism, personal Bible study, and prayer. When they returned to HBI ten weeks later, they reported to the group on how God had worked through their obedience in these assignments. While in training, we asked each church planter to survey 20 villages and identify five receptive villages around his main center with an objective to reach the people and plant churches where no churches exist. They have two years to prove themselves in the ministries of evangelism, making disciples, and church planting. If at the end of two years they had experienced no fruit from their ministry, we dropped them from the program. We believed that if God had called them, God would bring fruit from their faithfulness.

We also understood that most of these new believers had little, if any, experience with the basic disciplines of the Christian life— Bible study, prayer, confession, and accountability for character growth. Part of the training and accountability process focused upon teaching skills for personal piety and growth, and instruction on the cost of sin, and the blessing of righteous living. In each of the two-week training periods at HBI, we sought to reinforce this emphasis on character and commitment to obedience in Christ.

These church planters have endured and succeeded, first because of their calling by God and passion to tell others about Jesus Christ, and then because of their obedience to God in their daily lives and ministries. Many experienced trials, satanic opposition, persecution, and periods of stalemate in their ministries. Yet, more than 500 have persevered, have planted two or more churches, and continue to make disciples of those who have responded to the good news!

4. It requires financial support. We learned very early in the movement that most of the people God called did not have a financial base to carry out a church-planting ministry. With just a few new converts, the demands of teaching, prayer, counseling, and mentoring new believers exceeded the capacity of most leaders who worked as farmers or in other employment. We found that a minimal salary empowered these men to give their primary attention to evangelism and church planting, whereas without it, feeding the family became the focus of attention.

The American and European churches that partnered with HBI provided much of the financial support (80 percent) that enabled these men and women to follow the Lord in this ministry. Without these partners, the people God called to the movement would have staggered under such a heavy work load, they could not have planted these churches.

5. It requires contextualization. At this point in time we have encountered the walls of language and culture, and they have temporarily stalled the movement to reach the unreached in India. The training for cross-cultural missionaries has been more rigorous and challenging than we anticipated, and the numbers responding to God's call are too few for the magnitude of the task. Our vision of the centers through which HBI will equip a new mission force has great promise, but we are still praying and searching for the right people, and the resources to release them to fulfill this vision. We pray that the Holy Spirit will call churches, and individuals from around the world to partner with us to penetrate these cultural walls, and mobilize and equip new believers among these unreached regions to witness and to make disciples of their people for Jesus Christ.

The task of creating contextual materials to train indigenous leaders exceeds our capacity at this time. To reach the remaining unreached people groups we must equip a task force and release responsibility to them. Yet we lack the trainers and the materials to help them though the process. Unless the global church comes to grips with the realization that leadership must be localized and the

Word of God must be contextualized, we will fail to plant indigenous churches and to make disciples of the nations.

The national church in India must also recognize the multiple contexts for its ministries and face squarely its tendencies to parochial outlook and control. This ethnocentrism inhibits the mission of God by refusing to identify, develop and release leaders outside of its parochial traditions. When people are responding so rapidly to the gospel, we must make translation of Scripture and the development of contextualized materials for training leaders our highest priority. If translated Scripture and contextual materials are not available for the second generation of church leaders, the form of Christianity that will emerge will be foreign, and fraught with misunderstandings that corrupt the true meaning and message of the Bible.

Established churches must learn to work outside of their traditions, and to relinquish control of ministries to new believers who have grown in intimacy with God, and have proven faithful in the fire of practical ministry and leadership. They must make every effort to apply the knowledge of contextual ministry, resisting every desire for parochialism, and allow God, through the power of the Holy Spirit, to transform these people and leaders who have responded to the gospel. When the church mobilizes to disciple local leaders, and to produce culturally relevant Christian literature and training materials to empower them to train others, the church will be indigenized, and its people equipped to take up the work of making disciples in that people group and beyond.

6. It requires trainers of trainers. Today we know that the need for church leaders far exceeds our capacity to train them. Our church planters have caught the vision; the Holy Spirit has used these workers to bring in a great harvest; and we need thousands of shepherds to make disciples of the flock. We need gifted teachers to contextualize and translate existing materials, and to create new materials for pastors and teachers in the local church. We need gifted prophets who can discern the times and the movement of Satan to distort and destroy God's work, and challenge leaders and people to walk in obedience to Jesus Christ. We need apostles who can envision, facilitate, and empower evangelists, pastors, and teachers to keep the church on mission.

The demand for leadership training is an incredible opportunity and a terrifying threat for the future of the church. We desperately need men and women with formal seminary training and practical field experience who are humble enough to learn new cultures and then partner with others to meet this need. These master trainers may be Indian or expatriates, as long as they are willing to work alongside people with diverse ministry gifts and backgrounds, and learn from them. They also need churches that will partner with them financially to release them full-time to this training ministry. We believe this is the most urgent need for prayer and recruitment in the global church. The Spirit of God has gone ahead of the church, calling millions to respond to the gospel. The question before us is, who of the followers of Jesus Christ will mentor them, and teach them to obey all that Jesus commanded?

THE CHALLENGES FACING THE CHURCH

After watching what the enabling power of the Holy Spirit has accomplished through the church in India since 1987, we believe without a doubt, if the church continues to listen to God and focus on the discipling of the unreached peoples, India will have a church in every village and colony of every town and city by A.D. 2020. Yet even if the church is intentional in its strategies so that thousands of churches are planted, many people and locations may remain unreached. Further, if churches plant more churches, but the people bring little or no transformation into society, then the mission of making disciples will not succeed. Leaders must be intentional in their efforts to make disciples of the lost, inviting people into a powerfully transforming relationship with the Lord Jesus Christ, and forming new missional communities that bring spiritual, social, economic, and political transformation into their villages and towns. Satan has always battled against the Lord's people and sought in every way to derail the church from fulfilling its mission.

The first two decades of the 21ˢᵗ century portend a number of challenges for the churches in India and around the world in their efforts to fulfill the Great Commission. India has already witnessed increasing persecution of Christians and government pressure to prevent religious conversions. In other parts of the world religious, ethnic, and cultural conflicts have led to war, and sometimes attempts to destroy the Christian church. Church leaders must be vigilant in these times, and through a biblical theology of suffering prepare their people for a time of possibly severe persecution.

Church leaders must also think deeply about how to respond to the inhuman actions of people in power who seek to destroy Christians or any who resist their religious or political agendas. Which of a broad range of options—political activism, fundamentalism, liberationism, non-violent resistance, violent resistance, passive acquiescence—should Christians pursue? What are the theological issues we must address in the midst of rising insurgent movements among the tribal and religious communities of the world?

Tribal resurgence is another trend that will certainly test the church. While the globalization of world trade and international corporations might be interpreted to presage a world culture, the ethnic and religious wars of the Middle East, the terrorist campaign of Al Qaeda, and the hostilities of tribal and ethnic movements in Sri Lanka and Indonesia counter and rip apart any semblance of world unity and peace. One might also interpret the fall of the Soviet Union, the fragmentation of former Soviet Republics, and the breaking up of Eastern Europe in the late 20ᵗʰ century in similar terms. Tribal resurgence is visible in Africa, Indonesia, and certainly in the violent challenges of Iraqi groups in 2004 to the efforts of the United States to establish democracy in Iraq.

Church leaders should be compelled to ask, "What is the Holy Spirit telling us about the global phenomena of tribal resurgence and its import for the church?" and then, "How should we respond?" As early as 1910 God gave church leaders signs and warning that nationalization was just around the corner; yet the vast majority ignored the signs and continued to work as if colonial mission would never change. We must not make the same mistake today! What if India or Indonesia or Congo should disintegrate as nation-states, similar to the Soviet Union, or Yugoslavia? Could this unleash similar terrors of religious or ethnic cleansing, parallel to Bosnia, or Rwanda, or Chechnya? How might fragmentation pose a challenge to the church in the future? What should be our response and how should we prepare? Is it possible that the freedom we have could be lost? What strategy should guide us? Should we disperse our leadership training centers, diversify our leadership structures, build a stronger Christian presence in national governments and businesses, or organize Christians to facilitate peace making among hostile groups? We must explore all these options if we are to prepare for Satan's attacks against the church, and against humanity.

We believe the church ought to give very serious consideration to these trends, and network together for prayer. We must seek the wisdom of God to discern the times, and listen for direction from the Holy Spirit to insure the indigenous presence of a dynamic church, salt and light among the people groups of the world. By networking together in prayer, we may avoid the temptation to exploit one another, and develop the attitude of servants, working together to extend the reign of God in our worlds. Should we suffer as a result of tribal insurgence, by preparing in advance we may remain steadfast in the time of suffering, and continue to disciple the responsive into a powerful intimate relationship with Jesus Christ.

We live in a generation that has every potential to achieve the goal Jesus articulated on the mountain in Galilee, making disciples of "all the *ethne*" of the world. The doors in most places remain open, Christians have resources to give, people want to hear about Jesus, and thousands of leaders for church planting are available to work in the harvest. But we believe the church has not seen its opportunities. Thousands of potential evangelists and church planters need training, and support to get out and do the work. By telling this story, we hope and pray that many more churches and mission leaders will catch the vision, and join the task force.

Echoing the words of our Lord, we have seen the fields white unto harvest, and we implore our readers, take the responsibility for your church and your sphere of influence! Do (and partner with others to do) all that is necessary to train leaders, release them for the task of evangelism, plant indigenous churches, and watch God accomplish this task in our lifetime. It can be done, it ought to be done, and it must be done.

APPENDICES

PAUL GUPTA'S VISION FOR THE CHURCH IN INDIA

My father, Paul Venkateswami Gupta, was born to Hindu parents in a village called Thuganapali in the state of Andhra Pradesh. A high caste Hindu, he longed to have a relationship with God. His religion taught him that God came to save the righteous and destroy the unrighteous. He tried hard to be holy by performing all the religious rituals. He climbed the mountains, broke coconuts, chanted mantras, and dipped himself in the holy rivers, only to find out that all his efforts were in vain. His heart, mind, and ways were still desperately evil and he feared that the consequences of his wickedness would result in eternal destruction.

Hopeless as it was, one day sitting in his home, he heard a message from a speaker on the street: "This is a faithful saying, and worthy of all acceptation, that Christ Jesus came into this world to save sinners …" (1 Timothy 1:15, KJV). For the first time in his life he heard there was a God who came to save sinners. His Hindu gods came to save the righteous. He wanted to find out about this Jesus. He thought, "I am a sinner and if there is a God who came to save sinners I want to know this God." So he called his servant and sent him to see if the man had something in writing. The servant returned with a black book. It was a Bible and the speaker informed the servant to tell his master to read the book (Hunt, 1976:24-25).

My father opened the book with great expectations. He wanted to know all he could about Jesus. The very first verse he read was so compelling. Jesus said, "Come unto me, all ye that labour and are heavy laden, and I will give you rest" (Matthew 11:28, KJV). Soon, glued to the book, he found the words made great sense to his confused life. He came to understand that because he was separated from God, sin had taken hold of his life; evil had increased; deterioration had set in, and the only hope was salvation in Jesus Christ. As he continued to read the Bible, he believed that God's provision in Christ made perfect sense.

In 1937, understanding God's message of salvation, he accepted God's gift and committed his life to Jesus Christ. But for that decision he paid a great price. When he became a follower of Jesus Christ, he was cast out of his family and community. The tragedy of being turned out of his family into the street became God's first lesson of faith. Welcomed into the home of a Christian outcaste, God used this experience to teach my father God's love for him and for the lost. In this outcaste family, my father learned to be an evangelist. As an evangelist, he traveled all across the nation preaching Christ and he saw many people turn to the Lord.

He traveled a couple of years as a poor, wandering evangelist until God connected him with some of India's great heroes of the faith. They discipled him and taught him to preach the Word. As he matured in his faith, God opened his eyes to the thousands of lost people, living without an opportunity to hear the gospel. With a heart of compassion for the lost, his greatest concern was how would they hear? His favorite song was, "Everybody Ought to Know Who Jesus Is."

Ten years after his conversion the British negotiated the final stages for the independence of India. When it became apparent that India might soon be granted freedom, my father began to pray and ask the Lord, "Father, what will happen if we become an independent nation? Will we have the freedom to preach? Lord, keep the doors open for the missionaries. There are more than 450 million people! Lord, keep the doors open so they will hear and be saved."

One day while he was studying God's Word, the Holy Spirit spoke to him. Reading the first chapter of Paul's letter to the Philippian church, he heard Paul say that his imprisonment was for the furtherance of the gospel. The immediate question in my father's mind was, "How could Paul's imprisonment be for the furtherance of the gospel?" And then he read, "And many of the brethren in the Lord, waxing confident by my bonds, are much more bold to speak the word without fear. ...The one preach Christ of contention... but the other of love ... What then? notwithstanding, every way, whether in pretence, or in truth, Christ is preached" (Philippians 1:12-18, KJV). My father exclaimed with joy, "Hallelujah! The Lord says the gospel will be preached even if we get our independence. Thank you Lord!" That was a day of great joy because God had given my father hope for the lost.

Then suddenly, in the midst of all that joy, he asked the Lord, "Who will preach?" The Lord said, "Look at the Word" and the word said: "...those who are not preaching...will then begin to preach." Again my father asked, "Who are those who are not preaching?" The Lord said, "My followers in India."

From that day he prayed, "Lord, help the Indians to be burdened to reach our people." I heard my father say he would cry out to the Lord, "O Lord! Help my people to catch a vision for the lost. Help them to take the responsibility to preach the gospel and evangelize those who have not heard."

A NEW VISION FOR NATIONAL LEADERSHIP

One day while my father was praying, the Holy Spirit said, "Paul, I need you to help me reach the nation of India." My father said, "Yes Lord, what do you want me to do?" The Lord said, "I want you to start a training program to develop Indian preachers." Shocked, my father said, "Lord, are you sure you want me to do that? I am not trained! You need someone with all the degrees. How can I train anyone? I have not even completed high school. Don't you remember I was thrown out of my home?" The Lord responded, "I have a plan and your only qualification is obedience. If you are available and willing, leave the rest to me." My father responded with a yes! The rest of it led to the development of the first nationally-run, evangelical Bible college in India (Hunt, 1976:65-71).

God began to develop a vision in my father that was beyond his understanding, yet he never questioned God and just believed. God began to do miracles and wonders, heretofore unseen in his journey with God. By early 1948 he was on his way to the USA to be trained. Not fully aware as to what God would do, he simply trusted God. Although he was penniless, the Holy Spirit directed him to the Bible Institute of Los Angeles (BIOLA) and provided for his education. At BIOLA he faithfully studied God's Word and gained a greater vision for India (Gupta, 1992:86-87).

While in the United States, my father challenged the American Christians regarding the need in India. Fearing that the doors would be closed for missionaries, and many churches would be without a pastor, he sensed a great need to prepare many national pastors, evangelists, and cross-cultural missionaries to take the responsibility to disciple India for Christ. He shared the vision God placed in his heart to train one Indian to reach another Indian with the gospel. People began to pray with him and soon many committed to help my father train Indians. Together they formed a team to come to India for the purpose of training Indian Christians to reach the nation for Christ.

THE FOUNDING OF HINDUSTAN BIBLE INSTITUTE: VISION BECOMES REALITY

By 1950, God led my father and his new American friends to establish a board to form a mission society to send missionaries to India. But that same year the Holy Spirit confirmed to the board that they could not send expatriates to do the work of equipping nationals. The Government of India refused to grant visas for missionaries. At first, because it was not possible to send missionaries, the board nearly abandoned the mission. But then the Holy Spirit led my father to say, "You may not be able to go, but I can! If you will get behind me, I know God will fulfill His mission."

In 1952 God led the board to send my father back to India to the city of Chennai, which was then known as Madras. The mission of equipping Indians to reach India began in a rented building in Chennai with just five students and a borrowed missionary. They called the center "Hindustan Bible Institute" (HBI).

My father believed the best pastors were those who lived by faith, studied God's Word, and learned by doing the work of an evangelist and a pastor. He trained men to reach those who had never heard the gospel and to start new churches. He often said to his students, "Your pulpit is on the corner of the street." He proclaimed far and wide, "Hindustan Bible Institute will not produce pastors to take over the established churches. Rather HBI will develop evangelists and missionaries to pioneer in areas where Christ is not known and where no churches exist."

Within five years (1957) the training had gained broad acceptance among the established churches. As the need for emerging evangelists, pastors, and missionaries increased, students started to pour into HBI, greatly encouraging my father. By 1957 he searched for and found property to move the training center to a more permanent location. The new facilities had enough room to train 70 students, although his vision was to train 200. In the next 10 years he would develop the infrastructure to fulfill the vision and goal for 200 trainees.

By 1963 church leaders encouraged my father to accredit the program so they could send their candidates to be trained for the pastorate. Seeing the efforts of some of the graduates of HBI, many leaders decided that they would like to have their pastors trained at HBI. By 1966, more than a hundred students enrolled for study, a development that called for more infrastructures. By 1967, fifteen years after its founding, the college affiliated with Serampore University and was accredited by the Serampore Senate.

By 1974 HBI had exceeded its capacity with 230 students, at that time the largest school in India and Asia. God had blessed the ministries of HBI and in a short span of 22 years it had grown to have significant impact on missions and the church in India.

THE FRUIT OF THE VISION: NEW CHURCH LEADERS

From its beginning in 1952 until 2003, HBI has trained and graduated 8,185 men and women. Scattered all over India, in neighboring countries, and across the globe, they minister in existing churches and establish new churches. *The result of one man's obedience in a time of transition made a remarkable difference in the development of national leaders for the work of making disciples among the hundreds of people groups in India.* I will recount here three of the hundreds of stories of graduates who have become leaders for Christ's church in India.

CASE OF JEEVARATHNAM BURGA

One of the first five graduates of HBI, Jeevarathnam Burga founded the Bharat Bible College in 1969. The verse that inspired Dr. J. Burga's vision to start the Bible College was 2 Timothy 2:2, "And the things that thou hast heard of me among many witnesses, the same commit thou to faithful men, who shall be able to teach others also" (KJV). The college started with six students and a small faculty. It currently has 185 students and there are more than 800 graduates who serve the Lord in India and around the world. The college is now situated in Hyderabad, Andhra Pradesh, on a 25-acre campus. God has indeed blessed and multiplied this ministry for His glory.

CASE OF PAUL PILLAI

In 1958 an HBI graduate serving as a missionary in the islands of Andaman sent Paul Pillai, a converted Hindu, to HBI to be trained. Paul Pillai studied at HBI between 1958-61, and my father mentored and discipled him. After his graduation he committed to bring the gospel to the millions of Hindus in North India. His family and friends disowned him because he became a Christian.

In 1964 he founded the India National Inland Mission, and with his wife Annie, also a graduate of HBI, began working in North India. Evangelism and church planting are the primary focus of the mission. After leading many to Christ and planting several churches, he founded Grace Bible College in Haryana, North India, which today is the largest theological seminary and Bible college in India. Since opening in 1972, it has graduated 3,500 full-time ministers. Its graduates have formed 180 national missionary organizations. Another important part of the mission is the Bethesda Children's Home, an orphanage. Paul oversees the mission, the Bible college, and the children's home that has rescued more than 1,000 children.

CASE OF M. A. THOMAS

In 1963 M. A. Thomas, his wife, and three other graduates made a decision to give their lives to go to preach the gospel of Jesus Christ in the state of Rajasthan. To work in Rajasthan meant they would have to learn a new language before they could start their ministry. They knew that anti-Christian movements would challenge them and they would be persecuted. The church in the state is a minority and they had no financial support.

A friend of Thomas asked him, "Who is financially supporting the team?" He replied, "We will work as servants if necessary but God will provide." "How about your travel expense to Rajasthan?" The answer was, "God will provide and we are willing to walk to Rajasthan." "What if one of the children were to die as you walked this road?" Thomas replied, "We would dig a grave, bury the child, and keep going." A moment later he continued with tears rolling down his cheeks, saying, "If all of us died and only one of us crossed the border and put just one tract on the soil of Rajasthan, we would consider our mission accomplished."

On the day of their departure, God provided all the funds for their train travel. Every money order on that day was for them. They bought tickets and started their journey, but Thomas and his team had no idea of how much God would allow them to suffer. On the 17th day in Rajasthan they were physically beaten. Their Bibles and gospels were shredded. The militants threatened them and demanded they leave. They threw Brother M. A. Thomas in prison and the team thought they were finished.

Through such a traumatic beginning, God has blessed the faith and obedience of Thomas and the team. Faithful to their calling, Thomas and the team continued to witness to the saving grace of Jesus Christ, and many people responded to the gospel. As the ministry flourished, each of the team members expanded the sphere of witness to different areas of the state. All the team members have started multiple churches, developed a church movement, and have started at least one Bible college to train leaders.

God has blessed M. A. Thomas beyond all expectations. In forty years Thomas has started 19 Bible colleges, planted 4,000 churches, started 145 Christian schools, and is caring for 5,000 children through 103 orphanages. He started a nursing school and has a plan to start a medical college. On January 26, 2001, the President of India gave Dr. M.A. Thomas an honor called "Padma Shree" in recognition of his major contributions to advance the nation. This is one of the most prestigious awards given for service to India. Praise the Lord! What God can do if we are willing to listen to His voice!

These are but three stories of men God allowed my father to influence. As he discipled these men, and sent them out as workers for the harvest, God used them to accomplish great work. These stories can be repeated for almost every state of India. Hundreds of leaders in the church graduated from HBI. Some serve as bishops of churches, others as leaders of mission agencies and parachurch organizations. Today we can look back and see how God used my father to multiply leaders to serve the church that was going through the process of nationalization.

Today Hindustan Bible Institute is training nearly 1,800 men and women through its various leadership training programs in Chennai and around the nation. In this book you have seen how the Lord led HBI over the years to employ many different forms and methods for developing Great Commission leaders.

GOD MOLDS A REBEL
FOR HIS MISSION

I never imagined I would be the one God would have serve Him as president of HBI. If someone had told me I was headed to be the director of the school and mission I would have thought he was insane. I knew I was not smart enough for such a task. I also knew I was not good enough. I challenged my parents and rebelled against the faith and values that guided their lives.

My siblings matched the qualifications far better than I. They read books continually and one had a photographic memory. My older brother studied hard and graduated first in his class. My sister was just as intelligent. I could not pass my first grade without my father's influence. I failed my fifth grade three times. My older brother or sister had all the makings to be great leaders. Not me!

When something went wrong they looked at me! I often heard, "Bobby, you are good for nothing." I really believed that I was a zero, until I met the Lord. I was nobody and God turned me into somebody. He gave me identity and purpose, ability and skill. He had a plan for me, but I never believed for a moment it would be leading HBI.

In this chapter I will share how God worked to bring me to repentance, to change me, and to fill me with a vision and strategy that He would fulfill. I had to learn that my life was all about God and then allow Him to fashion me to accomplish His purpose.

GOD PURSUES A REBEL

As a teenager in 1970, I thought I knew it all. Rebelling against my family and God, I tried hard to finish high school but failed.

In absolute frustration I dropped out of school. Later I tried to complete high school by writing exams equivalent to high school, and every effort yielded a dead end. I no longer went to church and I was angry with God. In fact, I was angry with humanity and I despised myself. Like a vagabond, I lived life without any purpose and hope.

I still remember one Sunday morning, when my sister knocked on my door and asked if I would like to go to church. At that time I had not attended church in more than two years. But the previous night, I celebrated with a group and got so drunk I lost consciousness. My friends later told me they had decided if I did not revive by 4:00 a.m. they planned to drop me in the street for my family to find me. Thank God I regained consciousness by 4:00 a.m. that morning. My friends then ejected me, telling me never to come back again. I had almost lost my life! The near-death incident made me think of my future. I responded yes to my sister, not knowing exactly why.

While I waited for my sister to finish choir practice after church, I enjoyed talking with some old friends, especially a teacher who spent a lot of her time trying to help me find purpose in life. Dorothy, affectionately called Dot, invited me to attend a church picnic coming up on January 26. I knew I would feel like a fish out of water but I could not say no. She had done so much for me, I felt obligated to accept her invitation and planned to go.

When January 26 came, I attended the picnic as I had promised. (I was later informed that many prayed God would use the retreat to turn me around.) After the picnic, Dot asked, and I agreed to walk her home. As we walked together Dot asked me a question that I will never forget. Calling me Paul, she said, "Paul, what are you doing with your life?" I resented the question, avoided answering, and changed the topic. When we got to her home I was anxious to get away, so I said "bye." Dot looked at me and said to me, "Paul, I will be praying for you." The moment I turned to go, the Holy Spirit repeated the question, "What are you doing with your life?" and for the next three months it kept coming back. I tried hard to erase it from my mind but it kept coming back.

Finally, on a night in April 1970, lying in bed thinking, "What will happen to me if I die?" I realized I would go straight to hell. I had no hope and I was empty on the inside. I surrendered to the Lord that night, invited Him into my life and Jesus changed the direction of my life.

Suddenly, as clear as night and day, the moment I received Christ, the Holy Spirit reminded me of a commitment I made after I had failed fifth grade for the third time. Disgusted and disappointed with myself like the rest of my family, I said to the Lord, "If you take me out of the fifth grade you can have my life." To my utter amazement, the next year they moved me to the next class. Now I heard the Lord ask, "Do you remember that commitment? I have a plan. I want you to stop playing games. Are you ready for me to lead your life?"

I shared with my friends God's new direction for my life, expecting them to reject me. To my surprise they did not. Instead, expressing concern for the dangerous life I had followed, they encouraged me to keep faith. Surprised and shocked, expecting them to laugh and mock me, I got the opposite reaction. God slowly transformed me and helped me commit to His ways.

I wrote to my father, who was on a six-month trip in the USA, and told him what God had done in my life. I described God's call to me and expressed my desire to start preparing to serve Him. I did not expect my father to respond, but to my surprise, he sent me an audiocassette an hour and-a-half long telling me what I should do to have a strong relationship with the Lord. He also informed me that the only school that would admit me into Bible college was HBI, since I had not finished high school. I was not sure I liked that!

GAINING A VISION

In 1971 I applied to HBI, not knowing how the Lord would prepare me for the future. The teachers taught foundational knowledge, which helped me grow, but more importantly, three college seniors took me under their wing and discipled me to walk with the Lord. Every morning we spent time together in Bible study and prayer, allowing God's Word to transform my life. We shared our lives and concerns with each other. They taught me to pray and we saw God do miracles. I gained a new identity in Christ and began developing a burden for the lost. I learned to share my faith with others. They were incredible days of growth and maturing in the Lord that I will never forget.

In 1974 the Holy Spirit led me to make changes in my course of study. Thinking I would do a Bachelor of Theology, I planned to work as a pastor in India. But in the middle of my training, God pulled me out and took me to the USA to travel with my father. Although the direction was unclear, I sensed God leading.

My father was getting weak. We did not know it, but he had only three years before God would call him to Himself. His board had suggested that he begin developing leadership for the future. For six months I became my father's chauffeur and drove him all over the USA.

This was my first experience to see a different side of dad. He was truly a man of God, but I was so angry at the way he led his family I did not see or understand his passion. But I will never forget the privilege I felt driving him. Every day, I heard the story of how God called him and burdened him to reach India with the gospel. For some reason it never got old. I enjoyed hearing it over and over again. I soon found myself understanding dad and seeing his vision. I saw his passion for the lost. I heard him weep every day for the lost and the work God had entrusted to him. He knew names of graduates on the field and prayed for hours every day as though they were his children.

Dad had only one message, his story of how God saved him from darkness and called him to a mission. It did not matter what Scripture he read, the message was the same and the call at the end was, "If you have not met my Savior, He is a great God and He is waiting for you and if you are a child of God, get involved." I will never forget those days of praying with my father and listening to him. I developed a great respect for my father.

During those six months, God began to build a vision in my life. Working on my character and my vision, the Holy Spirit revealed that His plan for me was more than being a pastor of a church. I did not know whether I was ready, but God was getting my attention. After months of living with and hearing my father, for the first time I felt as if I had, as a rebel youth, lost much of his leadership in my life.

At the end of the trip as he prepared to go home, he said to me, "Son, I want you to go to school in the USA." His words triggered shock and dismay in me, because I loved India and wanted to go back. I was in the middle of a degree program at HBI and had not said goodbye to my friends. However, by this time, I was ready to yield to my father's leadership. He asked me to apply to Piedmont Bible College in Winston-Salem, North Carolina. I did, and was accepted with a full-tuition scholarship.

NEW FOUNDATIONS AND FAITH

The next three years I watched the Lord help me do the impossible—succeed in school. At Piedmont God reinforced the foundation to my theology. I remember studying with a friend, Bill Roberts, discussing the various approaches to theology and seeing the differences. I knew very little about liberalism, neo-evangelical, and evangelical theology. With God's help I soon began to understand the differences and develop an appreciation for His Word.

As I sat in the classes, I began to comprehend the role of a local church. I did not know the difference between Lutheran, Methodist, Baptist, or any other church movement. They all blended together, because in India these traditions were not an issue. The liberal denominations in the USA were evangelical in India, but study at Piedmont Bible College helped me understand what they believed and how they functioned in the U.S. I soon grasped the concept of the local church and its significance in God's agenda.

Perhaps the most important lessons at Piedmont were learning to trust God. I watched God provide for me as He had provided for my father, and I began to learn to trust the Lord for everything. I remember the many times God provided finances when I needed help. He also gave me a job and I learned to work and care for myself.

One of the critical faith moments came on the subject of marriage. Traditionally, Indian parents look for a bride for their son. My father decided it was time for me to get married and he told me he was looking for a bride. Almost five years before he made this decision, I had met Linnet Daniel, one of my sister's friends, on the occasion when my sister was departing India for the USA. At that farewell party Linnet and I got acquainted and from there we developed a long friendship. When my father decided to look for a bride, I asked him to visit her mother and discuss the possibility of our being married. They did, and she agreed, so they decided that Linnet and I would be married. Since I was living in the USA we applied for, and she was granted a fiancée visa. God provided a wife.

My parents lived frugally on a missionary salary and I did not want them to pay for anything related to our wedding. Wanting to trust God and move from dependency on my parents, I applied for a loan to help buy a ticket for Linnet to come to the USA. My supervisor, who had to approve the loan, looked at me and said "But, Bobby, you are not making enough to support a family." I replied that God had brought me this far and I was sure He would provide. He looked at me and laughed. Then I told him my father's story and said, "I believe in the God of my father." He recommended the loan, promoted me to a new position, and the administration approved the loan. Praise the Lord!

In 1975 Linnet arrived from India and we married. The week we were married God provided enough to pay off the loan and to pay for the next semester of school. From paying for our marriage to growing a family and finishing all our training, God never failed.

Another test of faith came from the cultural challenges and difficulties of studying in the U.S. Forced to make many cultural adjustments, I look back and see it was all part of God's plan to help me think cross-culturally. God was at work, developing me for leadership. I learned to trust the Lord, and to share the vision of HBI. Every time I shared the vision the Holy Spirit challenged me to think about the call for my life.

Two years into Piedmont Bible College, one of the board members spoke on the call of a minister and called for a commitment.

Feeling the Holy Spirit calling me to respond, I met the speaker and discussed the conflict going on inside me. He prayed with me, and that day I took a step forward to accept God's call, and to do whatever He wanted, including working with HBI.

In May 1977, after three years and the completion of my undergraduate studies, my parents and sister came for my graduation. I remember my father's joy, to think his good-for-nothing son had finished at PBC and was accepted for graduate study at Talbot Seminary in Los Angeles. I did not know that soon the Lord would call him to Himself.

In the fall 1977, just a few days after Mythraie, our daughter, was born, I had to leave for California. My brother Danny flew to North Carolina to help me drive. Linnet and Mythraie would join us after I had found a place for us to live. Like Abraham going into the unknown, I was not sure what the Lord had in store for us. Moving to the West Coast meant finding a home, a job, enrolling in seminary, and finding a church to worship. As my brother Danny and I drove across the country, I kept asking the questions, "Do you think we will find a home? What about a job? Do you think I will get one?" While I worried, God taught me more about trusting Him.

We reached California and within days I found a home and a job. While not the ideal job, it paid the bills. I had to work nights, go to school in the day, and sleep when I could. Soon the stress was overwhelming, so much so that Linnet and I asked the Lord to make a way out for me, so I could stay in school and not burn out. The Lord reaffirmed His loving care and plan for my life. The Church of the Open Door, Hindustan Bible Institute, and World Vision together made it possible for me to go to school and not work. I quit my job to concentrate on completing my Master of Divinity program. God was teaching me to trust Him for a greater task where my eyes must stay focused on Him.

STAYING FOCUSED AND LEARNING TO WAIT

In a few months, while everything seemed to be going so well, news came from home that Dad was in the hospital with a massive heart attack. It was a very sad weekend for our family, for within days the Lord called my dad home. My mother and family wanted me to go home, but I knew I was not ready. I did not want to go back before God led me to. I was very young and not ready for the plans others had. It was a difficult time in my life, but the Holy Spirit provided me counsel.

On my visit to the family after Dad had gone to be with the Lord, I met Victor Manogaram, one of the founders of Youth for Christ in India. When I was in Chennai on this trip, he came to visit me and said, "Bobby do not come home till you have finished what God took you to do. Come on the strength of the Lord and on your own grounds, you will be accepted. Do not come on your father's foundation." I will ever be grateful for those words, which encouraged me to work hard and stay focused.

In the next five years, I completed a Master of Divinity and a Master of Theology at Talbot Seminary (Biola University, La Mirada, CA) and all the coursework for a doctorate in Intercultural Studies at Fuller Theological Seminary in Pasadena, CA. After I completed the Master of Divinity degree my scholarship ended, forcing me to return to work in a bank. At one point in the process I worked for the bank, ministered in a church, and took courses at Biola and Fuller simultaneously. God used it all to fashion and remold me for the ministry God was leading me toward. As I look back, it is marvelous in my eyes that God gave me the courage and strength to stay focused and work toward finishing all my preparation for ministry.

LEARNING TO THINK OUTSIDE THE BOX

During the five years of training at Biola and Fuller, the Holy Spirit used some of the great men of God to mentor me in the field of missions and leadership development. They helped lay a strong biblical foundation for the vision, and I learned to trust God and think outside the traditions of the church in India. The impact of the Lausanne Conference affected the way Biola and Fuller faculty trained leaders for missions. They focused on the Great Commission and the command to make disciples as the end result of missions. This emphasis and value changed the way I understood mission–to have a lasting impact in our generation we had to make disciples and not just preach the gospel.

Mission leaders redefined the task of discipling the nations to focus on the unreached peoples and making disciples of every people group in the world. Dr. Ralph Winter at Fuller called the church to focus on more than 25,000 unreached people groups. Ed Dayton of World Vision emphasized the need to develop a strategy for evangelism with the end in mind and an intentional visible effort to achieve it. This required a strategy to grow churches. As I listened to these teachers at the School of World Mission, God prepared me to think strategically.

The faculty forced us to think outside the box of traditional mission practices. I began to understand the need for mission societies and churches to work together. I also learned the importance of contextualizing the message and the methods of evangelism. Missionaries in our classes, who came back after years of service, helped students from all over the world to understand why churches were not growing, why people were still not responding to the message, and how churches could grow if we contextualized the message and the methods.

Finally, we learned that developing and empowering national leaders to take ownership and responsibility were essential to accomplish the mission of God. Dr. Paul Hiebert helped me understand how institutions sometimes became an obstacle to this empowerment, and he taught me research processes and principles to help institutions to change. As I look back today, the training was a part of God's plan to shape me for the new vision and work of HBI.

BACK TO HINDUSTAN BIBLE INSTITUTE

By 1982 I had completed all the course work for the Ph.D. program so that only the application, testing of the theory, and defending my dissertation remained. I was ready, and the Holy Spirit led our family to return to India to begin the work He had prepared for us. I was young and uncertain of how the Lord would use us for His glory. We believed, however, that God's time for us had come, even though some in India would rather I did not return. God gave us a promise, "Fear not, for I am with you; be not dismayed for I am your God and I will strengthen you and uphold you with the righteousness of my right hand. I will straighten the way and make you a new and threshing instrument."

We returned to Chennai with a commitment to teach at Hindustan Bible Institute and be available to do anything they would like us to do. Our home church, Bethany Bible Fellowship, recognized God's call on our lives, and dedicated and released us to the ministry.

In the Epistle of Paul to the church in Ephesus, Paul writes we are God's workmanship. He is the potter and we are the clay in the hands of God. I learned over the years that God was working on and in my life preparing me to do His service. I had to trust the Lord Jesus, allow Him to go before me, and He would bestow His favor. If I would allow Jesus Christ to direct the course of my life, then He would accomplish His purpose.

Leadership development is the work of God. To lead effectively one must listen carefully to discern what God wants to do, and then allow God to work in and through us to be His servants. He will use people, information, structure, institutions, and any number of other things. It is our responsibility to become passive in His hand so that He can make us active for His purpose. I had to learn to let God bring transformation, vision, skills, and strategy to help me do what He wanted to do. I believe it makes a difference if we can learn to let God do what He wants to do through us.

REFERENCES

Barrett, David B., George T. Kurian, and Todd M. Johnson. *2001 World Christian Encyclopedia: a comparative study of churches and religions in the modern world*. New York: Oxford University Press. Vol. 1:842-843.

Chandrasekhar, S. W. editor. 1990 *All India Congress on Church Development, Hyderabad: Conference Manual, August 14-18, 1990*. Council on National Service, 86-89, Medavakkam Tank Road, Kilpauk, Madras, India 600 010.

CONS India. 1990 *The Hyderabad Declaration on Church Development*. Council on National Service, 86-89, Medavakkam Tank Road, Kilpauk, Madras, India 600 010.

----------. 1995 *Second All India Congress on Church Development, Madras: Conference Manual. January 9-12, 1995*. Council on National Service, 86-89, Medavakkam Tank Road, Kilpauk, Madras, India 600 010.

Dennison, Jack. 1999 *City Reaching: On the Road to Community Transformation*. Pasadena, CA: Wm. Carey Library.

Devanboo, Lemuel A, "Gujarat School of Evangelism, " *In CONS News Track: Official Bulletin of Council on National Service*. H. Lamech Inbaraj, ed. Vol. 1(4):10-11. Hindustan Bible Institute & College, 86-89 Medavakkam Tank Road, Kilpauk, Chennai – 600 010, India.

George, Timothy. 1998 *Faithful Witness: the Life and Mission of William Carey*. Birmingham, AL: Christian History Institute, Samford University.

Gupta, Paul Rajkumar. 1992 *Institutionalization and Renewal of the Hindustan Bible Institute*. Ann Arbor, MI: University Microfilms Dissertation Information Service.

----------. 1999a *The Unfinished Task in Karnataka.* Council on National Service, 86-89, Medavakkam Tank Road, Kilpauk, Madras, India 600 010.

----------. 1999b *The Unfinished Task in Rajasthan.* Council on National Service, 86-89, Medavakkam Tank Road, Kilpauk, Madras, India 600 010.

----------. 1999c *The Unfinished Task in West Bengal.* Council on National Service, 86-89, Medavakkam Tank Road, Kilpauk, Madras, India 600 010.

----------. 2001 "What Can We Do in our Generation to Fulfill the Great Commission in India?" *In CONS News Track: Official Bulletin of Council on National Service.* H. Lamech Inbaraj, ed. Vol. 1(1):4-10. Hindustan Bible Institute & College, 86-89 Medavakkam Tank Road, Kilpauk, Chennai – 600 010, India.

Gupta, Paul Rajkumar and Tony Hilton. 1995 *The Unfinished Task in Andhra Pradesh.* Council on National Service, 86-89, Medavakkam Tank Road, Kilpauk, Madras, India 600 010.

----------. 1996 *The Unfinished Task in Tamil Nadu.* Council on National Service, 86-89, Medavakkam Tank Road, Kilpauk, Madras, India 600 010.

----------. 1997a *The Unfinished Task in Maharashtra.* Council on National Service, 86-89, Medavakkam Tank Road, Kilpauk, Madras, India 600 010.

----------. 1997b *The Unfinished Task in Gujarat.* Council on National Service, 86-89, Medavakkam Tank Road, Kilpauk, Madras, India 600 010.

Hunt, Dave. 1976, 1999 *God of Impossibilities.* Honolulu, HI: Straight Street Publishing.

Huntington, Samuel P. 1993 "The Clash of Civilizations?" *Foreign Affairs,* Summer 1993, v72, n3, p22(28).

Inbaraj, H. Lamech, ed. 2001 *CONS News Track: Official Bulletin of Council on National Service.* Vol. 1(1), January-March. Hindustan Bible Institute & College, 86-89 Medavakkam Tank Road, Kilpauk, Chennai – 600 010, India.

----------. 2004 *Church Mobilization Department, Annual Report,* April 1, 2003-March 31, 2004. HBI Annual Report Documents. 86-89 Medavakkam Tank Road, Kilpauk, Madras.

Jebaraj, K., editor. 2003. *CONS News Track.* Official Bulletin Council on National Service. Vol. 3, No. 2. Published by Dr. H. Lamech Inbaraj, CONS National Co-ordinator, 86-89 Medavakkam Tank Road, Kilpauk, Madras.

Jenkins, Philip. 2002 *The Next Christendom.* Oxford University Press.

Johnstone, Patrick J. St. G. 2001 *Operation World 2001.* Paternoster Lifestyle (an imprint of Paternoster Publishing). CD-ROM adaptation by Global Mapping International.

Kolb, David. 1984 *Experiential Learning.* Englewood Cliffs, NJ: Prentice Hall.

Lingenfelter, Judith E and Sherwood G. 2003 *Teaching Cross Culturally.* Grand Rapids, MI: Baker.

Lingenfelter, Sherwood. 2005 "Power-Giving Leadership: Transformation for a Missional Church," in *Appropriate Christianity,* Charles H. Kraft, ed., Pasadena, CA: William Carey Library, pp. 275-290.

_____. 1998. *Transforming Culture.* 2d Ed. Grand Rapids, MI: Baker.

McGavran, Donald. 1970 *Understanding Church Growth.* Grand Rapids: Eerdmans.

_____. 1981 "A Church in Every People: Plain Talk About a Difficult Subject." In *Perspectives on the World Christian Movement,* Ralph D. Winter and Steven C. Hawthorne, eds. William Carey Library, Pasadena, CA. Pp. 622-628.

Ponraj, S. D. editor. 1988-90. *National Strategy.* A Quarterly News Bulletin of the Committee on National Strategy, Vols. 1-3. Published by Rev. E. Sunder Raj, the Secretary – CONS.

Ponraj, S. D. editor. 1993-95. *Church Development.* A Quarterly Bulletin of the Council on National Service, Vols. 4-8. Published by Rev. Dr. Paul R. Gupta, Chairman, CONS India, 86-89 Medavakkam Tank Road, Kilpauk, Madras.

Ramanathan, Joseph P, editor. 2001-3. *CONS News Track.* Official Bulletin Council on National Service. Vols. 1-3. Published by Dr. H. Lamech Inbaraj, CONS National Coordinator, 86-89 Medavakkam Tank Road, Kilpauk, Madras.

Raju, P.S. Shalem, editor. 1995-97 *CONS News Tracks.* A Quarterly Bulletin of Council on National Service (CONS), Vol. 8, Nos 6-8, and 4, No.1. Published by CONS-- Coordinator, 86-89 Medavakkam Tank Road, Kilpauk, Madras, India.

Sathiaraj, Daniel (editor). 2001 *Unreached Mega Peoples of India.* India Missions Association and FMC Research Team.

Sanneh, Lamin. 2003 *Whose Religion is Christianity? The Gospel Beyond the West.* Grand Rapids, MI: Eerdmans.

Singh, K.S. 1998 *Anthropological Survey of India.* "People of India" National Series Volume V.

Walls, Andrew F. 2002 *The Cross-Cultural Process in Christian History.* Maryknoll, New York: Orbis Books.

Weaver, Alan R. 2004 *Toward a Cross-Cultural Theory of Leadership Emergence: the Hungarian Case.* Fuller Theological Seminary, School of Intercultural Studies. Ph.D. 308 pp.

Winter, Ralph. 1981 "The New Macedonia: A Revolutionary New Era in Mission Begins," In *Perspectives on the World Christian Movement,* Ralph D. Winter and Steven C. Hawthorne, eds. William Carey Library, Pasadena, CA. pp. 293-311.

THE AUTHORS

Paul R. Gupta has been President and Director of the Hindustan Bible Institute (HBI) and College in Chennai, India, since 1984 and he also pastors New Calvary Bible Church in India. He holds a Diploma from HBI, a B.Th. from Piedmont Bible College, an M.Div. from Talbot Seminary, and the Th.M. and Ph.D. from Fuller Theological Seminary. He founded the Indian National Evangelical Fellowship in 1985 to spearhead the spread of the gospel throughout India, and he has led a number of All-India Congresses on Church Development and efforts to evangelize and plant churches throughout the country.

Sherwood G. Lingenfelter, Professor and Provost and Senior Vice President at Fuller Theological Seminary, previously served as Professor of Intercultural Studies and Provost and Senior Vice President at Biola University. He holds a B.A. from Wheaton College and a Ph.D. in Anthropology from the University of Pittsburgh. His field research includes three years in the Yap Islands of Micronesia, and short term research and consulting with Wycliffe Bible Translators in Brazil, Cameroon, Suriname, Papua New Guinea, Borneo, Philippines, Africa, and Latin America. He also contributes regularly to mission conferences, to publications, and to missionary candidate training for evangelical mission organizations. He is chairman of the board for Grace Brethren International Missions.

Endorsement

It is a delight to recommend Bobby Gupta's work. I have cited his experiences at HBI many times as a model for Bible training that bridges between theory and practice and between education as an academic exercise and a mission outreach. He has done excellent work in transforming HBI from a traditional institution to a pioneer in bringing education and mission together.

Breaking Tradition to Accomplish Vision is an excellent record of how a traditional Bible seminary has become a pioneer in breaking down the walls between academics and missions and between theory and practice. Built on solid theological foundations, the book reveals deep insights from both the humanities and the Indian context. It is essential reading for those around the world who are involved in higher Christian education and church planting.

– Paul G. Hiebert, Ph.D.